Centerville Library
Washington-Centerville Public Library
Center

D0628696

# Sealed with a Kiss

# Sealed with a Kiss

## an american love story in letters

### BOB ZIELSDORF

TWO SHORES BOOKS

Copyright © 2014 Bob Zielsdorf

All rights reserved. No part of this publication may be reproduced, distributed, or transmitted in any form or by any means, including photocopying, recording, or other electronic or mechanical methods, without the prior written permission of the publisher, except in the case of brief quotations embodied in critical reviews and certain other noncommercial uses permitted by copyright law.

All images from the author's personal collection.

Book design by cj Madigan/Shoebox Stories


ISBN 978-0-9913174-0-0

Printed in the United States of America

Two Shores Books
www.twoshoresbooks.com
www.bobzielsdorf.com

*To Fran, who first realized we were meant to be together. Without her devotion for more than half a century this book would not exist. And to our five children and ten grandchildren – all the result of an innocent kiss long ago.*

# INTRODUCTION

*T*HE TITLE OF THIS BOOK MENTIONS KISSING. BUT IF YOU'RE LOOKING FOR a story full of steamy encounters, you've come to the wrong place.

This book is about love, not about sex. In fact, the subtitle could be "I Married My Pen Pal." Fran and I met during the summer after eighth grade while I was visiting a friend in her town. We decided to write to each other. We kept it up for eight years, during high school and college, and then got married as soon as we graduated. Almost as remarkably, maybe, we both kept the letters we received from the other. Between us, we've preserved a total of 435 of them.

This book shares some of those letters, telling the story of the relationship that developed through their pages and offering a glimpse of the America that was growing up as we were.

During the time that we wrote to each other, Fran and I never went to the same school, lived in the same town, or even resided in the same state. In other words, we didn't have what would be considered a "normal" dating relationship. Maybe because of this, by the time we got married, we knew each other better than most couples who saw each other all the time. There's something about writing down one's thoughts and feelings that lets down barriers. As time went on, Fran and I did find ways to see each other more frequently, so our entire courtship wasn't entirely letter-based. But letters were certainly its foundation.

Until we were well into college, our letters weren't love letters. They were just newsy bantering between two average, middle-class kids about what was going on in our lives. We had ordinary dating relationships with others and were happy to tell each other about them.

Our candor was possible in part because we met in the 1950s. We thought about sex and talked about it with our friends, but sex outside of marriage was a social taboo back then. It's not that it didn't happen, but it was much more rare than today. Because our dating lives were fairly innocent, there wasn't a lot we couldn't write about.

Sometime in the middle of our college years, both Fran and I began to realize that we were in love, and our letters begin to take on a "love letter" tone. After that point, our commitment to each other changed the nature of our correspondence, gradually bringing it to an end. As we were finishing college and planning our wedding, we saw each other more frequently. The letters slowly became mere adjuncts to our in-person conversations.

This book, then, is both a love and a coming-of-age story. In addition, I hope it paints a picture, through the lives Fran and I led, of middle-class life in America at one of the country's most pivotal times. I don't mean to hold either of us up as paragons, or to suggest that every kid in America was like us. But I do believe the things we did and the way we did them offer a window into the life of that unique era. The late 1950s and early 1960s—a time of relative peace and stability—were characterized by a special innocence that was lost with the

Vietnam war and the sexual revolution of the late 1960s and 1970s. I feel fortunate to have lived through that era, and to be able to share a glimpse of it here.

For centuries love letters were a staple of the courting process. Today, love letters, and personal letters generally, are almost as passé as poodle skirts and bobby sox. Because Fran and I both cherish our letters from each other, we naturally feel that modern lovers are missing out. I think that email is one of the greatest developments of the twentieth century. I use it constantly—I even text with our kids and grandkids. But can texts and emails possibly feel as personal as messages written in ink on paper, or reveal the true depths of the person writing them, as well as handwritten letters?

I don't think so.

Call me old fashioned. Because I am.

## CHAPTER ONE

$\mathcal{W}$E MET BEHIND A BUSH, PLAYING A KISSING GAME AT AN EIGHTH-GRADE graduation party. I was 13. She was 14—an older woman by three months. If anyone had predicted then that eight years later Frances Jordan and I would be married, they'd have been accused of smoking dope. Well, maybe not. In the 1957 I inhabited, nobody except maybe weirdo musicians even knew what smoking dope was. But you get my point.

At the time we met, my family lived in York, PA. York in 1957 was an industrial town of about 55,000. I recall its downtown as much like the city set in the movie "A Christmas Story": a city square dominated by red-brick department stores and smaller shops of every variety. My school, St. Patrick's, was in the inner city, about a mile and a half from my home. Sometimes I had to walk to or from school, a trek I hated.

My father Frank ran a company called A.B. Farquhar, a division of the Oliver Corporation. A tall man, he was soft spoken except when his temper was roused and more comfortable with facts than emotions. As a teenager, I appreciated both his good advice and his willingness to step back and let me make my own decisions. He was a shrewd businessman who would much later become my own business partner, but during the years this story chronicles, I mostly felt resentful rather than admiring of the frequent relocations his career demanded.

My mother was a housewife—what is now referred to as a stay-at-home mom. In our middle-class world, hardly anyone's mom worked outside the home. Smart and ambitious, she always regretted the fact that she was sent to a small Catholic girls' college rather than the large university she had dreamed of. She felt she could have done bigger things, and had she been born a generation later I'm sure she would have managed them. Instead she poured her drive and energy into the accomplishments that were available to her. Impeccably groomed and dressed, she became an accomplished golfer and piano player, a great ballroom dancer, and a skilled amateur artist who designed both of the houses my family built over the years. Like my father, she was highly social—both of them loved to attend parties, entertain, and play bridge.

I was the only son, with three younger sisters whom I teased unmercifully. We all went to Catholic schools. My Dad wasn't a Catholic, so my parents were said to have a "mixed marriage." In those pre-Vatican Council days, in order to marry in the Church, Mom and Dad had to jump through all kinds of hoops. Among them, my father had to pledge that all the children in the family would be raised as Catholics. The Church taught that if you obeyed its rules, everything would be fine and you could go to heaven when you died. Unless, of course, you had the bad judgment not to be a Catholic. So Mom obeyed all the rules and Dad, I guess, hoped for the best. Catholicism was just one of the things I took for granted during the years this book chronicles, rarely in the forefront of my mind but always a presence.

When I met Fran, I had just finished eighth grade at St. Patrick's School. At 13, I was about five feet eight inches tall and, I thought, the world's skinniest kid. My parents could afford to dress me in the fashionable clothes of the day: khakis with a little buckle on the back, charcoal pants, pink shirts, and white socks. One exception was loafers. They were in fashion, but not for me. Mom said they were bad for your feet. Laced-up shoes it was, white bucks or black or brown leather. Sneakers weren't called running shoes yet. Not a status item, they were worn only for gym class or sports or working in the yard.

I was a daily reader of the newspaper but you wouldn't say I was politically aware. That year the daily edition of the *New York Times* cost five cents and the Sunday edition a quarter. Of course, I did know that in 1957 Dwight D. Eisenhower was President. Most people I knew seemed to think Mr. Eisenhower was doing a good job of running the country. About the only thing we kids were worried about was the Bomb. Our teachers told us that the Soviet Union might drop an atom bomb on us someday. They made us do periodic bomb drills, which required us to crouch on the floor under our desks until the drill ended or, as I saw it, they felt like teaching again.

Tony Beck was my best friend. Unfortunately, Tony's dad had lost his job as an executive with a company in York and had to relocate to his new one in Andover, MA. Tony had moved from York to Andover right after seventh grade. Eighth grade was really tough without Tony around. I had other friends but none who lived within walking distance of my house. I recall that as being a very lonely year. So the summer I graduated from St. Patrick's, my parents took mercy on me and said I could go to Andover to visit Tony.

I can't recall now how the arrangements were made. No doubt letters were written between Tony's parents and mine. And there must have been a number of phone calls to get all the logistics straightened out. This must have been quite a production for our parents, because in those days a long distance phone call was a major event.

Back then, everyone's telephone was black and weighed as much as a small dumbbell. That design was pretty much your only choice. You didn't go to a store and buy something—you took whatever Ma Bell provided. If you lived in a place with modern service, your phone had a rotary dial. Dialing, especially the higher numbers, was not quick. Waiting for the dial to unwind all the way back to the starting point seemed to take all day.

For a long-distance call, you dialed "0" for the operator. The operator, usually a woman, came on the line and asked for the number. You would then say that you wanted to make a long-distance call and state whether it was to be "Station-to-Station" or "Person-to-Person." With "Station-to-Station" calls you took a chance that the actual person you wanted to talk to would be there. If you were calling an adult and some kid answered the phone, you had to pay for the call even if the adult you were calling wasn't home. With a "Person-to-Person" call the operator would ask whoever answered for the particular adult by name. If he was there, great—you got connected. If he wasn't there, there was no connection and no charge. All long distance calls were expensive but "Person-to-Person" was astronomical. The whole thing was sort of like a bet with AT&T, which held the telephone monopoly for the entire country. Anyway, I can only imagine the cost in time and money for my mom and dad to set up this trip.

But even with the kind of hassle they had to go through, life in 1957 was much more straightforward than it is today. Phone calls might have been expensive, but telephone service was simple. For one thing, you only had one phone number to remember and for most people, it only had four digits. Today our household of two has six 10-digit phone numbers to keep track of, not to mention a variety of voicemail systems.

When the time came that summer to see Tony, I was put on a train for Boston, about 425 miles from York. I don't remember how long the train ride took, but it wasn't overnight. After Tony and his parents met the train in Boston, we drove the 20 miles or so to Andover. My visit lasted two weeks and included many memorable events, though some of them wouldn't be considered very exciting today.

I remember driving on a four-lane divided highway and being amazed at the smooth stretch of black asphalt and the speeds at which you could go. It's possible the road I'm remembering became part of I-95, but I don't really know. The interstate highway system hadn't been officially authorized until the year before. It was supposed to be completed in 12 years at a cost of $25 billion, though it actually took 35 years and $114 billion to finish.

There were dozens of other things I still remember about that visit, but the most memorable of all is the graduation party. It was held at the home of one of Tony's classmates, Paula. I was walking into a nest of strangers—except for Tony, I didn't know a soul. They made this new kid welcome and took an interest in me; no one treated me like an outsider, a kindness for which I was really grateful.

We were outdoors on a nice summer evening. Once I was introduced, everyone wanted to know what it was like to live in Pennsylvania (they eat cottage cheese with apple butter on it) and what it had been like to ride a train all the way to Boston by myself (bumpy and boring).

The highlight of the evening was the kissing game. Every boy removed something he was wearing and put it in a pile in the yard. Then the girls dove into the pile and picked something from it. Whoever belonged to the article a girl came up with was to accompany her behind a large bush (for privacy, of course—after all, this was New England) and kiss. As a man of the world at 13, I was no stranger to Spin the Bottle, but this was a great new twist!

I removed the scapular medal I was wearing and into the pile it went. Scapulars probably aren't very popular anymore, if they ever were. Basically pendants with religious symbols on them, they were worn around the neck, hidden under the clothing. In the 1950s, Catholic boys were encouraged to wear the wool versions because they itched; the resultant self-punishment was supposed to be "offered up" to God. But metal versions were also available.

Fran recalls that I was wearing a cloth scapular. I'm pretty sure that a couple of years earlier I had wised up and jettisoned the itchy cloth one in favor of the metal version, but that detail doesn't really matter any more.

What's important is that I removed whatever scapular it was and threw in onto the pile, along with the watches, identification bracelets, belts, and shoes the other guys had tossed in. At the appointed moment, laser-focused on that scapular, Fran elbowed out another girl to claim me as her prize.

I'm still not really sure why Fran picked me out of the crowd, except maybe because I was tall. I had no muscles, no coordination. I was always the last kid picked for a team in sandlot choose-up baseball. I had no interest in playing football. I was tall enough for basketball, but though I always tried out for the team I rarely got put in. Physically speaking, height was pretty much all I had going for me.

I remember noticing that she was tall and that she was blessed (from a guy's point of view) with a 36-24-36 figure. Okay, maybe not exactly, but that's what it seemed like to me. Both her height and her nice figure were rare commodities among 14-year-old girls back then, when girls reached puberty later than they do today.

Anyway, the moment when she picked me out was life-changing. What if the other girl had won? Existential questions aside, what I remember was Fran and I kissing behind the tree. It was an innocent kiss. But as far as eighth grade kissing went at that time, it was pretty good.

The next day, hopeful for an opportunity for a second kiss, I asked Tony if we could go visit Fran at her house.

It was a hard, uphill bike ride from Tony's house to hers, but luckily she was home. I'm sure she was surprised to see the two of us. God knows what her parents thought. She came outside, and we stood in her yard chatting for a while. She may have mentioned that she had a whole extended family inside, but she didn't tell me anything about them that day.

I quickly realized that this was clearly not a kissing opportunity. Even if I'd had the nerve to broach the subject, which I didn't, we were standing in her front yard in the middle of the day with her whole family inside and Tony right beside us. That didn't exactly conjure up a romantic atmosphere, but Fran did make me an intriguing offer. She playfully said she would pay me for my scapular medal. I was smart enough to know the currency would be another kiss. But I was too dumb to know what to do. I stammered around the subject long enough that nothing came of it other than the idea that we would write each other. We exchanged addresses and said goodbye, then Tony and I rode off down the hill.

When I got home to York, I actually did write her a letter. Amazingly, she saved it, along with all the others I wrote over the ensuing eight years. Even more amazingly, I saved hers, too.

August 20, 1957

Dear Frances,

I had a very nice train ride home. The train was nice and not dirty. I accompanied Tony's grandmother. That was a job!

Have you recovered from all those relatives yet? Things are quiet around here now because my sisters went swimming and my mother is playing golf.

I hope you are still not jealous of Clare. I don't even know her last name.

Andover certainly is different from York, with all the lakes and everything. The only thing around here is the Susquehanna River. My father has an island down there and a group of guys are going to sleep out there Friday night. By the way—I hope you can read this "handwriting."

Do you have a picture of yourself you can send me?

Well, I have to go now. I hope you will write me soon.

Love,

Bob

Though I mention her in two letters, I have to confess that neither Fran nor I remember who Clare is at this point!

In those days it cost three cents to send a first class letter. ZIP codes hadn't been invented, nor had two-letter state abbreviations. Andover was in "Mass." not "MA". York was either in "Pa." or "Penna.", depending on your mood. A letter usually took anywhere from three to five days to reach its destination. It might have been faster locally, but sometimes it was just the opposite. If you were mailing a letter across the country or internationally, it could take over a week, so it was often best to pay extra for air mail.

From the comment in my letter about my handwriting and the fact that I put the word in quotation marks, you can tell that I was a bit self-conscious about it. In spite of my teachers' best efforts to drill the Palmer method of penmanship into me, I never quite got it. My only bad grades in elementary school related to the fact that I had an uncontrollable scrawl. In the face of that glaring fault, I bravely sent off the first letter, not knowing if I would get a response. To make sure she was properly impressed, I covered the back of the envelope with cryptic letters intended to amuse and mystify her.

Something must have gone right because to my great delight, a response came, and much more quickly than I expected.

*August 22, 1957*

*3:15 P.M.*

*Dear Bob:*

*I was so glad to hear from you. I wasn't thoroughly convinced you were going to write.*

*Right now I'm watching "American Bandstand." It's just the greatest! It's a nationwide broadcast from 3 to 4:30 Monday—Friday. I see it on WMVR-TV in Manchester, N.H. Do you watch it? If you don't, you really should.*

*Early this afternoon I went downtown & met Geri & Honey. Sometimes Geri tries her hardest to make me feel like a 1st class fool & today was one of those days. I was so embarrassed 'cause she talks so loud & everything. I really like her a lot but sometimes she just pains me. Don't mind me, always complaining.*

*Honey O'Connor is having a party next Thursday. I sure wish you were here so I could ask you to go with me. (I wonder if you would after Paula's party?)*

*Monday I had most of my curls cut off & I look much better (not bragging) if you can imagine me looking good, ever!*

*Gee, looking this letter I realize my writing is very sloppy. Please excuse it but the paper is against my knees & is kind of wobbly.*

*I do have a picture I can send you but it's not handy right now so I'll send it the next time I write, OK? Send me one of you too!*

*Well I've got to go now. Think of me in your spare time if it's not too*

*boring a thought!*

*Love ya lots,*

*Fran*

Note that her letter is dated only two days after mine. That means my letter made its way from York to Andover in only two days, and that she didn't waste any time writing back!

And check out the back of her envelope. I thought I was being devilishly clever to put all those mysterious letters on my flap. That she outdid me with her response felt like a very cool thing.

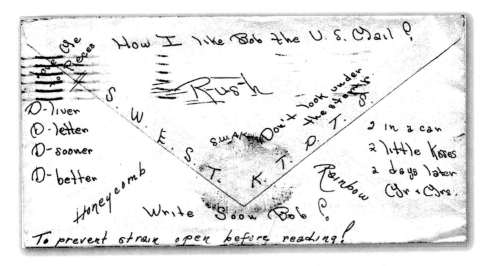

At our two brief meetings, there had definitely been chemistry between Fran and me. But now that we were writing, the physical had instantly been taken out of the equation. What mattered now was the intellectual and the emotional. Humor, caring, common interests, our true values, really—those were the kinds of things that counted in writing letters. We didn't put them in our letters at a conscious level. They just emerged as we reflected our lives in writing.

In retrospect I'm glad that no one, including ourselves, could have predicted what would happen as the years went on. If we had understood the powerful force that was drawing us together for a lifetime or contemplated writing almost 500 letters in total, we wouldn't have been able to relax and have fun. But blissfully unaware that anything "serious" was happening, that's exactly what we did.

*Bob at age 14, 1957*

# CHAPTER TWO

*I*N SEPTEMBER, 1957, FRAN AND I, BOTH NOW 14, STARTED BACK TO SCHOOL. We had lots of living to do. Our entire high school experience lay ahead of us and neither of us knew what to expect. Judging from our letters, we were not terribly concerned about that. I became a freshman at York Catholic High School. Fran left the Catholic school system to become a ninth-grader at Andover Junior High School.

Here is my response to Fran's first letter to me.

August 27, 1957

Dear Fran:

I took your advice and looked up "American Bandstand." We get it over WSBA -York from 3:00 to 4:30. I must agree, it's really good. Last winter on this same station they had a similar program called "Club 43." It was for the York area kids. There was one drawback though. You had to get tickets from different stores around town and by the time I got to one of those stores, the tickets would be gone. But a friend gave me some tickets once so I went up. Right now, they're playing "Honeycomb." It's a good song.

I am enclosing a picture of myself. It's not very good though. We had these taken in school this year. Don't forget to send me yours.

We start school on the 4th (curses) but the freshmen must go on the 3rd to see the school and everything.

Well, we finally had rain! It came on Sunday and it sure did a lot of good.

We should be moving in about 1 or 2 months. There have been about 2 or 3 offers for our house. The others were just curiosity seekers.

The country club is having a family night on Wednesday. They are lots of fun. There is a buffet dinner at 6:00 and an orchestra from 7:30 to 10:30 for dancing.

I thought Paula's party was a good one. Did you know that she taped it? That's a dirty trick I think but I would do the same thing.

Remember that "thing" I showed you at your house. Well, I put it on my bedroom floor and the maid came in and started to clean it up. And when it wouldn't clean, she started to bawl out the dog!

Well I gotta go now.

"It's Love, Love, Love,"

Bob

Life as we knew it went on. Like most teenagers, we noticed changes adults would call trivial much more than the big historic ones. By August 27, for example, I had become an "American Bandstand" fan. The program had started in Philadelphia in the early 50s and went national in August 1957. Hosted by

Dick Clark, it featured a studio full of teenagers—many of them regulars with whom fans formed special bonds—who danced to new hits and up-and-comers. A guest artist would also appear and lip-sync his or her hit song. Clark had the kids rate the songs, which gave it an interactive element that felt very cool to us then. The program started at 3:00 p.m., so many kids would rush home from school to watch. When American Bandstand came into my life there was no more rinky-dink "Club 43," my source for popular music before. Now I could tune into the same big time world of Philadelphia teens Fran could enjoy from Andover.

My school year was to start on September 4. As I said in my letter to Fran, "curses." September 4 is my birthday. It was always hard enough to get back into the routine of school, especially a new school. That year, to have to start that process on my own special day added insult to injury.

But the big news in this letter was about an impending move from York. That month, my father announced that we were going to move to Chicago and he had put our house on the market. I assume he was being transferred or promoted at the Oliver Corporation but I have no memory of the specifics. My real concern was the move. Its timing was terrible. I would have to start high school in York and then transfer during the school year. From my point of view, it would have been far better to move before school started, but the social life of a teenager was apparently not the Oliver Corporation's most pressing concern.

With his announcement, one of the continuing dramas of my adolescence began. My family's moves from place to place were frequent in those years. The disruptions to my social and school life sometimes made me resentful. I wasn't aware of it yet, but my correspondence with Fran helped give continuity to these years. Whatever else changed, she didn't—and because we never lived in the same place anyway, I never had to leave her.

One of the sillier references in the letter needs explaining. Ever the practical jokester and graced with the sophisticated sense of humor that all young teenage boys possess, I was the proud owner of a chunk of rubber dog poop—very realistic looking, too, may I add. Apparently I had shown "the thing" to Fran hoping to impress her with my suave jocularity. My reference to our maid sounds rather upper class and pretentious, and maybe that was the impression I wanted to convey. But the truth is much more middle class: we had a cleaning lady who came once a week. I still think it was pretty funny that our cleaning lady found "the thing" real enough to chastise my dog over it.

Fran's reply was postmarked on September 15. School for her had started on September 9th. She reported that "I just love it; the school and kids, not the terrible assignments they give you!" She told me about some of her classes: Social Studies with Miss Bisbee (Fran didn't like her), Mrs. Coleman's English class (reading "The Apprentice"), and of course, Home Room (with Mr. Bissett). She was going to a dance that night with 53 girls and 25 boys. She said "I can hardly wait!" (I don't know why. Didn't sound like good odds to me, at least from a girl's perspective.)

Before the letter ended, she said she had run into my friend Tony downtown, and that he was surprised I had written to her. Who knows why? My own surmise is that Tony just figured our meeting was a one-shot deal, and Fran tells me that he wasn't enthused about girls yet. Anyway, she added that she was glad I did and signed off "Love ya lots & lots." We were off and running!

In subsequent letters, I shared my own news. I told her school had been "running pretty smoothly. I get a ride in with a senior who drives her own car. I like all the sisters except Sr. Mary Patrick. Her I *non amat*." As is obvious from that reference, I was taking Latin that year. I also told her about a school dance with a live orchestra. "I'm glad it was good, too, for $1.00 a ticket," I added. That sounds like a tiny sum today, but back then a dollar was a whole week's allowance, not something to be spent frivolously. By way of context, gas only cost 35 cents a gallon, a postage stamp 3 cents. Anyway, I was glad to get my money's worth for what felt like a significant investment.

Our letters were honest and unselfconscious. From the beginning, I didn't worry much about what I was writing to Fran. I didn't feel that I had to censor my thoughts much, or be someone other than myself. Of course, I tried to impress her now and then, and sometimes a casual shading of the truth led to misunderstandings. For example, in a letter from that year I told Fran that I had spent the afternoon playing football. I have already confessed my total lack of interest in the sport, so what I was alluding to was some sort of backyard game with some of the guys. I probably mentioned it in a misguided attempt to add *machismo* to whatever image she held of me. It had the unintended effect of making her think I was actually on a football team. In her very next letter she asked what position I played. I responded by saying "In football I was quarterback. I was going to one of our games in Glen Rock tomorrow night but no one else is going that I know." Pretty clever, eh? Honest answer about the position I played in that backyard game followed immediately by referring to going to a real game. Fran couldn't possibly infer any longer that I was on the school team. There was no further questioning about my football career.

In another letter, Fran asked who I had brought to a dance. "Don't tell me you don't have a crush on some girl. It's fair and square to date someone else if your favorite friend is not handy. Right? That's the way I figure it." That remark seemed to set the tone for the next several years of our correspondence. We both agreed that we could be "favorite friends" and still date with impunity, so why not keep writing? Had either of us been more possessive, our correspondence would likely have imploded fairly quickly.

Over time, and without really planning to, Fran and I became committed pen pals. We didn't know it, but we were getting to know each other better than many kids who actually lived in the same place and went to the same school. There was something about sharing our lives in writing that allowed us to open up more freely than we might have in face-to-face communication. We weren't distracted by concerns about what the other might think or say, and peer pressure, the great bane of adolescence, didn't apply.

*October 14, 1957*

*1:15 P.M.*

*Dear Bob,*

*Please excuse me for writing to you on school paper. I know it's not the right thing to do.*

*I'm ordinarily in Art at this time but the Art instructor is sick so we have a study hall with Mrs. Partridge who is very nice. I don't have her for any subjects or studies at all. I think she teaches English and Latin.*

*We must be in school at 8:10 but classes don't start until about 8:15. We have 6 periods about 45-50 minutes long. We dismiss at 2:00 p.m.*

*Did I tell you I am taking field drum lessons? Next year I might play in the school band. Do you play an instrument?*

*Have you heard from Tony lately? Last time I saw him he said you were writing to "Clare" and that he never expected you to write me. Oh well, everything's possible.*

*The freshman football team is playing Methuen this afternoon at three.*

*Do you go to movies often? We (the girls) usually go every Friday. If*
*you want to see a "Great Movie" see "An Affair to Remember." You might*
*not like it but your girl most likely would. Another good one is "A Face in*
*the Crowd."*

*I can hardly wait to get our school pictures back. I'll bet mine came out*
*terrible. They usually do.*

*We are going to have class elections tomorrow morning.*

*Our first Student Government dance is around the first of November. I*
*think they might pair the couples off by putting names in a hat.*

*I'm not too sure if I'll be going to Virginia because I haven't heard from*
*my cousin in about two weeks.*

*Je crois de vous. Faire vous amer moi? J'espèrer vous faire. S'il vous*
*plait écrire a moi. Merci mon cheri.*

*Love you lots,*

*Fran*

This letter gave me some key insights to Fran and her life in Andover. Well, key
insights to a 14-year-old. To an adult, the things I learned might simply be silly
nonsense. But to us kids, these were important things to know.

First of all, I learned that she goofed off in study hall by writing letters instead
of doing homework. My kind of girl!

She had a shorter school day than I did. I went from about 8:00 to 3:00. How
lucky she was to have gotten out a whole hour earlier!

She had budding musical interests. (But she never did play the drum.)

She liked chick flicks, though the term hadn't been coined in 1957. Back
then we called them girl movies.

This letter also reveals that after only a couple weeks of school, her French was good enough that she could add a whole paragraph in that language to the end of the letter.

Since I wasn't taking French I had no idea what she said to me. I've translated now, and it reads: "I believe of you. To do you to bitter me. I hope to make you. Please write to me. Thanks, my dear." Something tells me that is not exactly what she intended to say, except maybe at the end. Perhaps it's best that Internet translators had not been invented in 1957. Without it, I could go on blissfully imagining whatever it was I wanted her to be saying.

We kept on writing, barely mentioning what was going on in the world outside our own lives. Only occasionally we did make references to current events. One such reference was my allusion to Sputnik in this letter:

Nov. 4, 1957

Dear Fran,

I have just finished my homework and it is my first chance in weeks to write to you.

Things have sure been busy around here. I fell down during a game of pitch and catch on Saturday night and landed on my head. I got a slight concussion.

Our football team won its last two games of the season to put us in about 4th place.

Somebody gave my name to the school paper for hearing "Sputnik" on my short-wave. They spelled my name Zealsdorf instead of Zielsdorf.

What did you mean by field drums? Are they like trap drums? I play a ukulele or at least try to.

Incidentally, I am not writing to Clare. Tony must be mistaken.

The "Hunchback of Notre Dame" just came to York and I hope I can

get to see it. Friday afternoon I don't have school, so I may see it then.

How was the Student Government dance?  Friday night at the Country

Club there was a Record Hop. It was supposed to be in costume but

when the four of us got there everyone was in khakis or Bermudas so we

went home and changed. It turned out to be pretty cool.

Can you do the "Stroll"?  They do it differently in some schools in York

than in others.

My French isn't so good but I'll keep writing to you and whatever else

you said.

Amo tu,

Bob

My paragraph about Sputnik was meant to convey a couple of things. First, I wanted Fran to know about my short wave radio. That year, I was an aspiring ham radio operator. By doing odd jobs around the house, and with additional contributions from my generous father, I had saved enough money to buy a Heathkit short wave receiver. I was learning to listen at the time. My plan was to master the technical side of transmitting but in reality I never got any further than the listening stage. With my short wave receiver, I could actually tune in to Sputnik's annoying beeps and hear them with my own ears. I felt very special to experience this historical event first-hand. But like my friends and most Americans, I was also frightened by what it could mean.

The Soviet Union had shocked the world by launching Sputnik, the first satellite ever sent into earth orbit. This little sphere, smaller in diameter than a basketball, was flying around us at 18,000 miles per hour emitting eerie electronic noises on a special radio frequency as it communicated whatever it had to say back to Russia. The whole country was on edge. Just what were the Russians' intentions? If they could send an object into earth orbit, surely they could easily start lobbing bombs at US cities. Even to us oblivious teenagers, the concern that the folks around us felt was palpable.

The second thing I wanted to convey was to point out to Fran that she, too, had been misspelling Zielsdorf, making the common error of putting the "e" before the "i". This subtle tactic worked, at least temporarily. Fran spelled the name correctly in her next letter, though she wobbled a bit after that. By the end of freshman year, she had mastered it.

It turned out that we didn't move to Chicago after all. In October, Dad announced that he had left his job with Oliver for a better one with Westinghouse Air Brake Corporation. We were going to move to Milwaukee, renting a house in the suburb of Whitefish Bay while my parents looked for a house to buy. I would be attending Dominican High School, which was also in Whitefish Bay. It was only about three quarters of a mile from our house, my parents told me, so I could walk to and from school. The four months from the time Dad announced the move until we actually relocated seemed to take forever. But somehow I got through it, Christmas and all. My first report from my new home was positive. Things were promising in Wisconsin!

Feb. 10, 1958

Dear Fran,

Well we finally moved. I am fairly well settled in everything. The new school is beautiful. It is one block long and has an auditorium, a gym with

3 basketball courts and a Little Theater. I take all the courses I did in York except General Science.

At our parties we just dance, raise a ruckus and go outside after curfew and a few other necessary things to liven it up. If you want to keep things interesting try inventing a new dance step. I have a real cool one.

The picture didn't come out right, so I am afraid you will have to wait for a while. The flash bulb caused a glare on the fireplace screen.

I have 3 sisters and a dog. The sisters are all little brats.

Did your snow ever melt? It has been between -9 degrees and +12 degrees for the past 4 days and we have 8 to 12 inches of the crummiest snow you ever saw.

How do you like French? I hate Latin and in 2 more years I will either take Spanish or French

The population of Whitefish Bay is about 20,000. Whitefish Bay is a suburb of Milwaukee with its own post office, police dept., fire dept. and shopping district. It is real neat. What is Geri's cousin's name? Tell Geri to tell her cousin to look me up. My phone number is WO 23631.

I will probably see Tony this summer. He hopes to come here and I hope to go up there also.

Yesterday I saw the Milwaukee Auto Show. It was tremendous. One of the models who was demonstrating an Imperial had a $15,000 dress on!

Amor,

Bob

Looking back at the letters from our freshman year in high school, I think they paint both a portrait of two youngsters getting to know each other and a picture of American life in the 1950s—from a teenager's point of view at least.

We listened to and commented on popular songs. Some of our favorites were "Dee Dee Dinah," "The Story of My Life," "Kewpie Doll," and "Skinny Minnie." We danced the stroll, the bop, and the chalypso. (The latter was a dance craze that combined the beats of cha-cha and calypso.) We went to school dances and parties and enjoyed bowling, skating, and sledding. And we still found time for our studies. Both Fran and I made the honor rolls in our schools.

Today's kids do many of the same things we did over a half-century ago, but not in the same way. There are still wholesome social events, but today's kids have to fend off pressures to try sex and drugs that didn't exist in the 50s. Back then, TV married couples like Ozzie and Harriet were shown sleeping in twin beds—the networks weren't allowed to show a couple sharing the same double bed, much less something racier. The songs we listened to and the movies we watched were much more innocent, too. Elvis Presley was considered profane for swiveling his hips when he performed. But contrast the words of, say, "Blue Suede Shoes" to practically anything by Eminem and you'll see a dramatic difference.

With so much less shown on screen, a kid could go to any top movie without having to produce an ID to prove he or she was old enough. Finally, most teens had little privacy in which to get in trouble. Mom was home after school. The Internet didn't exist—you might find racy material somewhere if you looked, but it generally required a trip to the library and a peek at back issues of National Geographic. Kids didn't have their own phones; you talked on the phone in the family kitchen or living room, which strictly limited not only what you said but the time you had to say it in.

Gradually, Fran and I filled each other in on our families. She learned that I have three sisters. I learned that she had a sister and brother, and that her maternal grandparents as well as an aunt lived in her household. I was really struck by her extended family. I knew that some people lived that way, but I didn't know any of them. My father's family in Wausau came close, but they lived in two parts of a duplex rather than in a single-family home. Fran's extended family home was neither good nor bad in my eyes, just different. Other than that, our families seemed fairly similar. She was an oldest child, her father was an executive, and her mother was a full-time housewife.

Our letters talked about what we got for Christmas, what movies we had seen, and when school was going to end for the summer. Our letters also discussed when we might get to see each other again, trying to make any opportunity work. Once, Fran told me that her family was going to Virginia to visit some cousins. In my thinking, Virginia had to be pretty close to York. Maybe they could stop by for a visit on their way. Of course, Virginia *isn't* actually very close to York—certainly not close enough for her parents to drive many miles out of their way just so a couple of pen pals could see each other.

Our best hope for an in-person meeting was that I would somehow get to pay Tony another visit. I wrote Fran several times that I was hoping that might happen; in response, she repeatedly asked when. For a short while, the plan was close to becoming a reality. But our hopes were eventually dashed when Tony called off my visit. I guess his parents weren't ready to play host again. Whatever the reason, a visit in the summer of 1958 was not to be.

When would we see each other again?

It was an unanswerable question to two 14-year-olds.

# CHAPTER THREE

*I*N SEPTEMBER, 1958, OZZIE AND HARRIET WERE IN THEIR SEVENTH YEAR on television and Fran and I were 15. The wholesome, clean-cut Nelson family had been with us half our lives. They were as familiar to us as some of the real people we knew, and no doubt they had shaped our characters in subtle ways. Needless to say, the show didn't accurately reflect the complexities or the dark sides of "real life." Back then, no television show did. But it did reflect life as we *thought* it was and thought it would always be.

That fall, Fran entered Andover High School as a sophomore. She wrote soon after school began.

> *Wednesday*
> *September 3, 1958*
> *Dear Bob,*
> *How's everything up North? Everything here is running smoothly, with*
> *school starting Monday and all. In a way I'll be glad to get back because*

we'll be in the new high school and with a different crowd of kids. When do you start school? What school is it this fall?

So glad you recognized me on the post card, but really I was only joshing you.

How did the swim meet turn out? Did you win a medal? How long did you stay with your cousin in Wausau? Is it a male or female cousin you visited?

Dad has been taking a lot of pictures this summer, another of his hobbies. If and when they are developed I will send you one of myself. I'm not destroying yours, it's a good picture. Who took it?

What's your new house like, s'il vous plait? When do you move in permanently? I'm getting confused with all your addresses!

Dad is teaching me to drive. He bought a '57 white Ford Skyliner—you know—hard top and convertible and that's what I'll run around in when I get my license next June. I'll be 16 the 5th of June & will get that slip of paper about 10 days later!

My sister starts seventh grade this year and it seems unbelievable! It seems odd that I'll be a sophomore too!

The boy next door just turned 16 and all he does is bomb up and down the street in his car. What a racket!

Boy, if I was talking to you I'd be all out of breath, this is such a windy letter.

Write soon and be good.

Love always,

Fran

In Milwaukee, the Zielsdorf family housing situation remained in transition. The house my parents had bought in the suburban village of Fox Point had not yet been ready when the lease was up on our first rental house in Whitefish Bay. So, during the summer, my family had moved out of rental number one and into rental number two. Finally, sometime just before school started, we left the rental world and settled into our new home at 317 East Acacia Road, Milwaukee 17, Wis.

Changing houses three times in nine months didn't faze me as much as I'm sure it did my parents. And as it turned out, I didn't miss York at all. Maybe it was because I was so happy with my new friends and my new school. Because Dominican High drew from a wide geographical area, I had friends all over. Where I was living at any point in time wasn't important.

In her first letter of the fall, Fran was already focused on that teenage dream: getting a driver's license. The magic day was still nine months off for her and even longer for me. But it wasn't too early to start imagining what life could be like with licenses in our pockets and access to the family cars.

317 E. Acacia Rd.

Milwaukee 17, Wis.

Nov. 19, 1958

Dear Fran,

I am very sorry that I have not written to you in so long. Tony wrote and said that you wondered what happened so I thought I'd better write.

I am doing this in study hall so that what's with the casual paper. It's kind of noisy. Everybody is throwing pennies—that's the latest fad for study halls.

How's it going in Andover?  What subjects are you taking?  I am taking Biology, Latin II, Religion II, English II, Geometry (plane), and Spanish I.

My aunt is coming from Wausau, Wisconsin for Thanksgiving. I am going to try to convince her to sell me her 1950 Ford next summer. She said that she wants to get rid of it. Keep your fingers crossed.

When is your birthday?  I am taking it for granted that you are still 15.

How about sending me a picture?  I have got several coming up of me and I'll send you one. They should be better than that last one you got.

It is now 8:10 p.m.

The bell rang at "got." Right now it is 9:10 in Andover. We are on Central Standard Time.

Tomorrow is the day when they give out letters and numerals awards to the football teams. I am getting a minor "D."

There are some dances coming up. I wish you were here. What is the latest dancing rage in the East?  It is various forms of the jitterbug here. Also the "jack" still rates pretty well.

I was just thinking, are you still willing to "pay" me for that medal?  I didn't realize a good thing when I had it, then.

Don't forget that picture. Write soon.

Whole lotta lovin',

Bob

By this time I had abandoned the practice of covering the backs of my envelopes with indecipherable letters and had gone the more sophisticated gold seal route. Unfortunately, when I ordered the seals I didn't know how to indicate the order of my initials properly. The seals were delivered with my middle initial, L, rather than Z in the dominant position. They had cost me too much to toss them out and start over, so I proceeded to use them up, as ridiculous as they were. To her credit, Fran never mentioned the mistake.

As my letter shows, I was planning ahead to the driving stage, too, and even hoping to get my own wheels. Aunt Lucille's 1950 Ford would have made quite a statement in 1959 Milwaukee. Of course, I had no idea how I would have found the money to buy it, but it was fun to think about.

My letter includes another mention of football: the casual reference to getting a football letter. I was probably hoping this would make a big impression and that Fran would overlook how I had earned it.

As the world's skinniest kid, I wouldn't have made much of a football player even if I had been interested in the game. Instead, my friends who played had talked me into being the team manager. Usually, the position involved little more than doing errands for the coach, helping with whatever chores he needed. But I had lucked out. Needing a "spotter," the stadium announcers asked me to fill that role. I got to sit with the announcers in the press box during our games, helping identify the players on our team so the right kid got credit for making a play. It was fun. And since the announcer's booth was enclosed, it was a lot warmer sitting in there than standing on the sidelines!

In a burst of hormone-driven chutzpah, I closed my letter by asking Fran if she would be willing to "pay" me for my scapular medal. I was referring, of course, to the kiss she had offered to give me the day Tony and I had visited her house. As I wrote this letter I had no idea how and when we would ever see each other again, so there would have been no way to collect payment. Still, the thought was strong fuel for a teenager's fantasies.


*180 Chestnut Street*

*Andover, Massachusetts*

*November 25, 1958*

*1:30 P.M.*

*Study in Cafeteria*

*Dear (forgetful) Bob,*

*I was so glad to get another letter from Wisconsin that I decided to answer*

*it immediately. (Jan just looked that word up in her dictionary for me.)*

*(My spelling & penmanship are getting worse every minute.)*

*Here's hoping your aunt decides to let you buy her car. I sure wish I*

*could have one of my own, but guess I'll have to be satisfied driving our*

*1957 white Ford Skyliner. I will be sixteen on June 5th, 1960.*

*How tall are you now? Last time I saw you I was a little taller than you. I'm only 5'7" at present.*

*Since you wrote to me during study I figured you wouldn't mind me doing the same. We get out about noon until Monday. How long do you have out?*

*This year I only have four subjects to worry me: French II, Biology, English II, and Algebra II, plus extra-curricular.*

*When will you get your license?*

*You asked for a picture but my school pictures, that were taken in early October, are all gone. I'll send you one when I get a good one of myself. Please send yours along anyway, O.K?*

*The teacher in this study is called "the Hawk" and anyone can plainly see why, despite the fact that her name is Miss Hawksworth. She is gigantic & is wearing "desert boots." She is standing over me & makes me very nervous.*

*You asked about payments on a medal. Do you charge interest over a period of weeks, months or years? Anyway, I guess it would be my duty as a solid citizen to pay for that which I have taken.*

*Pen running out of ink! I put a new cartilage in my pen.*

*Do you play football, basketball, etc.?*

*Wish you could come & see Tony (& me) during the Christmas holidays!*

*The dismissal bell is about to ring so I shall sign off.*

Amour toujours,

*Fran*

P.S. Écrive-moi bientot!

*Tuesday*

*Hi,*

*I forgot to mail this, so since I have nothing to do during this study just thought I'd say "hello." Don't forget to write.*

Wow! Obviously Fran knew exactly what I meant by payment for the medal, so maybe she remembered making the offer. I couldn't have asked for a better response. I'm sure my imagination was thrown into overdrive at that point.

There was so much going on in that letter I probably didn't notice her comment that she had put "cartilage" in her pen. Most pens then were fountain pens; the easiest to use accepted ink cartridges. You bought a box of cartridges, placed one in the barrel of your pen and screwed the pen point into it. When the cartridge ran dry, you just replaced it. The alternative was to refill your pen using a bottle of ink. You had to make sure the bottle top was on tight, tilt the bottle to fill the well at the top of it, dip the pen point into the well, and squeeze a tube in the barrel to suction ink into the pen. The invention of cartridges made filling a pen faster, easier, and cleaner, and greatly reduced the chance you would spill ink all over in the process.

Amazingly, in my next letter I never mentioned the kissing "payment." I suppose I was so tongue-tied I didn't know what to say. With no idea of where the subject was leading, it must have felt wiser to drop it. Evidently I had already begun to live by the adage that it's better to remain silent and be thought a fool, than to open your mouth and remove all doubt.

317 E. Acacia Rd.

Milwaukee 17, Wis.

12/9/58

Dear Fran,

My aunt will sell me her car if she hasn't sold by the time I want it. Now I'm

not sure if want it because I will always have a car or two of the family's to

drive. Right now we have three cars: A '57 Merc station wagon, '56 Ford

convertible, and a '59 Ford Skyliner. You said you'll be 16 on June 5th,

1960. Does that mean that you are 14 now or did you mean 1959?

Right now I am 5'10" and going strong still.

I am eligible for my license on September 4, 1959. I just hope that

they don't pass a certain law saying that you can't drive until 18 before

then. Some jerk cooked up that idea.

If all goes well my picture will be in my next letter.

What does "écrive-moi bientot!" mean? My French isn't so good.

You asked about basketball. I went out with 45 other guys for

the varsity team. Only 15 made it. Guess who got cut with the unco-

ordinated. We have stupendous teams this year. The varsity hasn't won a

football or basketball game yet.

Well it's 9:15 p.m. and I'm running out of stuff to say so I'll cut out.

Remember '57!

Bob


Cars and driving were still hot topics in our minds. It clearly felt to both of us

like it was taking forever to turn sixteen. Fran had inadvertently added a whole

year to the wait in her letter; she would turn sixteen in 1959, not 1960.

I was one of the youngest in my class, which meant a lot of my pals were already driving. To make matters worse, at that time some politicians were floating the concept that the driving age should be raised to 18. I was terrified that they could change the rules before I had a chance at the freedom a license would offer. Oh, the injustice! Two years represented a whopping one-eighth of my lifetime. I could hardly stand to imagine my friends with licenses safely secured while I was sentenced to another two years of waiting for the same privilege. Fortunately, driving at 18 was an idea ahead of its time, and all my worries turned out to be unfounded.

As our letters indicate, height was also an important issue to us at the time. I don't remember Fran being taller than I was when we met, but she does. In any case, I had shot up in the intervening year. At a little over 5' 10", I was now among the tallest in my class. At 5' 7", Fran was among the tallest girls in hers. Fran would only grow another inch in the years that followed, but I would eventually reach six feet, two inches.

The December letter printed above wrapped up our correspondence for 1958 and marked the halfway point of our sophomore years. A letter from Fran kicked off the new year of 1959.

*Monday*

*January 5, 1959*

*Dear Bob,*

*Here's hoping you have recovered from Christmas and your strenuous vacation, New Year's Eve of course, too!*

*Getting up for school this morning was a terrible task as I had not been up before noon since December 23rd when vacation started. It was rather a dull vacation because nothing was doing except New Year's Eve when I went to a great party! As is expected on this particular night some of the more daring boys were drinking. One, named Robin, was so thirsty that by 12:30 he was out in a cold stupor lying on the floor! He was really something to see!*

*What did you do New Year's Eve? (Hope you can remember!)*

*Sorry about my mistake. I will be sixteen June 5th, 1959 and surely hope to have my license by the 20th so I can take the car to school before we get out for the summer, which seems so far away at present.*

*Dad is watching a western on T.V. so if you see a few bullet holes through the paper you'll understand.*

*Your varsity sounds amazingly like ours! We won three football games but not one basketball game so far and we have played seven.*

*Don't forget your picture in your next letter! Do you have my newest school picture?*

*Saw Tony at a Catholic Youth Organization dance recently. He's still as funny as ever.*

*Our mid-terms start three weeks from tomorrow. We have them for one week, after we have three more weeks of study, then a week's vacation sometime in February. I can hardly wait!*

*Well, be good and don't do anything I wouldn't do!!*

*Love & stuff,*

*Fran*

*P.S. Écrive moi, bientot!*

*(translation – write soon, Bob)*

I responded quickly.

Jan. 8, 1959

7:38 P.M. (C.S.T.)

My Dearest Fran:

How's that for a beginning? Glad to hear from you. Thanks for the Christmas card. Your sleeping hours for vacation sound strangely familiar. My sleeping hours were on the average from about 1:30 to 11:30. Our vacation started Dec. 23 too. The last day was Dec. 20.

What I did on New Year's Eve is to be kept under your hat. If it ever gets back to Milwaukee some people will be ruined.

I couldn't go anywhere on New Year's Eve except to a friend's house. His name is Jim. His parents were at a party at our house. This is a long story. My girl lives in Shorewood. That is a neighboring village and there was no transportation to her house. But, we wanted to see each other so a little before midnight, Jim, who doesn't have his license, and I took his dad's car and went down to Barb's house. I ran in, gave her the traditional New Year's kiss, ran back to the car and got back to Whitefish Bay— where Jim lives—in time enough that his dad never caught on. Wow! That took some saying.-Your party sounded like a real blast. I got along pretty well with the joy juice, but not enough to get as boozed as your friend Robin.

I had a terrific vacation—3 dances and two parties plus other amusements.

I don't have your latest picture. I hope I can find one of mine for you.

By the way, what wouldn't you do so I know my limits. I have been pretty active and that doesn't necessarily mean I've been good.

And now, from the elevator shaft of the Grand Batz Hotel, this is Harry Nostrils, with a warm good-bye to all.

With ardent love,

Bob

P.S. How's that for a closing?

P.P.S. Letter or something coming with large, lousy picture.

As an adult, I'm embarrassed to show you this letter. But back then I was only 15 and starting to feel my oats. Kindly overlook the "sophomoric" greeting and closing; now I understand where that word comes from!

Instead, focus on the New Year's Eve caper. It really happened. Though I didn't mention this, I recall that it had just snowed, leaving the roads slippery. There we were, two unlicensed and inexperienced high schoolers, off on a major adventure late at night and in bad driving conditions. Given how many bad things could have happened but didn't, I truly believe the Lord was looking out for us. Who knows why? Whatever the reason, there was no accident. No being stopped by the cops. No parents arriving home early to catch us red handed. Just the adrenaline thrill of the forbidden ride—and a quick New Year's kiss with my girlfriend, Barbara.

I had started going with Barbara earlier that year. She and her identical twin sister, Kathy, were the youngest of a large family and the only ones still living at home. Barb was a lot shorter than I, and had medium length brown hair. She was also one of the smartest kids in our class, an A student but not a nerd. Barb was fun to be with; we liked doing the same kinds of things, dancing and bowling, sock hops and beach parties, necking to Johnny Mathis. She was also one of those girls who could get along well with many different people, and for that reason she was widely liked.

My letter about the New Year's Eve adventure implies there might have been some alcohol involved. I actually think I put that reference there in hopes of impressing Fran with my manly ways. I don't recall drinking anything that night. In the letter, I also brag about "not necessarily" being good. But, hey, other than abetting car theft, I was actually well-behaved that night.

There was one law which I broke with some regularity that year, though I did it more or less with Mom and Dad's blessing: the one making it illegal to hitchhike. Barbara lived on Newton Avenue, in the suburb of Shorewood, about four and a half miles south of my home on Acacia Road in Fox Point. To visit her, I would walk the half block from my house to Lake Drive, the major north-south road along Lake Michigan, and then thumb a ride.

Even in those days, hitchhiking was never completely safe. But in areas like the North Shore suburbs of Milwaukee, it was relatively common and problem free. Today's news is full of far too many stories about missing kids to believe that there is any safe haven for hitchhikers. Whether or not any of the victims were thumbing rides isn't as significant as the fact that the world seems to have somehow spawned a huge number of predators.

Thumbing a ride to and from Barbara's was rarely a problem. I never felt threatened—in fact, I met some very nice people along the way. I only had one unpleasant experience. I just couldn't get a ride one day and, as I walked along with my thumb out, I was stopped by the Whitefish Bay police. Naturally, they looked at me like I was nuts when I kept repeating that I lived in Fox Point. They kindly refrained from giving me a ticket or even a formal warning, but they did tell me sternly that no matter where I lived, I had better not be hitchhiking in

Whitefish Bay again. Good boy that I was, I wound up walking all the way home. Man, did I ever want that driver's license!

When she responded to my January 8 letter, Fran answered my flippant question about "limits."

"Of course I don't mind if you go out with other girls. I certainly have lots of dates myself, but please don't forget me!" She added, "Do you think that you may possibly grace Andover with your presence here this summer? I surely hope so."

As this suggests, we continued to think about how and when we might see each other again. Travel to Andover was always high on my wish list.

"I hope to come to Andover this summer if I can talk Tony into it. I'd sure like to see you again. It has been almost two years. I'd like to have you come out here sometime but it might be tricky to arrange," I wrote that year, adding, "Tony turned 16 so you might see him driving up telephone poles in their '59 Olds. I managed to transfer the white paint of our garage door to the coral paint of our car door."

For the balance of the school year and through the summer we wrote once or twice a month, mostly just trading information and joking with each other. For example, Fran wrote: "Do you have Spring fever yet? They say a sure cure is a date with a terrific kid!!"

Referring to a trip I had taken with my family, I told her, "Florida was terrific. I did see more than oranges—real peaches. We drove down and flew back. Dad is bringing the car back and making business calls on the way. Don't panic with the frogs [in biology lab]. Don't bite them and they won't bite you. I don't have spring fever yet because it's not Spring-like yet."

I also tried to explain my emerging philosophy of dating. "As near as I can come to it when I go with somebody it's not just 'pot luck.' I like to pick the cream of the crop, so to speak. That's why I've been writing to you for nearly 2 years and going with Barb for 4 mo." As I said earlier, I was definitely feeling my oats that year!

More prosaically, I told Fran that my school subjects for next year were to be Chemistry, Advanced Algebra, English III, Religion III, US History, Speech II, and Phys. Ed. Fran told me that hers were English III, Plane Geometry, French III, Chemistry, and US History. She also mentioned that she had made the Honor Roll, adding that "Oh, we're still working on those frogs, their insides, yet! I've taken your advice and they haven't bitten me yet." She was going to go to the beach during her mid-April holiday after an all day picnic and dance. "We got our boat out of storage last week and are giving it a new coat of white paint. We got new water skis too." "What do you and Barb do for fun?" she continued. "There's absolutely nothing to do around here especially if it doesn't cost too much."

I answered Fran's question. Barbara and I had stopped seeing each other for a time, so my answer was in the past tense. (I don't remember why any more. I have some vague recollection that I asked another girl to a party and Barb got mad.) "What Barb and I do for fun is sort of hard to say. But when I wasn't at her house we went to movies or bowling or walked down to the beach or something. We always found something to do that wasn't too expensive mainly because I am broke most of the time."

I also returned to the subject of getting together. "I asked my father if you could come out alone this summer, but he said no," I wrote. "Doesn't trust me I guess. It looks like I won't see you unless I go to Tony's or if you can talk your parents into a vacation in Milwaukee. This summer will make it 2 years since we met and I think that it is high time we got together again." The comment about my dad not trusting me was a throwaway jest. In reality, the amount of trust my father placed in me was remarkable. I had the freedom to do many things at a much younger age than anyone else I knew. At least in part, this was because I didn't abuse the privileges he granted.

As summer vacation approached, there was some talk about the possibility that my father would make a business trip to Boston and that I might get to go along. But that never happened.

Fran wrote two letters that summer, filling me in on what she was doing, and I responded once. Fran's letters were especially fun because she wrote on Nebbish stationery. More about that in a bit. These are the letters we exchanged before school started once again.

*Sunday, Aug. 9, 1959*

*6:00 P.M.*

*Dear Bob,*

*How's everything? Things here are sort of dull because it's been raining so much this weekend.*

*I got your letter while I was at the lake. Mom sent it up. I stayed an extra week with a girl I met up there. I've sure had a fabulous summer. Wish it wasn't almost over.*

*I still can't ski on one ski yet, matter of fact I haven't had enough nerve to try. But I can jump the wake, sort of.*

*Went sailing last Saturday. We went up for the weekend and Steve Wingate took me. It was fabulous but so rough that all of a sudden the tiller snapped and we hardly had anything to steer with. We had to take the jib off and try to get back to his house. It was sure fun, though quite wet.*

*What have you been doing? Has your father been to Boston yet? If he hasn't, be sure you're with him when he comes.*

*Do you have your license yet? When is your birthday?*

*I get the car almost every day and last week we got caught in the rain twice with the top of the Ford down of course.*

*When we were up at the lake, I got caught on a dead stump going to my girlfriend's over an old dirt road. We had to have the left front side repainted and everything, but dad was real good about the whole thing. I got the car the very next day!*

*This past week has been sort of dull except for last night. Wally and I went to Hampton Beach Casino and saw Lester Lanin. Boy, he is just fabulous, the greatest. I got sort of mangled trying to get one of the felt hats he passes out at the end of the night but I still managed to grab two of them.*

*What are you doing for excitement? Dating lots of beautiful girls?*

*I really think it's wonderful that we have written for two years without seeing each other, but I know I enjoy it tremendously! How about you?*

*Well, guess I'll hit the road. Be good & try to get to Andover. I miss you still. Write soon when you have a free minute or two.*

*Love ya lots,*

*Fran*

*P.S. Think a picture of yours truly may be in next letter, you poor boy!*

I responded promptly.

8.18.59

8:30 P.M.

(all is well)

Dear Fran,

How's life? (Stupid question, isn't it?)

I'm glad you've had a good summer. Things have been duller than #%*&. Tomorrow starts a 5-day canoe trip which should liven things up a little.

I went up to Big Cedar Lake with some kids (a girl I know had a cottage up there) and went water skiing all day. I tried one ski skiing & could do it for 50' or so. Then I fell, hard and fast right in the kisser.

My father isn't going to Boston so I guess I haven't got an excuse to come see you this summer. I'd sure like to though.

I got a temporary permit for Driver's Ed class & will get my license Sept. 8. My 16th birthday is Sept. 4.

School (now I have to get my mouth washed out) starts the 10th.

I am sort of going steady with Barb (I have now for 8 ½ months) but still go out with someone else occasionally.

Football practice starts tomorrow. We better have a good year. We got a new coach so I guess we will. Our last year's record 0-8. Our coach's team last year was 8-0.

Please write me soon and send that picture if possible.

Much love,

Bob

I loved Fran's new Nebbish stationery. Nebbishes were a huge cultural icon in the 1950s, especially in the East. Created by Herb Gardner, they caught on in a big faddish way. Originally a Yiddish word, "nebbish" meant something similar to today's "nerd": someone without much personality, who just can't *quite* get it together. Anyway, reading these letters was double the fun: I got to find out what was going on with Fran, but I got to enjoy the hip Nebbishness of the letter paper too.

Fran's summer highlights were clearly based around Lake Winnipesaukee, a huge and beautiful body of water in New Hampshire located about two hours north of Andover. It was exciting for me to read about her adventures. She was already driving and, lucky her, got to use the family car frequently. She was going out with a guy named Wally, sailing and water skiing with her family and other friends, and just generally having the time of her life.

Fran's father did things I would have liked to do, but couldn't because they weren't among my own dad's interests. I had learned to sail, and once almost bought myself a little nine-foot sailboat, but most of the boating I did was with people outside of my family. Our neighbor was an expert sailboat racer, and I learned to sail crewing for him in Lake Michigan races. And when the St. Lawrence Seaway opened in 1959, I would stand on the beach and imagine that just from a block from my home I could travel by boat all the way around the world. I loved the fact that Bob Jordan was a serious devotee of boating and that Fran's family constantly enjoyed the use of their boat during the summer. By contrast, my own chances to enjoy this pastime were quite rare.

But my summer wasn't so bad. I was taking Driver's Ed in eager anticipation of my sixteenth birthday in September. I was dating Barb again, but not exclusively. I got to visit a lake and try my hand (and the rest of me) at water skiing, too. Neither Fran nor I became accomplished skiers that summer, but we enjoyed ourselves. Neither of us had summer jobs, so life was easy. But in the midst of all our separate activities, we both held onto the dream that we might somehow, someday, get to see each other again.

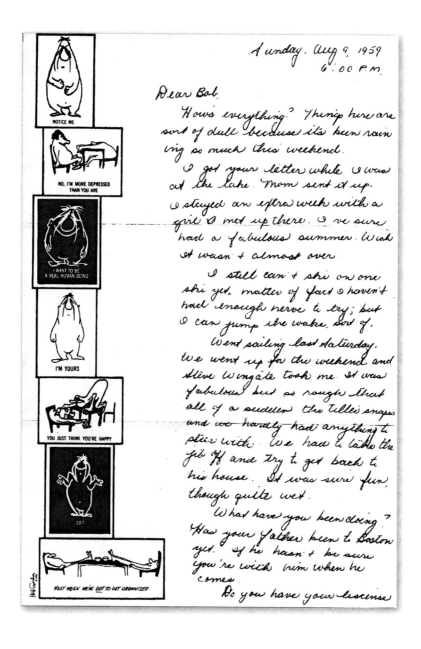

Sunday, Aug 9, 1959
6:00 P.M.

Dear Bob,

How's everything? Things here are sort of dull because it's been raining so much this weekend.

I got your letter while I was at the lake. Mom sent it up. I stayed an extra week with a girl I met up there. I've sure had a fabulous summer. Wish it wasn't almost over.

I still can't ski on one ski yet. Matter of fact I haven't had enough nerve to try; but I can jump the wake sort of.

Went sailing last Saturday. We went up for the weekend and Steve Wingate took me. It was fabulous but so rough that all of a sudden the tiller snapped and we hardly had anything to steer with. We had to take the jib off and try to get back to his house. It was sure fun, though quite wet.

What have you been doing? Has your father been to Boston yet. If he hasn't be sure you're with him when he comes.

Do you have your liscense

# CHAPTER FOUR

*I*N THE FALL OF 1959, FRAN AND I WERE BOTH 16-YEAR-OLD HIGH SCHOOL juniors. In my first letter from that fall, I announced that I was a half an inch over six feet and weighed 145 pounds. Braggart that I was, I probably pushed the scales at more like 142 or 143.

Sometime during the summer, I had again broken things off with Barbara. In one letter, I told Fran that I had met a new girl, Lisa. Lisa went to Whitefish Bay High School and was a year behind me. I had met her late that summer at an impromptu party at the house of one of my friends. Mom had asked me to pick up some bread while I was out, so I showed up at the gathering with a loaf of Wonder Bread tucked under my arm. There were a number of kids there I didn't know, but everyone wanted to meet the bread guy and find out why I was carrying the thing around. One of those kids was a cute girl named Lisa with a long pony tail.

Lisa seemed different from the other girls, somehow. Not different in the sense that they had two heads and she had one; different because they were familiar to me by now and Lisa was new. Being from another school made her seem somehow exotic as well.

I became immediately infatuated. I don't know why anyone falls in love at first sight. At 16 I'm sure I didn't even know what love was. But I felt an immediate and powerful chemistry—a reaction I had never experienced before. A bolt of lightning? A ton of bricks? Whatever hit me, it left me with the intense feeling that I just had to get to know this girl better.

She was about 5' 2", so she literally looked up to me. That night she was wearing blue jeans, a white blouse, and sneakers. She was funny, teasing me about the bread. It had obviously made an impression on her—a favorable one, I hoped. With her slightly prominent front teeth, you wouldn't say she was pretty, but she was attractively self-confident and witty. After we talked for a bit, I made sure I got her phone number and her permission to call. And call I did, the next day.

As we started spending more time together, I learned she had an older brother and sister who had already left home. I don't know what her father did for a living but they lived in a modest two-story house in Whitefish Bay. Her parents were Finnish—Lisa claimed to be something like 47th in line for the throne of Finland—but in reality they were an unpretentious family. Lisa had a certain amount of street smarts. Without pretense or sophistication, she just knew what was in and what was out, what was hip and what was square, what to wear and what would never do.

Lisa was an avid student of modern dance. I wasn't sure what that was exactly, but I found out it took a great deal of her time and energy. Driven as she was to perfect her dance skills, she was carefree in other respects. Though she wasn't an A student, she wasn't a slacker, either. Very relaxed socially, she mixed easily with everyone and was quite self-confident. I enjoyed her quick wit and her broad sense of humor. Her personality had a bit of Sandra Dee's Gidget in it, along with a little Audrey Hepburn romance. Being madly in love for a 15-year-old boy was more hormone-driven than it was something carefully considered. All I knew was that I really liked this girl. We had a lot of fun being together. We went to parties, we danced, we necked, we cruised around town in my car with her sitting not at the passenger-side window but right next to me on the bench seat. We talked about how we saw life and about our hopes for the future—all the things that young love meant in the 50s.

She frequently called me "Robert," not "Bob" like everyone else. She had long hair which she wore in a pony tail 95 percent of the time. She would frequently pull it over her shoulder and play with it, or move her head so it flipped around a bit.

She could be very headstrong and she definitely had firm ideas about right and wrong, about what she liked and didn't like. Although she was a Lutheran and I a Catholic, we shared the same core values. As our friendship grew she began to look up to me not just physically but in other ways as well. That was a heady rush at my young age. I was a year older and a year ahead of her in school. When I was with her I always felt liked, loved, and respected—but also like I was the one in charge. I never took advantage of that, which is probably why she permitted it.

I spent a lot of time after school and on weekends hanging out at her house. Her parents would always greet me warmly, and then disappear into some other room so Lisa and I could have the living room to ourselves. Going with a girl from another school gave me a certain cachet at my own. For some reason, dating someone from another school was considered a "cool" thing to do. Virtually overnight I had morphed from a regular guy to a cool guy.

In one fall letter, I told Fran that I was taking a full class load of college prep courses and had decided to try out for the basketball team. I also told her that I had quit smoking. I don't actually recall being a smoker then, but I'd have picked it up honestly. Like so many Americans of this era, both of my parents were hard-core smokers. Our house was full of second hand smoke and road trips were even worse. Most 1950s cars, including ours, weren't air conditioned; their fresh air ventilation systems weren't strong enough to remove the clouds of toxic smoke generated by two adults puffing away in the front seat with the windows up. The only smoking I remember doing in those days was an occasional cigarette, which I'd bum from someone and smoke in secret, without inhaling. On the other hand, Fran was a true smoker. I found out later that she had started smoking regularly that year, following in her mother's footsteps, I guess, since her father had never picked up the habit.

I also admitted (or maybe "bragged" is more accurate) to Fran that "beer is the hardest thing I drink." In Wisconsin, it was legal to drink beer at 18. A younger kid who looked 18 could usually buy some—the dangers of teen drinking weren't really on the national radar yet, so IDs were rarely checked back then. But if that was impossible, there was always an older brother or friend around who wouldn't mind doing the buying for a party or other beer-drinking occasion. Easy as it was, though, drinking beer was still fairly rare, at least in my circles.

Fran and I exchanged only five letters before the end of that fall. Besides our school work and activities, we were busy dating others.

Being smitten with Lisa didn't preclude my pen-pal relationship with Fran, however. I wrote to her in early October, but I didn't hear back from her until mid-November. When she finally responded, I got the feeling she had never read my previous letter. Looking back at the letters now, I notice that she frequently wrote while she was in study hall or class, which would explain her distraction.

Her mid-November letter asked if I was still going out with Barb or dating anyone else. She wanted to know if I had my license, what car I was driving, and if I had taken up smoking or drinking. I had already told her all of those things, but I guess her mind was somewhere else—maybe on her own boyfriend, Wally. "Wally and I are still going out together but at present he is sort of mad at me for some reason or other. Tell me, do boys always get cross more with girls they like than is usual?" she asked.

The question inspired me to write back quickly.

Nov. 20, 1959 A.D.

12:17 P.M.

Dear Fran:

I decided to "Do unto others, etc." and write you a letter from study hall again. If I don't finish it I probably won't write for four more days, because Saturday morning I am going to go camping with a bunch of guys up north. Saturday night will be pretty cold so I better invest in some long underwear.

I have my license—to answer a question. I've had it for about 3 months. I'll be driving a '56 Ford convertible. It's black with black & white interior. We are going to get a black '60 Bonneville convertible, red interior & bucket seats. I told Lisa about the bucket seats & she wondered if I thought she was a contortionist. We are also going to get a '60 Ford Galaxie, blue.

The great philosopher will now philosophize or whatever it is that philosophers do. You asked me about guys getting cross with girls they like. I don't want to incriminate Wally, but I have found that when a guy has been going steady he gets in a rut that is hard to break out of. And one way to break out of it is to act like an ass and hope she'll tell you to get out. This may not be true, but it happened to me with Barb. I finally told her we were through & haven't seen her since.

Lisa is the girl I went steady with for 5 weeks. Then I decided it wasn't worth getting in the rut again so we broke up last Monday. So now we're going "steadily," not steady.

Now that I have bored you on that subject, I'll try it on school. Nice going on those grades. I got A in Religion, B in Chemistry, also Algebra & English, and a C in History. That's what I get for not studying.

I might have a chance to see you next summer. I'm going to France to live with a family over there for the summer. I would like to stop in Andover for a couple days at least, on the way home.

Your T-Bird sounds like a sharp car. I'd like to drag it with my Ford, sometime.

There's the bell—write soon.

Love,

Bob

If my "great philosopher" insights hit the nail on the head for Fran, I never found out. She didn't acknowledge my comments, and she and Wally continued to date. Philosophical musings aside, my letter was full of references to things that tell the tale of American life in 1959.

Most boys then were Cub or Boy Scouts. But many dropped out as they turned 14, the age at which you became an Explorer Scout. That included me. I had quit earlier, maybe around age 13. I don't recall having any friends in York who became Explorers, so at first I thought it was weird that my new friends in Milwaukee were doing it.

I wasn't sure about joining their Explorer post when they asked me. But when they assured me that the group was really just a bunch of guys from our class who liked doing stuff together outdoors, with Louie's dad as its leader and no requirements for uniforms or merit badges, I agreed to join. Despite my insistence on being cool, I did work sufficiently on merit badges to become a Life Scout, just one rank away from the vaunted Eagle Scout designation. Our late fall camping trip to northern Wisconsin involved sleeping on the snow-covered ground in tents, cooking on an open fire, and freezing our "patooties" off. But we thought it was great fun. A guy thing, no doubt.

In the car and driving department, I was truly fortunate. Dad had kept the 1956 Ford convertible that had previously been our family vehicle, so I had a car to drive. He made it clear that the Ford was not "my" car, but as long as I used it responsibly he was willing to give me driving privileges. It was a perfect car for the times and for a guy my age: sharp-looking, quick, and roomy enough to hold five friends.

At the time, Dad was Vice President and General Manager of the LeRoi Division of Westinghouse Air Brake Company. He was entitled to a company car, at that time a 1960 blue Ford Galaxie. A boxy family sedan, the Galaxie had some advanced design features, but it was still quite ugly in a 1960s sort of way.

That didn't really matter to me, as company rules wouldn't have let me drive it even if I wanted to. In contrast, the 1960 Pontiac Bonneville convertible on order for my mother was a long, low-slung, wide-track, high-powered behemoth of Detroit iron. I knew I would rarely, if ever, get to drive it myself. But I couldn't wait for it to arrive, and once it came, it was exciting just to have it in the garage.

Since the custom has since fallen out of favor, my reference to going steady with Lisa might warrant some explanation. Many if not most kids did this back then. The usual practice when a couple decided to "go steady" was for the boy to give the girl his class ring. She then wore it on a chain like a pendant to show the world she was spoken for. In some places and groups, going steady allowed a couple to go a bit further in terms of necking and parking than an uncommitted couple might, but neither Lisa nor I had that expectation.

Unfortunately for my going steady plans, I went to a school run by nuns. They considered class rings akin to graven images and golden idols, and also probably realized they would mainly be used for going steady, a major no-no in "nundom." I therefore didn't have a ring to give away. But I wasn't the only boy chasing after Lisa—and being madly infatuated, I needed to discourage the other "dogs" from sniffing around. In an era when most kids had steady boyfriends and girlfriends, not tying her down in some way risked losing her to someone else.

My buddies and I decided that I didn't have to give Lisa a class ring. Any ring would do. One afternoon a bunch of us piled in the Ford convertible and drove across town to a store where I could buy a man's ring cheaply. I found one that would work: gold (plated I'm sure) with a black, onyx-like stone. With that ring in hand, I asked Lisa to go steady. To my surprise and consternation, she wouldn't answer right away. She didn't really want to be "formally" committed, to me or anyone else. She also worried about what her parents would say. For two days, as she thought things through, I was in a state of panic.

Finally, we had a heart-to-heart talk. She had decided that she was ready to let the other guys go by the wayside and just go with me. She agreed that wearing a ring would be the best way to keep them at bay, so she agreed to accept mine. We were formally "going steady." In the short run, the strategy worked, as the other guys backed off. But neither of us was ever completely comfortable with the idea of a formal commitment. After a few months, we ended our going steady arrangement, but we each continued to go out only with the other.

It's hard to say, so many years later, what the source of our discomfort was. For her, perhaps, it was fear of parental disapproval, although her parents continued to treat me with the same friendliness and respect they always had. More likely, it may simply have been that the idea of being committed in any formal way didn't fit her. For me it would have been that my parents didn't approve of the idea. They liked Lisa, but no doubt they feared that going steady would eventually lead to dangerous behavior. In other words, in the minds of all parents, sex. Mom and Dad were willing to tolerate my arrangement, but they were keenly on guard. And to my surprise, going steady made me feel a bit more restricted than I liked. The ring had gotten the job done. Everyone knew Lisa was "my" girl. So it wasn't necessary any longer.

The real bombshell in the letter was my casual announcement that I would be traveling to France come summer, perhaps with a stop in Andover along the way. This was truly an epic event for any teenager, but for reasons I no longer remember I barely gave it any mention. In her next letter, written during Thanksgiving vacation, Fran was understandably curious.

"Your trip next summer sounds simply fantabulous. How did it all come about? Who are you going with? Why are you going, other than pleasure? Please tell me all about it," she wrote.

I answered her letter just after Christmas but I ignored the trip to France in favor of more ordinary things. I told Fran that we had gotten a "Stereo-Hi-Fi" for the living room for Christmas, on which I was listening to Kingston Trio and Peter Gunn albums. The Bonneville convertible had arrived. It had snowed 12 inches and I'd obtained permission to drive 30 miles north to ski, only to have the snow melt before I could leave. I had been elected junior class president. Finally, I told Fran that my friends were stocking up on booze for our upcoming New Year's Eve party. Who knows why I never mentioned France?

I heard from Fran shortly after the start of the new year of 1960.

*Friday, Jan. 8, 1960*

*Dear Bob:*

*Sure sounds as though you had a fabulous Christmas! I especially like the description of your new Bonneville convertible. Wish you would drive over to see me some time.*

*Congratulations on being elected president of your class. I'm positive you'll do a great job. Hope you do well on your mid-year exams, if you have them. Our exams start the twenty-sixth and continue for three days. I'll have to begin studying pretty soon if I want to get good grades. They count as much as a whole term of 8 or 9 weeks when added into our final average.*

*Please forgive my writing again on school paper. But at present I am in French III. Yesterday I hadn't done my homework so I told Miss Smith I* had lost my book. Since I didn't have time to do my homework again last night, I just left my book at home until Monday. She just called on me to translate anyway.

Tell me what you did New Year's Eve? Wally and I went to a party (couples) at Jay Ogakway's house. He goes to Phillips Andover so there were a few PA boys there too. Things were pretty dull until about 10. But then Wally put a big snowball down my dress which did cause a little confusion.

At 12 everyone start kissing everyone else, especially Wally. But I got my share too. I was home at 1:30 & still sober of course. Did you stay _fairly_ sober? A lot of kids here were really drunk, out cold in fact.

Wally and I can only see each other once a week according to my father's new restriction, which started Jan. 1. Actually I don't really mind. I was getting tired of seeing him every day & most every night. I hardly had any time to call my own. Wally gave me a scarab & pearl bracelet for Christmas. I gave him a sweater.


Sunday Jan. 20, 1960

Hello again!

French classes aren't as long as they used to be. I didn't have a chance to finish the letter. Hope you had a nice week-end. Wally took me to see "The Miracle" last night. It was really fabulous. Have you already seen it? If not you should.

Would you answer me another question? (You don't have to if you think I'm getting entirely too personal.) Since you've gotten your license, have you taken girls parking? Does everyone do it in Wisconsin? What do *you think about girls who you take parking? Finally, what do you do???*

*There's been a lot of talk about it here recently & I was just wondering*

*what someone who doesn't live around here thinks? Try to answer in your*

*next letter.*

*We voted on class rings the other day. They are really nice. Wally wants*

*to wear mine when I get it but I doubt if I'll let him. I want to wear it*

*myself (for awhile anyway.) Do you have class rings?*

*Bob, do you suppose you could send me another wallet size or larger*

*picture? I haven't sent you one for ages but we took a lot around*

*Christmas, so you're sure to get one. Please write soon & be good.*

*Love always,*

*Fran*

Fran's questions about parking were quite a surprise.

At the time, the word meant kissing or "necking"—finding a dark, quiet, out of the way place where you could park the car and make out. It may surprise today's teens to learn how risky pre-marital sex seemed back then. Even "heavy petting" wasn't a casual thing to do. The "if it feels good, do it" mentality of the 1960s hadn't yet begun to emerge. Strong social taboos—and for many, even stronger religious ones—still held sway. Though the Pill had recently been introduced, birth control was neither easy to get nor anonymous, and God help the poor girl who found herself "in a family way." (The word "pregnant" wasn't considered proper in polite company, so numerous euphemisms were used.) Rather than suffering the shame and ridicule of having a pregnant female under their roof, a family would send their daughter off to a home for unwed mothers or to some out of state relative's house until the baby had been born and put up for adoption.

Many a girl's reputation was ruined by guys who would lie or exaggerate about what she would do or how far she would go. Fran herself was victimized by this. Even I, hundreds of miles away, had been told that it was said she would let a guy go farther than just kissing. Though he didn't believe it himself, Tony had passed on this cruelly unfair and unfounded rumor, which dogged her through most of high school.

Anyway, at the time of Fran's letter, I knew that what kids actually did while parking varied greatly, but it hadn't yet occurred to me that there might be regional variations. Among the kids I hung out with, things rarely got past the kissing stage. For my part, they *never* got past the kissing stage. Not that I wouldn't have liked them to, but there were so many pressures against premarital sex it had never seemed a real possibility. I had my own principles on the matter, so when I got Fran's letter I couldn't wait to weigh in.


Thurs. Jan. 15, 1960

After school

Dear Fran,

Hope you had fun with Wally over Christmas. It sure sounded like it. Our exams are the same times as yours are. Needless to say, I'm not looking forward to them.

Your class rings look real sharp. Since Dominican is a new school we haven't had class rings. And as class president I was asked by my "fans" to talk to the top brass about it. I argued it out with the principal for

20 minutes. And I guess she won. For reasons still best known only to herself, we aren't going to have class rings.

Your New Year's Eve sounds like it was a real blast. Believe it or not I did stay sober (I was about the only one in the crowd, and it <u>was</u> a crowd.) I figured as long as I was driving I might as well forego the booze. I still had a lot of fun. I was with Lisa and didn't get home until 2:30, even though the party broke up at 1:30.

I'd like to stop in Andover for awhile this summer, before or after I go to France. Maybe we can work something out.

At the present time (that just means maybe) it looks like I'll go over on the Queen Elizabeth and fly back. I hope that is the way it'll work. Sounds like a blast.

For Christmas, I gave Lisa a black kitten to replace one that ran away. I brought the thing in, in a box wrapped up. I told her to open it right away because it was pretty perishable. When it jumped out of the box, she nearly fainted.

You asked about parking. That I'll be glad to answer. Naturally I have parked with girls. And naturally I think it's fun—to a certain extent. You see, around here almost everybody parks along Lake Michigan in certain parking lots which parkers have taken over. It's real nice especially in summer when the moon is out, etc. The only trouble with this deal is that cops come around every once in awhile to make sure everything is "O.K." To make a long story short, the most passionate times are had at parties. Of course I park most with Lisa, and most of the times right in front of her house. I don't think much of girls that try to run the show completely, but they usually know when to stop. If they don't I do. Sound easy?

How about the same info about Andover? It's probably pretty much the same from the sound of Tony's letters.

I didn't realize how windy this is getting.

The enclosed was originally from a friend of mine at Annapolis. That probably will explain some of the questions.

I haven't got a picture right now but when I get one I'll send it. I'd like one of yours soon. The freshman shot I have of you is probably pretty out of date. Write soon.

Lots of love,

Bob

My response pretty much sums up the attitude of the times. Knowing when to stop was paramount. Boys were expected to try to "go too far" and girls were expected to prevent them. Human nature being what it is, mistakes happened, but "no" was the norm. I could get into some pretty passionate kissing, enough to steam up the windows of the car, but I never expected things to go beyond that.

In a brief mention of the France trip, I started to fill in the blanks, though an explanation of the story behind the trip was still to come. In the meantime, I was more interested in answering Fran's question about parking and in joking around. My letter contained a form, painstakingly typed, with the words "Application for a Date" at the top.

The story went that the form had been created by United States Naval Academy midshipmen. It wasn't hard to imagine some date-starved guys at the Academy, sitting around trying to cook up some way to meet girls and coming up with this application as the answer. To use it, all you had to do was identify some attractive female (maybe your roommate's cousin or next door neighbor)

APPLICATION FOR A DATE

I have , by one means or another, attained knowledge of the fact
that you are quite nice and vry good looking. With no effort on my part,
I have decided that I would like veyy much to meet you. Since it is impossible
for me to follow the proper channels in order to make your acquaintance, I am
attemting to overlook several laws of social etiquette and persue the desired
end. If I have succeeded, please fill out this form and return it.

and send her the application. She fills out the form, sends it back and, bingo, you'd made a connection.

I don't know how I happened upon it, but I thought it would be cool to send it to Fran and see what she said. Ever up for a joke, she completed the form and returned it forthwith.

In the letter sent with it, dated February 3, 1960, Fran also wrote this. "Well guess what? Wally and I broke up last weekend. This time ring and everything went back. He doesn't speak to me unless he has to during school but he occasionally calls at night. We both have dates this weekend and strange enough our dates are people we have both dated before. It sure seems funny to be without him after almost 1½ years."

That news, together with her properly suggestive answers to my questionnaire, were all music to my ears. I wasn't really jealous of Wally, but I must have been at least a little green with envy. In my return letter, on February 17, I tried to be philosophical. "I imagine you are happy without Wally by now. I had more fun when I broke up with Barbara than when I was going with her. I still see Lisa a lot but every once in a while I take someone else out, for variety." I'm not sure any more whether that last statement was true or just bravado. Maybe I did have the odd date or two with someone else but I really only remember Lisa at that point of my life.

A typical date would have involved "doubling" with another couple, cruising the main street of Whitefish Bay, pulling into the Milky Way drive-in for

1. Name in full _FRANCES ANNE JORDAN_ Age _16_ Phone # _GRS-1752_
Address _180 CHESTNUT ST. ANDOVER, MASSACHUSETTS_

Residence(check one) Home _✓_ apartment ___ Hotel ___ Trailer** ___ Dorm ___

2. Height _5_ ft. _7_ in.   Measurements:   Figure (check one)
Weight _130_ lbs.

Color of eyes _GREEN_          Bust _36_          ( ) OO-la-la

Color of hair _blondish-brown_    Waist _24_          ( ) Sensational

Length of hair _to shoulders_     Hips _36_          ( ) Repulsive

                                  Ankles _8"_        (✓) _Call it what you want!_

3. (a) Do you dance _yes_ ( ) Jitterbug ( ) Waltz ( ) ___ (✓) Close

   (b) Do you smoke? _yes_          Favorite brand _Marlboro_

   (c) Do you drink? _no_           How often _(New's 4 years Eve)_

        ( ) beer   ( ) Gin   ( )Kickapoo joy juice   ( )Everything   (✓) _Coke_

   (d) Do you neck? _yes_   How often? _not too_   With whom _someone I like a lot_
   (I know if you mean about the room !)
   (e) How late will you stay out? _12:30-1_ Why _Because my curfew is 12:30_

   (f) Will you try anything once? _no_   More than once? _sometimes_

   (g) Do you like moonlight rides? _yes_   Secluded country roads? _yes_

        Suppose the moon isn't out, then what? _turn on your head lights_

   (h) If in school, denote which one. _ANDOVER HIGH_   co-ed? _yes_

   (i) Do you believe in love at first sight? _yes_   By mail? _yes_

   (j) Does your father have a gun? _yes_   Does he hunt? _no_
        Where is it kept? _cellar - bedroom_   Is he a good shot? _yes_

   (k) If you live at home, indicate the position of the following:

        Most comfortable sofa _in playroom in the cellar_

        Closest light switch to above _12 inches away from end of sofa_

        Best courting spot _in the playroom_

   (l) The most expeditious route (in case of emergency) from:

        Your bedroom _out door, down stairs though front door, up street_

        The parlor _though dining room - to kitchen, out kitchen door, down street_

        The front porch _down driveway, across street, over fence to sanctuary_

   (m) Do you have a car? _yes_   Make? _Ford skyliner_ Year _1957_

   (n) Do you have a good job? _yes_   Salary $ _.50 hour_ Hours _7:30 - 2 AM_
                              _babysitting_   (over)

fries and a shake. The Milky Way, known as "The Milk," was reputed to be the inspiration for Arnold's Drive-In on the "Happy Days" sitcom. After seeing and being seen, we might head for Lake Michigan and park for a while. Then it was back home, generally by midnight on a weekend night.

(o) Do you like men? _yes_ Rebels? _yes_ Yankees? _yes_

(p) Do you collect men's jewelry? _no_ What type? _____

(Q) Your favorite color?*** _✓_ Navy Blue Army grey_____
Warning: This may be held against you.

(r) Do you have a boyfriend? _yes_ Is he big? _5'9" 160 lbs_
Does he get jealous? _yes_ Does he carry a gun? _no_
How often does he take you out? _once a week (Dad's new year resolution)_

(s) Would you like to be married? _yes_ Stay single? _____
Why? _love, security, home, family_

(t) Do you prepare for the worst on a date? _no_ Do your escorts? _I hope not !_

(u) What kind of lipstick do you use? _revlon- honey_ Taste good? _very_
Does it smear? _no - it's guaranteed_

(v) Do you think you know how to kiss? _yes_ Would you like lessons? _o k_
Describe your kisses: ( )½ second (✓)½ minute ( ) French Maid ?
( ) French General ? (✓) from soul ( ) motherly ( ) _____

(w) What do you say most? Check one:
( ) yes ( ) why not? ( ) maybe ( ) later
( ) Welllll... (✓) why? ( ) no ( ) _____

(x) Will you bring a chaperone? _no_ Friend? _sure_

(y) Do your best friends dare tell you? _tell me what ?_

Bonus Question:
What is your percentage according to the Kinsey Report? _I've never read it._

General Remarks: _Please tell me how I rate. Of course you could answer a questionnaire like this + send it back to me also. If you would_

Signed _Frank Jordan_

Enclose SNAPSHOT or PHOTO, PLEASE

Return to:
_Bob Zieledorf_
_317 E. _____ Rd._
_Milwaukee 17, Wis._

NOTICE: This offer void if not returned within twenty (20) days.

In this letter, I finally got around to explaining France: "I am making an attempt at learning French for my trip this summer, "I wrote. "Maybe I should have started out: *Ma cheri Françoise*. It's not guaranteed to be correct but the average bear should be able to figure it out. You asked about my trip. Well, I am going over alone on the Queen Elizabeth (at least I have applied for reservations) and will live with a family over there. We know this family through my father's business and the son of this man might come over here the following summer."

The Westinghouse Air Brake Company had operations in Europe. On an earlier visit to our home in Milwaukee, a Paris-based executive named Yves Perrin had noticed my curiosity about France. He suggested that I come and stay with his family for a summer; as I told Fran, we hoped that his son, Blaise, who was about my age, would come to America another year, in a kind of informal exchange. I thought it was a wonderful idea and to my delight my mom and dad were willing to go along with it.

My future hosts, M. and Mme. Perrin, spoke English. But since none of their four children did, it was important for me to learn some French. I only had about nine months to do it, and French was not offered in my school. I bought a Berlitz French course and studied it on my own at home. Of course, this was long before the invention of cassette tapes, CDs, DVDs, iPods, or programs like Rosetta Stone. The course consisted of an LP record and a workbook. I would sit by the hi-fi, place the tonearm on the record, and listen to the teacher speak some words, following along with them in the workbook. Then I would have to lift the tonearm and repeat the words. It was far from a perfect system but it was the best I could do. At least the built-in deadline helped me muster the discipline to stick with it. I would be far from fluent when I finally got to Paris, but at least I could tell a taxi driver where I wanted to go and I could order a basic meal in a restaurant.

The Queen Elizabeth must have rejected my application, because I never got to sail across the Atlantic. Instead, the urgent question of the moment became whether I would be allowed to go to Andover on my way to Europe.

While that question burned in my brain, Fran went off with her Catholic Youth Organization group on an overnight ski trip to Mount Cranmore in Conway, New Hampshire. In a letter dated March 11, she confessed to a major blunder.

"There were twelve girls in our room and a couple of us had brought a little liquor (guess who?) and we got caught," she wrote. "Two of us were confined to our room for the remainder of the trip which was exactly 24 hours. Of course I told my parents as soon as I got home so they wouldn't hear it from somebody else. Naturally I'm being punished. I can't date for a month (15 days left) and I can't drive the car until Easter. Pretty stupid, huh? Oh well, practically everyone has forgotten it."

Apparently, what had happened was this. After a party her parents had given, she had drained some unfinished cocktails into a small jar and smuggled it along on the ski trip. Neither she nor her friends ever drank any of it. Nevertheless, they were caught red-handed with the contraband, and she was paying the price. Her girlfriends were angry and decided as a group to keep their distance— something that hurt Fran more than she wanted to admit—and she said she had never seen her father so furious.

In the same letter she let me know she was now dating someone named Donnie Anderson. "I saw Donnie practically all weekend and so my science project (compulsory) wasn't ready for today. I can't understand Wally. He still calls me, talks to me in school but continues to try and hurt me even though he appears to like Sandra. I must bore you with all my problems."

Actually, I have to admit that such discussions *were* a bit boring to a 16-year-old guy. I really didn't much care who she went out with, although Wally sounded like a jerk. I had my own girlfriend, Fran was hundreds of miles away, and I didn't know any of the guys she wrote about. But I did have to wonder how, if she was still grounded, she managed to see Donnie all weekend—even to the point of ignoring a compulsory science project. Often, questions like this were never addressed, and others were never answered. It didn't really matter. At this stage, we were just happy to find letters in the mail box once or twice a month.

My March 18 letter had big news, at least from my perspective. "We got a color T.V. set the other day and I've discovered the number of lousy shows they put on in color," I told Fran. In 1960, color television was just beginning to come into its own. Hardly anyone had a color set yet, so most shows were still broadcast in black-and-white. NBC had aced out its competitors in the color arena. In 1960 its main color broadcasts were the weekly "Bonanza" and the "Bell Telephone Hour." It was really neat to watch "Bonanza" in full color, but that Western was the only thing on that interested me.

To my mind, the really amazing thing was the fact that we actually owned a color set at all. Dad was not what would now be called an "early adopter" of new technologies. I had been in second grade before our family got TV. That first set, a DuMont, had featured an enormous console cabinet with a round screen that was probably no bigger than fifteen inches in diameter. Still, I had thought it was great! Since all my school friends had TVs at home, the talk at lunchtime was always what they had seen the day before. Once we got our TV I could join in the conversation.

Four or five years after that first TV, it came time to replace the DuMont. We got a Sylvania with Halo Light, a fluorescent light that surrounded the round screen. Most people in those days watched TV in the dark. In response to the theory that doing so was bad for one's eyes, Sylvania built a light right into the set, which could be turned on when the room went dark to ease the eye strain. Halo Light was as adventurous as our family got in the electronics realm until the color TV showed up. I don't know what amazed me more—being the first in my class with color or the simple fact that Dad had actually done it.

I also shared some prom news in that March 18 letter. The prom was always the social highlight of the year in high school. Earlier, Fran had commented that she wished I could come to hers as her date. I said: "Our prom is going to be on May 6. This is our first one, since we are a new school. As class Pres. I've got a real job on my hands to get this thing going. It looks like quite a wild affair tho. If that was an invitation in your letter, I'd be glad to come out to Andover for your prom. Just say when & if it's o.k. I think we would have a ball."

Of course, I was unlikely to be able to make good on this promise, but I talked a good game. A couple of weeks later, she wrote, again asking if I would come to Andover for her prom. My parents wisely said no to the idea for reasons of cost, logistics, and school schedules, among other things. Staying home spared me what would undoubtedly have been a most uncomfortable experience. As she wrote me, after the CYO trip fiasco her girlfriends had abandoned Fran. To make matters worse, she was now juggling things between two jealous boyfriends. I was just as glad not to have stepped squarely into that rivalry.

*Wednesday*

*April 6, 1960*

*6:00 P.M.*

*Dear Bob:*

*Figured I had at least 45 more minutes to wait for dinner so thought I'd write while I had the chance.  Naturally I'm late in answering your letter but guess you expect that by now. I was calculating the other night. Do you realize it will be three years this summer since I met you and we started writing?  Too long since I've seen you, though?*

*Just ate dinner, excuse me s'il vous plait. Looking through an old letter box this afternoon and happened to come across some of your old letters. Just as interesting and funny as recent ones!*

*I have so many problems. Ever since the ski trip Charlene, who was my best friend before we left, hasn't spoken to me except an occasional yes or no when I ask her something. Our little group of six has all split up and I'm on the outside it seems. I wish I had never gone. Things are all so different, but you know how girls are, don't you?*

*Another thing not exactly a problem is boys. On this one you can help me n'est-ce pas?*

*You see, ever since Wally and I stopped going steady about nine weeks ago I have been dating Donnie Anderson. Last weekend I went out with Wally again on the night Don was working. This weekend I'm going out with Wally Friday (the night Don's working) and Saturday with Donnie. The thing is, how long can I do this?  They're both jealous as anything and one will see me walking with other in school and bango.... Of course Wally is dating someone else too, but just for a good time, he tells me. Donnie, on the other hand isn't. He sees a girl from Lawrence occasionally but has never dated her. They both ask me about each other, and what can I say? I really like them both. Then to top it all off is the prom. They both asked me—and I asked you. Wally asked me last year and keeps reminding me. Donnie asked me about three weeks ago. Oh please help me, what can I do? Actually it's all sort of stupid. I could always move out of town?*

*Now about our prom weekend, June 3-5; do you really think you could come? Would your parents let you? How would you get here?*

*That date application was a panic. Put me down for the week of the 4th. Naturally, bring your car with the good back fender.*

*Dad bought the boat home this weekend. Boy, it sure looks great. Can hardly wait to go skiing again. But my water skiing is really bad. I realized that after viewing some home movies. Oh, well guess we can't be an expert at everything. But why not just me?*

*Are you still going out with Lisa? How can you keep all your other fans away? Enough flattery. Your head will get too big for your Easter hat!*

*Have been trying to talk dad into a new car, but no soap. No new car either. Oh well, the Ford will do. By the way, Dad gave me the car two weeks ago, 3 weeks earlier than he had promised.*

*This house is so confusing. My sister is chasing my brother through here, and my mother is chasing them; the radio's blaring; my grandmother's doing the dishes, (I'm supposed to); my aunt is yelling to Bobby. However, my father and grandfather haven't arrived at this crazy little palace yet. Any minute… Oh God!*

*We get out of school next Thursday the 14th, and don't go back until the 25th. Welcome relief. Dad's contemplating getting a new lawnmower, you understand, one with a shift, seat, etc. (of course)!*

*Our latest saying around here is "KAK". Can mean almost anything.*

*Who are you playing for President of the US? Kennedy, natch!!!*

*My mother is planning to go to New Orleans for about 10 days the end of May. Wish I could go but just the "women" are taking off. What do you do for laughs over the weekend? I've run out of exciting ideas. Almost forgot, couple of the drive-ins are opened for the season. Saw "Solomon and Sheba" last Friday. Pretty good, although gory in part.*

*If you've got through this letter with your eyes still straight more power to you. My writing is almost as bad as the guys'. No insult made, honest.*

*Well, I'll close and let you do your homework or eat or telephone or something. Please write soon, and try to answer some of questions. Thanks.*

*Love you always,*

*Fran*

I wrote back on April 28. In the interim, I had called Fran to tell her I would not be able to make the Andover High prom. My letter said, "It was nice to talk to you after 4 years. I can dial you direct—no operator—by 617 and then your number. Really amazing." The phone call was truly a treat. Even though the call could be placed without operator assistance, long-distance calls were still expensive. My parents limited the amount of time I could talk so we couldn't waste precious minutes saying nothing. But after so long, to hear Fran's voice with its lovely Bostonian accent was a huge thrill.

Of course, she was disappointed that I couldn't come for her prom. We were still searching for the opportunity to actually see each other again, and we talked about how and when that might happen. I would be heading east for my trip in July. We thought that was our next best possibility and hung our hopes on it. In my April 28 letter I said, "I hope to fly out to Andover (if my arms don't get too tired) this summer before France. That makes it sometime in the middle of July."

Also, in that letter I told Fran that Mom and Dad had broken the news to me that we were going to move yet again. The business Dad ran had three manufacturing plants in three different cities. It made sense to consolidate them into a single operation. For that purpose, they had bought an empty factory in an Ohio town called Sidney. That's where we were going.

The language of the letter didn't express my true feelings about moving. What I said was "It's going to be bad news moving before my senior year but I shouldn't have much trouble." What I felt was anger. This would make three high schools in four years, not to mention the fact that I loved living in Milwaukee and didn't want to leave.

I had actually been born there. We had moved away when I was four, then come back midway through my freshman year. The two and a half years I had spent there this time around were the highly important years of high school. To this day I tell people I grew up in Milwaukee; it feels true, because I came of age there in those critical high school years.

I loved everything about my life there: Dominican High School, my girlfriend, my school friends, the city, the lake, the beach, being a big shot in my class, and all of my activities. To have to leave all that and start over for my final year of high school in some small Ohio town was too much. I begged my parents to let me stay behind somehow, but we had no relatives there and no friends we could impose upon. I gradually became resigned to my fate, but never happily.

There was one particular event that junior year that I never wrote about. But when she later learned about it, Fran said she found it especially endearing. In many ways, it typified the innocence of the times and, I suppose, said something about me, as well. I didn't intend to hide it from Fran—I knew she would love to hear about it. It's just that I was too lazy to try to explain the whole thing in a letter.

It began when the guys in our class decided to play an April Fool's Day prank on the community. The idea arose during lunchtime cafeteria bull sessions. The brainstorming took place over a period of weeks and evolved into a firm plan in time for April 1. We were going to stage a gangland-style murder in the middle of downtown Whitefish Bay on that night. It took careful and highly detailed planning and a couple of walk-throughs, but we pulled it off flawlessly... almost.

The main street of Whitefish Bay, Silver Spring Drive, was a typical suburban village downtown. It was lined with all kinds of shops including a movie theatre. Running parallel to Silver Spring Drive was an alley. There was a vacant lot between the alley and the street, so someone positioned in the alley had a clear view of the movie theatre. We checked the movie schedules to learn exactly when the late movie would end. Before the start of the early movie, we parked a car on the street directly in front of the theatre. There was no metering at that time of day, so it wasn't a problem to leave it there for several hours.

I was to be the hit man. Our volunteer victim was Dan Harrigan. John Kemmet's dad had the perfect gangster car, a black four-door Buick, so he was the designated driver, and I rode with him. The other major players were four other classmates who had an important role.

The beginning went according to plan. Fifteen minutes before the late show was to end, Harrigan stationed himself on foot in front of the theatre, pretending to be waiting for someone. Kemmet and I waited in the black Buick in the alley, watching Harrigan. The other four guys were lurking down Silver Spring Drive.

When the movie was over and people started flooding the street, Harrigan checked the traffic light (which we had timed) and scanned the scene for cops. When the timing of the light was right and the coast was clear, he signaled us by taking a swig from a vial of fake blood we had concocted. At the signal, Kemmet raced the Buick down the alley, around the corner, down Silver Spring Drive, screeching to a stop in front of the theatre.

I was holding the murder weapon, a blank starter pistol I had borrowed from the track coach. I pointed it out the window, yelled, "Harrigan! You rat!" and fired the gun two or three times. The gun emitted blue flame, white smoke and loud noise. Taking off, Kemmet and I cleared the green light at the corner. Harrigan dropped to the sidewalk, fake blood spewing from his mouth. As bystanders yelled and screamed, the four lurkers ran down the street, picked up the body, and threw it in the back of the planted parked car. They were to take off through the corner light before it turned red, but that's where the perfect plan hit a glitch.

The car wouldn't start! So the driver started madly cranking the engine and the guys in the back with the body tried to cover by slapping Harrigan around a bit. Of course, half the school was hanging around watching. Someone quickly figured out the problem. He pulled his car alongside, they lifted Harrigan's "body" out of one car and into the other, and off they went.

It didn't take the Whitefish Bay police long to track us down. They were quite stern about the whole thing, but we could tell they were trying to hold back their own laughter. They took down everyone's name and address in case we caused any more trouble. We were strongly advised to keep our practical jokes private. "Someone could have had a heart attack, you know. As it was, we had to take one lady to the police station to get her calmed down," one of them said. The next day, out of curiosity, I went into a store on Silver Spring and asked a clerk if she had heard anything about a murder the night before. "Oh, *yes!*" she said. "It was *terrible*. A bunch of boys came by and shot another boy right in front of the theatre." Ah, music to my ears.

Silly as it was, it was also one of those memorable shared experiences that build lifetime friendships. Sadly, Dan Harrigan passed away recently. Until then, I still saw him once in a while, and we stayed in touch periodically by email. A few years ago he invited me to a Dominican High School reunion. I saw people I hadn't seen in over 40 years. Not surprisingly, the April Fool's gag was one of the main topics of conversation.

When Fran learned about the prank later on, she said that she got such a kick out of the imagination, creativity, sense of humor and daring of the stunt. She didn't know anyone else capable of pulling that kind of thing off, and Milwaukee seemed much less conservative than her prep-school town!

It was a month before I heard back from Fran on May 29. I got all her prom plans: "How was your prom? Did you go anyplace after? Our junior prom, 'Song of the South,' is this coming Friday. Guess who I am going with? Wally. Oh, well, things could be worse. At present he is going steady with a bleached blonde sophomore named Karen. Honestly, she is the sexiest thing on two feet—and ½ the time her feet are off the ground! I'm very happy for them both. Donnie is going to the prom with Pat. She's really cute and also a great kid. I sure hope things work out this weekend." She went on to detail the expected round of pre- and post-prom parties, one of which her parents were going to chaperone.

The festivities would pick up the following day with a trip to the beach and a night at the drive-in movie. She added, "Usually my parents won't let me go to the drive-in but this is special, especially since it will probably be the last time I'll see Wally." And then she asked me to tell her about the "fabulous time" at my own prom.

There is no letter indicating that I ever answered that question. But some memories are still very vivid. As junior class President I would automatically be the head of the prom—we didn't elect kings and queens. It would just be me and my date leading the "promenade," followed by the other class officers and their dates. There was one major problem, however. The good Dominican Sisters of Sinsinawa, Wisconsin had decreed that in order for someone from another school to attend the prom, he or she must be a Catholic.

The fact that Lisa was Lutheran created a situation that called for some creative thinking. Fortunately, she hadn't been to enough Dominican events for the nuns to know her name, let alone her religious affiliation. She talked a Catholic friend of hers from Whitefish Bay High into letting her assume the friend's identity for prom night. It was a pretty high stakes gamble. If the ruse was discovered, Lord only knows what troubles would have befallen me. But we got away with it. Lisa was "Cathy Jones" (or whatever) that night. The whole class was in on it but no one ratted us out.

As far as prom activities went, we were not nearly as evolved as Andover. There was no pre-prom party, though a group of us did go to a restaurant for dinner before the dance. Afterwards, there was a post-prom party somewhere which broke up around 1:00 a.m. Finally, some of us went to the home of one of the girls for the obligatory late-night carrying-on. Mostly, we were too tired to carry on at all, pretty much hanging around like zombies until it was time to go home. I can't speak for the whole school, but among my group of friends there was no booze, no sex, certainly no limos—just a bunch of 16 and 17 year olds enjoying a special dress-up night.

School was nearly over for the summer. Fran wrote me on June 10 and asked if I was really going to come to Andover. She also told me about her first summer job working as a waitress at the Cedar Crest restaurant in Lawrence, a city just north of Andover. I didn't write to her, or if I did, the letters are gone. But I had about six weeks to work and earn some spending money for my trip to Europe. Dad put me to work at LeRoi microfilming company documents in preparation for the move to Sidney. I sat in a huge room full of filing cabinets stuffed with correspondence, interoffice memos, invoices, and records of every imaginable kind, size and shape and fed each document into a microfilm machine. I was all by myself. It was eight hours a day of crushing boredom. But it meant a weekly paycheck that I got to keep and bank for spending in France, so I stuck it out until mid-July before taking off.

I was able to make arrangements to fly to Boston to visit with Tony Beck before going on to New York for my flight to Paris. Tony was just the excuse— seeing Fran again was going to be the main event. I don't know which I was more excited about—seeing her or going to Paris! But when I arrived in Boston I learned that my meeting with Fran was to be very different from the reunion I had been dreaming of for almost four years.

When I saw Tony, he informed me that Fran had had a serious automobile accident and that she was in the hospital in Danvers, MA. Fran's friend Bill Dalton owned an Austin Healy Sprite, a small British sports car known for its bug-eyed headlight design. One night they had gone out and Bill had let her drive the Sprite. Being unfamiliar with a stick shift, she hit the clutch instead of the brakes on a sandy curve and rolled the car over. She had broken her neck and she was in traction.

To say I was stunned was an understatement. I had been happily going along, thinking that when I got to Andover I would get to see the Fran I had been writing to for years. In my imagination, we would spend hours talking and catching up on our lives. And of course, I was looking forward to more of the kissing that had started this whole thing. All of a sudden the world was turned upside down. I still couldn't wait to see her, but now I realized our meeting would be substantially different from what I had imagined.

Fran had been paralyzed for a while but traction was doing its job. By the time I saw her, she was beginning to move her arms and legs. Visiting her in the hospital was a bit awkward, but more so for her than for me. It was still wonderful to see her, even in the state she was in. Tony and another friend, Tom Kelly, were in the room with me; Fran's nurse Regina was keeping a close eye on things to make sure she didn't do anything to hurt her progress.

When I entered her room, she was lying in a special bed with her head covered. She explained that anchors had been drilled into her skull, to which cables were attached. Weights at the end of the cables were stretching her spine to take pressure off it and allow healing to occur. It sounded gruesome to me and she was no doubt self-conscious and embarrassed. But I barely noticed. I was just so happy to actually be in her presence again, to talk to her in person. I couldn't touch her for fear of doing further damage, but I was still hoping to get in at least a brief kiss.

Fran's attitude was good and thankfully so was her prognosis. It was hard to see my pen-pal in that condition, especially after imagining our first reunion and how I would be "paid" for that medal. I couldn't stay long. We made teenage small talk for a while. Then Tony, Tom, and Regina excused themselves. Finally alone, I bent over her and, very carefully, we kissed. It was a soft and tender kiss; it had to be, given her treacherous condition. But it was another memorable one, much like the first one behind the bush almost four years earlier.

Then, sadly, it was time to leave. The next day I finished my visit with Tony and headed off for "Gay Paree".

During my trip that summer, I had plenty of time to think about my life. I mostly thought about Lisa and about how much I dreaded the upcoming move to Ohio. But sometimes I thought about Fran. We had by now spent three years writing letters to each other, and I had just left her in terrible shape in a hospital bed. At that age you rarely expect the worst to happen, so I was naively optimistic. But I thought about how special it was to have seen her again, even in that scary condition. I began to recognize that there was more to Fran Jordan than met the eye. Talk about courage under fire! She was trying to recover from a serious accident, one that easily could have killed her or left her permanently paralyzed. Yet during our meeting she hadn't shown a single sign of self-pity or anger. She was just happy to see me, and girlishly self-conscious about how she looked. To me, that was a wonderfully lovable combination. I definitely wanted to see her again, if only I could.

My summer adventure was magnificent. Although the Queen Elizabeth crossing hadn't worked out, I had the thrill of flying over the Atlantic Ocean on a jet. Jet airline service in 1960 was relatively new. I flew on a TWA 727; their first regularly scheduled trans-Atlantic jet flight had occurred less than eight months earlier.

My first activity in Paris involved meeting up with a group of Marquette High School boys from Milwaukee who were touring Europe. Dad had arranged for me to be with them for the three days they were in Paris. So I got to tour the city with a bunch of other American tourists, not a bad introduction.

The Marquette group soon moved on. I took a train to Bern, Switzerland, where Lisa was studying dance for a month or so. She was staying in a girls' *pension* with rigid rules and strict supervision. I got a hotel room nearby, and we spent a little time sightseeing together before I left the next day. This all happened less than a week after my reunion with Fran in the hospital, but I have to admit that I wasn't giving Fran much thought at this point. At the time, Lisa was my girlfriend, my first love. I hadn't seen her for a couple of weeks and was missing her a lot. It was great to see her and certainly a treat to see the city of Bern. But her schedule and strict rules didn't allow us an opportunity to get into any trouble—which was the whole point of her living arrangement, of course. It was a short visit, but an exciting sidebar to the story of my European adventure.

From Bern, I took a train to Brussels, where I was to meet and stay with a relative of my maternal grandmother. "Nana" had been born in Belgium and she still stayed in touch with some family members. Most memorably, I met an uncle, older than my parents, who charmingly took me under his wing for a weekend. He introduced me to Belgian beer and showed me the sights of the city.

"Robert (he pronounced it *Roe-bair*), you want to learn to speak French?" he said one day.

"Yes", I said.

"Then when you get back to Paris you hire a prostitute. You spend three days with her. When you leave you will speak perfect French."

Today when I tell that story, people always ask me if I did. I just tell them, "Je parle français parfait." But the truth is I had neither the time nor the money.

Back in Paris, I became part of the Perrin family for the next five weeks. We spent the balance of July at their apartment in Paris. The Perrins lived near the beautiful and expansive Jardin du Luxembourg. That central location meant we could walk everywhere we went. A great host and tour guide, Blaise escorted me to most of the fabled landmarks of the city: the Louvre, the Eiffel Tower, and the Champs Élysées, among others.

He had a lot of studying to do for some important tests, so we weren't together all the time. When we were together one-on-one, communicating was tricky. My French was still quite limited, although it improved immensely as the summer went on. Blaise's English was pretty much nonexistent. But we usually could make ourselves understood with a combination of simple French and English words, hand gestures, and a French/English dictionary.

There were some occasional misunderstandings, however. For example, an American slang word of the day was "crazy," which meant "cool." "It's crazy, man" indicated something was particularly good. I introduced Blaise to the word, and we went around Paris with me exclaiming that everything I saw was "crazy."

About three weeks later, we were with some English kids. Blaise was listening to our conversation when someone referred to another person as crazy, in the sense of being a loon. Blaise caught the word, and he could tell that it was not complimentary. He asked me what was said and I told him that it meant the person was insane. He went ballistic, thinking that I had been denigrating everything he had been showing me in his beloved hometown. Eventually we got him to calm down enough to understand the semantic differences. But it got pretty tense for a while. If there are troubles in the United Nations, it isn't any wonder.

Along with nearly every other family in France, on August 1 the Perrin family migrated to the country for the month of August. They had rented a house in a Normandy village, Jullouville, about 215 miles west of Paris. Luggage for a month, including what I had brought, was loaded into the family car or shipped ahead. The drive from Paris took about four hours. The house was situated about a block or two from the beach where we spent a lot of time hanging out. I met lots of other kids, all of whom were summer visitors. I especially enjoyed being with the kids of an English family staying nearby. It was great to be able to speak English with someone my age.

The Perrins were wonderful hosts. They took me to see the Normandy invasion beaches and the American cemetery. We saw the magnificent monastery at Mont Saint-Michel, although only from a distance. Only a short drive from Jullouville, this extraordinary place is built to be accessible only when the tide is out. When the tide is in, it is completely surrounded by water. When we passed it the tide was in, so I didn't get to visit.

From the Perrins, I learned about drinking French wine and the apple brandy of the region, called Calvados. Wine was a fixture at nearly every evening meal. We kids were allowed to drink it, but only diluted to about half strength with water. The Calvados was occasionally served as an after-dinner liqueur. We kids were allowed to have some, but we didn't drink it. Instead we soaked a sugar cube in a small amount of Calvados and sucked on the cube.

The stay wasn't without drama. One evening, Blaise went into the bathroom to take a bath. I was in my bedroom, reading, when I heard something large thump the bathroom floor. It turned out to be Blaise. The hot water for the bathtub (there was no shower) was provided by a gas-fired water heater on the wall over the tub. When you wanted a bath, you lit the gas, heated the tank of water, and emptied the tank into the tub. Apparently when Blaise turned on the gas, it had failed to light properly. The bathroom filled with the unburned fuel and Blaise soon passed out. At the thud, his mother ran to the room and asked through the locked door if he was okay. When she didn't get an answer she called for her husband, who broke the opaque glass window in the door to open it.

When I heard the glass breaking, I ran to see what was going on. Blaise was lying on the floor, motionless. His parents were pleading with him to breathe. I had completed an American Red Cross lifeguard course, so I knew exactly what to do. We pulled Blaise out of the room and turned him onto his belly. I proceeded to administer artificial respiration. In the days before CPR, this was how you resuscitated someone who wasn't breathing. Blaise quickly came around and was soon his old self.

While I was certainly enjoying my foreign adventure, I was anxious to get home. I knew that once I got to Milwaukee I wouldn't have much time with Lisa and my buddies before I had to move to Ohio. And although I didn't want to admit it, I was a bit homesick. I missed speaking and hearing my own language. Not being able to understand everything people were saying was mentally exhausting. I missed hamburgers. And strangest of all, I missed round doorknobs. Really. All I knew in the US were round doorknobs, while in France it seemed all doors had lever openers. It was a small touch of culture shock that symbolized the foreignness of my surroundings.

But I had adapted more than I knew. When it was time to go home, M. Perrin took me back to Paris the day before my flight. I had a chance to take a final walk in the city by myself that evening. Along the way, a Frenchman stopped me and asked, in French, for directions. I answered him in French that I was an American, a stranger, and couldn't give him the help he wanted. He seemed quite startled. Usually an American could be spotted quite easily. Over the summer I had changed the way I combed my hair and had acquired some new clothes. Somehow, on a Paris street, I was mistaken for a local. It was a gratifying conclusion to my visit.

When I got home from France, there was a long letter from Fran waiting for me.

*MASSACHUSETTS GENERAL HOSPITAL*

*BOSTON 14*

*Wednesday*

*8/10/60*

*Dear Bob,*

*How's the tourist? I'll bet your vacation was strictly the "end." Thank you so very much for the gift. I love it. Many thanks also for the post cards and letter; I'm glad you had time to remember me. Did you see much of Lisa during your stay? It was so wonderful to see you again after so long a time. You looked great! Sure wish you lived closer to Andover. I'd help you keep busy. My mother thought you were very nice—much better looking than your pictures—and wants me to invite you up for a few weekends during the school year. Naturally, I'm not arguing the point. Isn't Sidney, Ohio closer to Andover than Milwaukee by about 200 miles or so?*

*Billy Dalton got his Sprite back from the repair shop last Thursday. It really looks great. He had silver racing stripes put on & the car is sort of a bright turquoise, more blue than green though. Dad won't let me ride in it yet.*

*You're probably wondering where this stationery is from & how I got it. Well, so many things happened after I saw you it's almost too much. Are you ready?*

*The Friday after I saw you, they removed the tongs & put a very uncomfortable iron & felt brace on. I was to wear it six weeks, with a remote possibility of an operation at the end of that time. I wore it 5 days and then, because it was rather unstable, my neck dislocated again. Of course they didn't tell me. I still thought I was going home in three days.*

*The next day, Friday, my doctor informed me I was going to Boston to be looked over—a slight shock! Two hours later I left in the ambulance for Baker Memorial and Dr. Marten Smith-Petersen. I was operated on Monday, July 25th. They removed a bone from my right hip and fused it to my neck; they also wired the vertebrae. It only took them 5 hours with 2 doctors operating.*

*Two weeks later the doctor removed all my stitches (34), all of which were on the sides of my head where they had put more tongs in. I just came home last Wednesday. Now I feel great. The incision on my hip is still a little uncomfortable, but nothing bad. All in all, I guess I'm just lucky. I don't even think of what could have happened. It's all over now.*

*I have a new brace to wear, it's much better than the old one. I have to wear this one for 3 months. I guess it takes that long for the bone to fuse. One good thing, I lost 10 lbs.*

*Wally and two of his friends came up. The only stayed a little while. I still see him every so often even though he is going steady. Donnie is going out with someone else. I didn't like him too much anyway, and this way no one was hurt.*

*My mother just brought the mail in. There was a card from you, from Normandy. Sorry I didn't write while you were in France, but I was afraid the letter wouldn't reach you as I wasn't sure of the address.*

*Hope you can read my writing. My hands aren't real steady yet.*

*The kids in my class (about 40 of them) chipped in and bought me a huge stuffed dog with big floppy ears. He is so soft that he feels like velvet. I named him Ichabod but my little brother persists in calling him "Bozo." Oh well, he's happy anyway.*

*While I was in the hospital in Boston I met one of the O.R. orderlies. He left for Greece three days after I was operated on. He was about 20, but he went with his parents, not alone. Not as lucky as you I guess. Oh—to be rich!!!*

*Tony and Tom came down again about a week after you left. I was still at Hunt but in a different room.*

*The summer has just flown by. It doesn't seem like we'll be back in school in about four weeks. Do you know what subjects you'll be taking? What school are you going to? I'm taking English, World History, Trig, Physics and possibly French IV. I'll be busy—no dating this year. Ha-ha!!*

*Did you meet Billy? He was the boy whose car I was driving. He's awfully nice. Maybe I'll go out with him when school starts.*

*Do you think our parents will let you come for weekend during some school vacation? I'm looking forward to seeing you.*

*Will you keep Lisa's ring when you move? Does she have something of yours?*

*I won't be able to drive until about November. Hope I don't forget how. My father will probably decide to teach me again anyhow!*

*Well, guess you've worked through enough scrawl. Please write to me*

*soon & send me your new address.*

*I miss you very much.*

Je t'aime, *

Fran

*P.S. *Surprising what you can learn in three years of French—but I mean it.*

What a summer that one was! For Fran, her first summer job, then a life-threatening accident, a major operation, weeks of hospitalization, and hours of time to reflect on what could have been.

For me, a once-in-a lifetime experience that very few teen-agers ever get: the chance to travel abroad without one's parents, and to be temporarily immersed in a new family, a new culture, and different language. Then home, soon to be uprooted, moved to a new city, a new school, and a new life.

And for us both, the chance to have seen each other again, face-to-face, after three years of writing letters.

That long letter from Fran contained news that ran deeper than I was prepared to plumb at the time. I definitely didn't fully understand the seriousness of the surgery she had undergone while I was in France. But I was flattered by the fact that she said I had looked good and that her mother wanted to invite me to visit. I was floored by the fact that she said she meant it when she said "Je t'aime." I was really too absorbed right then with my own situation to take this in, and its true importance managed to escape me.

Mostly, I was pleased to hear that the worst was behind her, that she was healthy and ready to get on with her life. I took time to fire off one quick final note before leaving Milwaukee.

August 27, 1960

Dear Fran,

This will have to be short, I'm afraid. We are moving Wednesday and I have lots to do. Actually, my family is moving, but I am staying until Labor Day with some of my buddies. Sorry to hear about your second operation but glad you are pulling out of it. Tony wrote me about it in Europe and I was really worried until I got your letter. I didn't get home till about the 18th. Hey, it is about a week later and I'm still unpacking my stuff.

Lisa has her ring back and I have mine. We're still going together though.

If you care enough to write before you get anything hefty from me, my new address is: 1806 Port Jefferson Road, Sidney, Ohio.

It'll be another 2 weeks until things will be back to normal. I'll write a long letter as soon as I can.

Lots of love, and a few other things,

Bob

Well, that was it. Wrapping up the end of my life as I knew it in Milwaukee would take another week. Then I was off to Sidney, OH, and God knows what. It was going to be the start of a new era for me. I could only hope for the best.

CHAPTER FIVE

*W*HEN THE INEVITABLE TIME CAME TO LEAVE MILWAUKEE, DAD AND I drove my car to Sidney so I could be there for the first day of school on September 7. I would enroll in Sidney High School for my senior year.

The trip took about seven hours. I was angry the entire time. I didn't have much to say to Dad. Intellectually, I knew he was doing what was best for his company, but emotionally I was convinced he was simply ruining my life. These feelings would persist well into the school year but amazingly, none of this angst ever manifested itself in my letters to Fran. She was a thread of constancy that ran through my life. As I moved—first York to Milwaukee and now Milwaukee to Sidney—she was there, even though she wasn't. As I've said earlier, since I never lived near her, I never had to leave her. She was a constant in a world of change.

On September 4, she wrote: "I was so glad to get your letter. Our mailman was beginning to be afraid to come without a letter for me. I was afraid you wouldn't get my last letter as I wasn't sure when you would be home from France.

I'm also glad Tony told you about me. I was going to write to you in Paris but I wasn't sure of the address."

Sounding like her old self, she mostly talked about school, a sign she was recovering well: "How's this for easy living? Our principal (sp?) said I only needed to go to school 4 days a week until I felt well enough to stand-up to a full schedule. Huh—me, never!!! Maybe this will be a good year after all—fake headaches, etc."

She asked if I had met Bill at the hospital. "He's the boy who let me drive the car I wrecked, his car, only six weeks old! Well, anyway, he has it back now, painted a different color but just as nice. He had been coming up to see me almost every day since I came home—had even taken me to the drive-in movies a couple of times—then he up and started dating Carolyn, one of my best friends. Boy, wait till I get this collar off. Am I going to give someone a rough time!"

In the letter, she indicated that she thought I wouldn't be interested in hearing about her problems, and that her letters were too long and boring. She wondered if I would still be seeing Lisa now that I've moved. Then she concluded: "I'm listening to the Stereo Hour on the radio and every time the violins go high up my arm jumps—that's why my writing is so jerky. Be good and I'll love you always."

It was a most welcome and extremely timely letter. I wrote back as soon as I got it.

Sept. 8, 1960

Dear Fran,

I was glad to get your letter yesterday on my first day here in Hicksville. My parents moved on the 31st but I stayed in Milwaukee with some friends and my car until the 7th.

Yesterday school started. I have 16 study halls a week! Physics, Civics, Trig and English 12 are my trouble-makers this year. You sound like you have a tough one ahead of you, also. The school is nice—a brand new building. The kids seem too friendly, too. A couple guys just left my house, as a matter of fact. They stopped by to say hello. As far as I can see, my dates will be few and far between because I haven't seen any attractive girls (as yet)!  Believe me, I'm looking.

Our house here is still being remodeled, so we have a trailer in the driveway!  My dad and I sleep there now, but we'll trade off with everyone as our rooms are completed. They are air-conditioning part of the house and might even put in a swimming pool!  You'll have to bring your Mercedes down to add class to the place. (Our Bonneville is dirty.)

Speaking of cars—my dad tried to sell my Ford while I was in Europe but prices were down & he kept it. I'm glad of that.

As I might have told you, our house is on a river, but at this time of year it is impossible to see it and almost as impossible to reach it. This fall when the leaves and underbrush die, I think I'll hack a path to it. I forged my way down there with my dog yesterday and when we got back it took a half-hour to get the burrs off me and a whole hour to get them off the dog. It is very sharp down there. There's an island in the middle of the river, and down about a half-mile is a boat club.

They even have a ramp for skiing. About a mile up the river it really gets wild. The kid next door takes his boat up there and goes hunting every once in a while. I guess he built a shack or something there. I understand that we have to watch for raccoon and deer in the woods here. In fact I thought I heard a 'coon out in back a little while ago.

Almost everybody here talks with a hillbilly "twang"—mainly because almost everyone is a hillbilly. I just hope if I pick up an accent, it is southern and not hillbilly.

How is your romance with Billy coming? I did happen to meet him and he seemed like a nice guy. I hope your neck is O.K. after you jerked it.

When I said "a few other things," I didn't mean anything in particular, so you can take it as you want it.

I'd love to come up to Andover this year. Just say the word on what weekend(s) it'll be handy to have me, and I'll do my best. Do you think you could ever get down here? I would like to have you and I have plenty of room.

As for Lisa—of course I'll be going back to see her. I hope I never have to choose between you and her, though, because it would really be a tough decision.

I think I'll go "check the lower 40" and turn in for the night.

Much love,

Bob

P.S. I gave you a bum steer—my address is <u>1608</u>, not <u>1806</u>, not that it makes any difference in this town.

That letter pretty much speaks for itself. Sidney = "Hicksville" = hillbilly twangs. But also friendly kids, a nice new school building, and a new family home under reconstruction. In retrospect, one remarkable thing stands out. In her previous letter, Fran had signed off, "Be good and I'll love you ... Always." For whatever reason, I completely ignored this breakthrough and simply signed mine, "Much love." I guess I'm a slow learner.

We wrote 11 letters before Thanksgiving. Mostly, they were newsy riffs on what was going on in our lives, lives that revolved around school and dating. From these accounts, we began to learn not only how we each lived but also what was important to the other. For example, Fran told me she was having a tough time with her academic course load in school. She wound up dropping French IV and Trigonometry in favor of Problems of Democracy and Review College Math. Maybe her recovery was proving to be more difficult than she expected.

She casually mentioned Hurricane Donna, a storm that set records for its strength, duration, and destruction. In early September of 1960, it hit every state along the east coast of the US and killed over 360 people. A Massachusetts observatory recorded gusts of 145 miles per hour. Since she only gave it casual mention, I assumed the Jordan family was not badly affected. But since I was safely hundreds of miles away, Donna was more of an abstraction than a reality. Hearing from her about it, even if only a brief mention, made it seem more real.

I found out that Fran became resigned to her friend Billy and her best friend, Carolyn, going together. She claimed to be giving up boys but threatened to make up for lost time once she got rid of her cervical collar. And, in fact, she continued to go out with Donnie.

There were silly little things, too. She asked me to tell her my middle name and for details about the school I was attending. She kept me up to date on the performance of her high school football team and said she was wearing out her new Everly Brothers album from playing it so much. She was back to driving the family car almost daily and said she went to a dance with a guy (not Billy) in his Sprite. I had to admire her courage for getting back into a Sprite. Maybe it was like getting back on the horse soon after you get thrown, a way to conquer your fear.

I didn't have as much to say about school and academics as she did, although I did tell her I started taking a Journalism course to cut my 16 study halls per week down to 11.

I was an extremely fortunate kid and was excited to share my adventures with Fran. For example, I got to occasionally fly to Milwaukee in the LeRoi Company plane, if it didn't mean missing school and as long as there was an empty seat. In the process of phasing out production in Milwaukee and phasing it in to Sidney, executives had to be shuttled back and forth frequently. So the company had purchased a twin-engine Aero-Commander for the purpose. The pilot was an ex-military pilot named Jack Kelly. Most of the time it was just me and Jack on board so I got to fly in the right co-pilot's seat. It didn't happen often, but it did give me the occasional chance to stay connected with my Milwaukee friends, especially Lisa, who I missed more than anyone.

As far as Sidney went, I was quickly getting acclimated to my new life. I was enjoying school, making friends, and even had the occasional date. The house we moved into was a large center-hall Colonial. It had been built around 1918 and needed substantial remodeling. Living there while the work was going on posed particular hardships. As a sop to offset our family's collective suffering, our parents started talking about installing a swimming pool in the backyard come summer.

I mentioned in one letter that my folks were having part of the house air conditioned. In truth, that was a bit of an overstatement. In the 1960s, central air conditioning was still a rarity. In older homes like ours with hot water heat, it was virtually impossible due to the lack of ductwork. The affordable solution was window air conditioning units. That was the route we took. Known colloquially as window shakers, they would, if large enough, take care of the room they were installed in and sometimes part of the surrounding area. I was assigned a bedroom on the third floor of the house. Because heat rises (as any high school physics student could tell you), my room was practically uninhabitable in the summer. So I lucked out and got one of the four window shakers my parents opted for. The other three were located in the kitchen, the family room, and the master bedroom. I don't recall my sisters protesting but unfortunately the budget did not allow for units in their bedrooms.

I later learned that Fran's father, a known "heat-o-phobe," was an early adopter of A/C technology. Her house was completely cooled with a large central system. Her father was very proud of the fact that he could maintain what he referred to as the ideal temperature year-round. In his book that was 70 degrees Fahrenheit. It didn't matter that 70 air conditioned degrees feel much colder than 70 heated degrees. Visiting there in the summer was like living in a meat locker. Everyone put on sweaters and complained bitterly. But he could never be persuaded to change the thermostat.

About the end of October, I received a letter from Fran officially inviting me to pay her a visit at Thanksgiving. On November 5, I answered. "Your invitation for Thanksgiving sounds really great. I'm brainwashing my parents and Dad is checking plane schedules. If I can make it, I'll be there. I'll let you know as soon as I can. By the way, are your game and dance both on Thanksgiving?"

I also added a short update on what I had been doing, offering my sincere empathy for her physical troubles: "I'm glad you are all better by now. You know you were very smart to pile up somebody else's car instead of your own. Think of how mad your father would have been." I was not exactly a model of compassion, but as always she was a great sport about my jokes.

That wasn't much of an answer to her invitation, but it was the best I could do. Today these things would be handled in seconds with phone calls, emails, or texts. But in 1960, plans like this took time.

Soon Fran wrote again, saying I was welcome to stay at her house and detailing the plans for the holiday weekend. I finally answered her on November 13, two weeks after her initial invitation and only ten days before Thanksgiving.

ROBERT L. ZIELSDORF

1608 PORT JEFFERSON ROAD

SIDNEY, OHIO

November 13, 1960

Dear Fran,

By the time you get this letter, your collar should be off for good. How does that feel?

Guess what? After a highly skilled and thoroughly prepared brainwashing operation, my sister succeeded in getting my parents to let me come see you. All kidding aside, I can come. On the Friday after Thanksgiving, my parents and I will fly in the LeRoi company plane to Holy Cross College to look it over. My parents will go on to New York, where my father has a business meeting, and I'll get to Andover in time for dinner Friday. That I'll have to write more about. The pilot has reserve duty in New York and he'll pick me up Sunday. It is too bad that I can't be there for the game on Thursday but it is out of the question. Besides I look like hell right now anyway. I have some kind of skin infection (non-contagious) and I look like a three-year supply of pimples. The doctor is valiantly doing all he can though, and most of it should be gone by then.

This weekend I succeeded in breaking up two kids who had been going together for 4 years. Ann asked me to a party to make Mac jealous because he had been taking her for granted. Now she likes me and is through with Mac for good. That's the breaks.

How is your love life coming? I doubt that it is suffering any.

I suppose it is up to you and Tony where I sleep. I'd prefer to sleep with you (wait...I'll rephrase that). It would be more convenient to stay at your house, but do what is best.

Thanks for sending your school paper. I'll send you mine as soon as I have a good article in it.

Thursday I have to give a talk to the Y-Teens Club about my trip last summer. What fun!

Please excuse the sloppy handwriting, but a weekend of breaking up lovers exhausts me.

I'll write about how and when I'll be in Friday. I might have to take a train from Worcester to Boston or something.

Write soon.

Love, etc.

Bob

P.S. I'll let you guess for a while about the "etc."

So it was official. I was bound for Andover. At the time I saw the trip mainly as a welcome relief from small town life in Ohio, though I was also anxious to see Fran again when she was not in traction. It would be fun to see her standing upright and with full use of her arms and legs. And, of course, seeing my old buddy, Tony, would be fun too. He and I were maintaining a correspondence, but it was winding down as my relationship with Fran was ramping up.

In my letter, the suggestion that "I would prefer to sleep with you" was meant to be facetious, an obvious joke in the context of the 1960s. In today's world, given the enormous change in sexual mores, it might be interpreted as a direct suggestion. But in our world at the time I had no such hopes. Desires, yes. Hopes, forget it. At best, from my teenage boy's point of view, the comment might open the door a bit to something beyond kissing.

My allusion in the letter to "some sort of skin infection…" was an attempt to prepare Fran for the worst. The fact was that since arriving in Sidney, I had developed terminal acne—terminal because every time I looked in the mirror I wanted to kill myself. I didn't just have the run-of-the-mill red spots like most kids. My face had huge cysts the size of watermelons. Well, okay, maybe not quite that large, but they might as well have been as far as I was concerned. No doctor could tell me what caused it, but I'm sure now it was a combination of hormones plus the stress of leaving my beloved Milwaukee and adapting to life in Sidney.

This disease plagued me for the rest of high school and well into college. Amazingly, I was still able to make friends and girls seemed to be happy to go out with me. Maybe it was because I made up my mind not to let it force me into a shell. I was determined to overcome any social resistance by sheer force of personality. That was far easier said than done, but I didn't know what else to do. Over the years I saw several dermatologists but none could offer the silver bullet that would put me out of my misery. I did what I could and learned to live with it.

And then it was time for the trip. On the Friday after Thanksgiving Mom, Dad and I flew from Sidney to Worcester, MA in the LeRoi company plane (known as the "Flyin' Lion" thanks to the company logo blazoned on its side). We got there in time for me to look at Holy Cross College and have an interview with its admissions department before my parents flew on to New York, and I somehow got myself to Boston. I can't remember any more how that happened, but Tony Beck and his friend Tom met me and drove me to the Jordan home in Andover.

Their house was a very comfortable one-and-a-half story gray Cape Cod with a finished walk-out basement. This was home to Fran and her parents, her younger sister and brother (he with Down syndrome), her maternal grandparents, and her paternal aunt.

Her Mom and Dad were gracious hosts and went out of their way to make me feel welcome. Fran's parents were an interesting contrast to mine. She had a strong-willed father and a mild-mannered mother, while in my home those roles were reversed. Bob Jordan was a banker, a smart, athletic man who loved cars and boats. Living in a household dominated by women, I think he appreciated the male company I offered. Fran's mother, Marion, was a striking woman, quiet and yet strong, sociable yet dedicated first to family. From the beginning I found her easy to talk to and enjoyed being in her company.

Of course, I was more than eager to see Fran again. The last time I had seen her, she was flat on her back in a traction bed with weighted cables screwed into her skull. Now I saw her as she wanted to be seen. Her traction was long a thing of the past and her neck brace was gone too. The surgeon had done his job beautifully and so had the good Lord: other than a scar down the back of her neck, hidden by her long hair, she showed no signs of ever having been injured. She was a tall, blonde, green-eyed beauty.

I can no longer recall the precious moment I first saw her again. Chances are good that it was in the presence of her parents and that we shook hands rather than kissed. But it was obvious to me that she was thrilled to see me, and I hoped it was obvious to her that I felt the same.

After some introductions and a bit of settling in, her family excused themselves. Tony, Tom, Fran and I sat down in the dining room for a dinner of leftover Thanksgiving turkey. It was a fun chance to renew acquaintances and get caught up all around. I talked about life in Sidney and my summer trip to France. The others filled me in on life in Andover and their respective schools. Somewhat late in the evening the guys left. Fran and I joined her folks to talk a bit more before going to bed.

I was assigned to her aunt's room in the basement. Her aunt and her mother both had to move to make room. Clearly, sacrifices had been made to accommodate me.

On Saturday, Fran drove me around Andover, showing off her town, her school, and her favorite haunts. That evening, her parents took Fran and me to dinner at their favorite restaurant. It was customary then to dress for dinner out, so her dad and I were in coat and tie. Fran wore a plaid wool skirt and jacket, her mother a brand new cashmere suit. During dinner, her mother admired the watch I had purchased during my brief visit to Switzerland. To better show off my shiny Omega, I proudly thrust my arm towards her. On the way across the table, my fist connected with her mother's water glass, spilling its contents all over her beautiful jacket and into her lap. Fran and her father were horrified. I turned bright red, mute from embarrassment and humiliation. But her mother handled it with aplomb, assuring me that it was nothing. Her suit would be just fine. Her calm reaction diffused what could have been a disaster, and dinner continued as though nothing had happened.

After dinner, Fran and I went to a large party given by one of her classmates. I was a bit self-conscious, being an outsider, but just as during that first graduation party, her friends were welcoming and friendly. I can't remember any more what time we were expected to be home, but we left the party in time to find a quiet place where we could park and be alone.

We took advantage of that time for some kissing, and also some talk about the things we had been corresponding about. It felt so good to fill in the blanks of the previous three-and-a-half years. In the process, something amazing happened. We realized that we both had feelings that went beyond platonic, pen-pal friendship. We were in love with each other.

It came as a gradual dawning rather than as a bolt of lightning. We seemed to recognize it simultaneously. Why such a big change, so suddenly? I can only say that it was probably the combination of our growing maturity, the cumulative knowledge we'd gained about each other, and the unpredictable magic that is love. It was probably me who was the first to voice it, to say "I love you." But Fran didn't hesitate to say "I love you, too." I remember that she took off her class ring and asked me to have it. I was happy to, and only wished that I had something with which to reciprocate. But the fact that I didn't was of no consequence. We had both reached, and recognized, a huge milestone in our lives. Somehow, we managed to get home early enough to stay in her parents' good graces.

The following day, the Flyin' Lion picked me up at the local airport. My heart filled with new emotions, I was off to Sidney. On the plane ride back I had time to mull over what had happened. Falling in love with Lisa was like getting hit by a truck. Falling in love with Fran was like a long ride in a limousine: smooth, relaxed, thoroughly enjoyable. I knew it was where I was meant to be some day. Fran had it all. She was smart, a good student but not bookish in any nerdy way. She already knew where she was headed in life—college, and then teaching. She was gorgeous, as I've said. She had a sense of humor and she appreciated mine. Our families seemed to be about the same place on the social scale, and I truly liked her parents. Having exchanged at least a hundred letters over the past three-and-a-half years or so, I had developed a strong visceral sense of who she was. What I sensed about her was now proven by actually being with her. It was love, but in a way I had not experienced love before. I lost no time in writing to tell her so.

ROBERT L. ZIELSDORF

1608 PORT JEFFERSON ROAD

SIDNEY, OHIO

November 28, 1960

Dear Fran,

Well, how did you survive the weekend? I really hope you had as much fun as I did. I am still in a state of shock from seeing you again. I guess I was actually in it all weekend. (Don't get the wrong impression. I meant good-type shock.)

I broke up with Ann this afternoon. When I showed her your ring she went all to pieces. That's the breaks! And, it was fine. Now the next step is to break the news to Lisa. I'd better wait until I see her again, though.

(If this letter seems to ramble, it's only because I am in a good mood for a change.)

You might be interested to know that Jack Kelly thought you were real sharp. He offered to exchange "black books" for awhile. I told him to get lost, of course.

I wish I could have talked to you for a couple hours this morning, but…

The flight home was smooth but took longer than we expected. We hit some strong headwinds that really held us back. We landed at Harrisburg at 7:00, had dinner, took off again at 8:30 and landed at Sidney at 11:30. Harrisburg is not far from York, Pa., where I used to live.

Now I realize what a blind fool I must have been for the last 3 years and a half, or 3 ½ years or whatever you are used to saying. It finally took you and a moonlit night to make me realize that I love you. I mean it and I'll say it again and again if you want me to. I love you, I love you, I love you, and I always will feel that way. I only hope that you will too. I want to tell you, also, that my respect for you jumped up about 100%. When I came out I still had that rumor in the back of my head and I didn't exactly know what to expect. Don't get the idea I am a prude though—I'll take what I can get. I just wanted you to know that, and hope I said what I meant to say.

I haven't seen my new car yet. It got delivered to the wrong place so I'll have to wait for a day or two.

There are lots of things that I would like to say, but I don't know where to start. When I read over this letter I'll probably want to tear it up and start over, but I'm not going to. Just lazy, I guess.

I hope that I can see you again soon. Every month is going to seem like a year now. Don't get your hopes up for Christmas, but it might be a remote possibility.

Have fun and write soon. Remember that I have your ring and am still wearing it.

Love, etc.,

Bob

P.S. I love you.

When I traveled to Andover I still had in the back of my mind the rumor I had heard about Fran—the one about how far she might go sexually. I had no idea if it was true. So, while we were parked under that moonlit sky, I made a move to find out. I learned in no uncertain terms that the rumor had been false. She was a good kisser but no more. Kissing. Period. End of story.

No doubt that rumor, like so many others, was started by someone who exaggerated (or outright lied) about what happened on a date to impress his buddies and to blow up his ego. It was good for me to learn the truth. And it was good for our future relationship to be able to go forward unencumbered by any doubt.

Very soon, I had a response from Fran.

*Friday*

*December 2, 1960*

*6:00 P.M.*

*Dear Bob,*

*I love you and I miss you very much. I sure wish that it was this time last Friday. Last weekend was wonderful. I can't ever remember when I've been so happy. I sure hated to see your plane take off. My sister is still teasing me because I was so upset. Oh well, little sisters are made for that.*

*Every day someone at school asks about you, all my girlfriends thought you were sooo nice and real cute too. Naturally, I agreed.*

*Billy sends his best hopes you come back to Andover soon. He wants to have a small party, but promised me he'd rather wait until you would be here.*

*I've read your letter over a dozen times; it was so nice. You said everything I'd ever hoped you would. I was kind of afraid that once you left Andover you would forget everything you told me. I'm glad you haven't, because I never will. It meant so much to me that you thought enough of me to say it.*

*Guess I survived your visit although it took me four days to descend from cloud #9. Now I'm right back up there!*

*I'm sorry about Ann. I hope it was what you really wanted to do. Anyway, that's what I would have liked you to do – guess I'm pretty mean, huh? I'm waiting to find out what happens with you and Lisa. I'll just hope for what's best for you & I hope me.*

*This letter must be pretty confusing but there are so many things to say that my mind goes faster than my pen. Hope you can understand what I've been talking about. Maybe this will help: I love you & I love you & I love you & I love you & I love you and I still love you. Told you I'd do that someday, didn't I?*

*We got our report cards the Monday before Thanksgiving—I just showed it to my parents this Tuesday. My marks weren't too hot.*

*I just ate dinner, had to have fish this week. Do you like fish? (What a stupid question!)*

*This week promises to be quite dull. There is absolutely nothing up tonight—a lot of the boys are going to Central but the girls usually don't. Tomorrow night there is a basketball jamboree at the high school. Eight schools participate, each playing about two eight minute periods. About nine of the gang are going up together. Hope I can get the car. I have had it for school every day this week, with the exception of Monday, because my mother has been sick. She's been up today but still looks sick. I'm finally over my cold, guess cutting down on cigarettes would help matters. I smoked much too much while you were here but I was a little nervous and unsure of myself. I doubt I will be next time we see each other.*

*Has your mother or anyone mentioned my ring? My mom hasn't said a word but I know she knows it's gone. Jan and Louise mentioned it. Wish I had something better to give you, maybe someday, if given the chance, I will.*

*I'll be getting my class pictures in about 10 or 12 more days. I had a colored one (5" x 7") made up for you. Would you want me to write something on it? Please send me yours when you get them.*

*There's a dance at the high school tonight but I don't feel like going. Maybe I'll go babysitting with Louise and Mo. Exciting, huh?*

*I am having an interview with the director of admissions from Lake Erie tomorrow afternoon in Boston. Only one thing wrong with that college is that you have no vacations long enough to go anywhere over 200 miles*

*(if you fly). You don't even get the chance to go home for Thanksgiving but*

*if I make it there, I'll cut classes and go to Sidney! Or Andover anyway!!!*

*Well, you must be thoroughly bored by now. I write as much as I talk.*

*My father brought the Corvette home Wednesday night and took me for*

*a ride. It was the most powerful car I've ever been in. He had it up to 73 in*

*first gear! But all good things like cars must end, according to dad. So he*

*returned it the same night. He evidently talked himself out of it.*

*My parents liked you very much and would like to have come again*

*soon. I hope to see you real soon. Christmas would be so uneventful*

*without you around.*

*"Wonderland by Night" is just playing on the radio. Right now that*

*could be Andover because there is a huge yellow moon shining. Wish we*

*were under it together.*

*Well, I must do some errands for my mother. Please write soon and*

*never forget that*

Je vous aime, toujours et a jamais

Fran

*P.S. Just re-read this epistle; hope you don't think I'm foolish or*

*over- sentimental.*

*I love you again.*

*P.P.S. Just noticed that I wrote the envelope up-side down—I'm all confused!*

We wrote six more letters before the end of the year, each one professing our true love for the other. Mostly, they contained news about what was happening in our school and social lives. Socially, since we were again hundreds of miles apart, it was business as usual. We continued to date others, trying to sort out the confusion of feelings we were experiencing. If we were in love with each other, how could we still have feelings for the others we were dating? There was no simple answer. We just had to have patience and trust it would all work out.

That Christmas I gave Fran a gold locket. She gave me a silver ID bracelet. She told me about her family Christmas celebration and the parties she was attending during the school break. I told her about my gifts from my parents (an *oo-gah* horn for my car and various ski equipment).

Amid the trivial news, I told Fran that Lisa had visited Sidney for a few days after Christmas. The trip had been arranged several months before. Lisa drove the six hours by herself so we could see each other over the vacation. In spite of now being in love with Fran, I continued to have strong feelings for her. Not at all sure of what was going on with my own feelings, I was just going with the flow. I wasn't ready to completely break things off with Lisa, but I knew what I felt for each girl was different. It was too ephemeral to grasp in any meaningful way so I just put each relationship in its own compartment and tried to go on.

Still, I wanted to be open and honest with each of them. Fran knew about Lisa. Lisa knew about my pen pal in Massachusetts. Now she was learning that there was more between Fran and me than letters. During this visit, I broke the news to her about how I now felt about Fran.

It happened when we were out one night during that visit. I eventually found a quiet place so I could talk to her. I was nervous. I still liked her and dreaded hurting her, but I felt compelled to come clean.

I told her that I had Fran's class ring. Afterward, I reported to Fran that "Your ring didn't go over too well with her. Everything is working out for the best for us, and you don't have anything to worry about." As vague as that comment was, it was the best I could do. I honestly believed that things would work out for the best; I just didn't know what that outcome would be.

Later, in January, I told Fran again not to worry about my relationship with Lisa. I wrote, "You couldn't want to know all the sordid details about how she cried and everything. I just told her about you and how we gradually fell in love over the years that we have been writing. Even if I go to Marquette next year, I said I didn't want to date her."

It was a bittersweet change for me. Lisa and I had been close friends and first loves for more than a year. This would require us both to adjust to a new reality. We agreed we would continue to see each other when possible. But we both knew that things wouldn't be the same.

So the year 1960 wound to a close. Fran and I had reached a new level of closeness. But we were still just kids, living hundreds of miles apart. While we knew we shared something strong, we were determined to live normal lives in our communities, schools, and families. So dating others was still no problem. We simply carried on with our lives, knowing we held each other in a special place in our hearts.

# CHAPTER SIX

*F*RAN AND I WERE NOW IN THE FINAL HALF OF OUR SENIOR YEARS. CLASS-work was still important, but we could feel the pressure for grades easing off as graduation approached.

Fran's letters were full of queries about my dates and questions about why I had not been answering her questions. For example, "Now, after three years, will you please tell me what <u>etc.</u> on your every letter means?" I had developed the habit of signing my letters "Love, etc., Bob." The truth was, it didn't mean a thing. It was just something I thought added a bit of mystique that Fran could interpret any way she wanted. But I never explained that and, to stoke the mystique, I ignored the question whenever she raised it.

As the pressure on grades eased, the pressure of college selection intensified. Having already given the subject a great deal of thought, we had both already applied to several colleges and universities. Fran had told me in the fall that she was considering Lake Erie College in Painseville, OH; Goucher College in Towson, MD; and Boston College, which her father had attended.

Naturally, Mom and Dad were my major consultants on college selection, hugely helpful to me in sorting out the many possibilities. They had offered to pay my way wherever I decided to go. Surprisingly, that "blank check" made it harder to choose. When I asked Dad how to go about picking a school he gave me sound advice as always. "Think about where you want to live after graduation. Most businesses recruit from local schools. If you think you'd like to live in Milwaukee, go to college there." Though I eventually chose a school for other reasons, his guidance was always welcome and his wisdom always sound.

My college selection thinking turned out to be heavily influenced by a Sidney High classmate, Chuck Eisenstein. Chuck and I had become good friends since my move to Ohio. We shared many of the same classes, interests, and friends. I liked Chuck, I trusted his judgment, and he thought he knew *the* college to attend.

For years I had set my sights on Georgetown University in Washington, D.C. I was also still considering Holy Cross in Massachusetts and Marquette University in Milwaukee as second choices. Then, thanks to Chuck, Notre Dame entered the picture. Chuck had always wanted to go there, and he had begun to intrigue me with the idea. The more we talked about the school and the reasons he felt it was the right choice, the more I became enamored with the idea. My parents were open to the idea, so I sent an application to the University of Notre Dame.

In retrospect it might seem odd that, since Fran and I were so much in love, we didn't even think about going to the same college. The answer boils down to our tacit business as usual philosophy. As much as we cared for each other, we were not so thoroughly committed that our relationship would influence our college decisions. When we narrowed down our choices, we found ourselves headed in different directions. She picked Lake Erie, a small women's college, because it offered a semester in Europe for every junior. Studying abroad was an important goal of hers and this was an affordable way to do it, since the term abroad was included in the college tuition. In those days study terms abroad were rare compared to opportunities today—and when they were available, they were usually quite expensive.

It's interesting to me now that all my primary choices were Catholic institutions. I wasn't overtly religious. But I had spent most of my school years under the thumb of various orders of nuns–not all happy experiences, yet ones that had obviously instilled in me a trust in religious schools. Eventually I picked Notre Dame because I knew I'd get a first- class education there, and I loved the campus and the traditions. The Notre Dame mystique was the lure that intrigued me—the football traditions, the famous name, the academic prestige. When I later visited the campus and saw its iconic university buildings and grounds, was introduced to some of its students, and met with faculty and administrators, I knew this would be my home. The only question that remained was whether Notre Dame would pick *me*.

On February 15, I sent Fran the card pictured on the following page.

"I'll have you know it cost me 50 cents," I told her. It was a Gibson Studio card, which in those days cost a quarter. The additional quarter went to pay the parking ticket I got when I stopped at the card shop—an amount that seems tiny today, but was a hefty fine in 1961.

Later in February, I wrote Fran about my continuing quest to get into Notre Dame. "On the 22nd I had an interview in Columbus with a guy from U. of Notre Dame. He told me I <u>would</u> get in. Then he told me what I had to do to stay in once I got in. Anyway, I sure hope he is right about getting in."

The man who interviewed me was an alumnus who volunteered to screen the applicants who were getting serious consideration. His sage advice was a basic "nose to the grindstone" talk, tailored to the unique aspects and traditions of the University. He made sure I understood what I would be getting into: rigorous studies, tough discipline, and serious social regulations. But he also highlighted the positives: a top education from a nationally respected university, a storied football program, and many activities available to fill the social gaps. I knew that I was ready for it all.

In early March I heard from Fran that she had been accepted at Lake Erie College. That was big news, and I was truly happy for her. Besides the announcement about Lake Erie, her letter was full of updates on her school and social life and, of course, the usual questions.

*Wednesday*

*March 8, 1961*

*Dear Bob,*

*How's my boy? It was so good to get your letter last week, I'd thought you had forgotten me. As for my writing, I can't remember when I've been so busy. Anyway, I still think of you all the time. As usual I have a million and one thoughts to tell you—but don't panic, I won't tell you all of them. First and to me most important, is my acceptance to Lake Erie College in Ohio. You'll never get away from me now. I still haven't heard from B.U. or Rosemont but they're not important now.*

*How is your class play? Ours is well under way and should be a great success with my dramatic ability. We're doing "Ask Any Girl." It's fairly funny and not too long.*

*Two weeks ago the Andover Teen Center opened. This is a project the kids have been working on since January. We used an old two-story building and spent our entire week's vacation washing and painting*

walls, sanding and waxing floors, getting the latest records and selling
memberships. For all my work, I was elected vice-president of the Youth
Council, which is the governing body of the center. Billy is president. It's
going over pretty big—hope it stays that way.

I'm so far behind in school work, I'll never catch up. Between play
practice, newspaper and yearbook and youth council meetings, there's no
room left for homework. Guess what? I have a 93 average in Physics. I'm
really proud of myself.

Glad you're keeping yourself busy over the long lonely weekends.
Haven't you exhausted the supply of girls at Sidney High yet? Do you still
wear my ring? Just yesterday my mom asked if you had it. She must have
known all along. Hope you still love me, too. Blunt, aren't I?

Did you ever receive the Andover High School emblem I sent in my last
letter? You seldom answer my questions, so I never know what's happening.

Do you write to Lisa, still?

I bought the most fabulous album yesterday. It's "What'd I Say" by Ray
Charles. He's really wild.

The boy I have been going out with is named Bob, too. He's awfully cute
and has a white MG, one of the older ones with the continental back. He
picked me up for a meeting last night & he had the top off and I nearly
froze to death.

Was just looking out my bedroom window – you should see the sky – it's
dark gray with big black clouds rolling back and forth. It's real eerie—all
kinds of weird shadows and whistling sounds from the wind. Darn, it's
supposed to snow tonight. That's very annoying because for the past three

*weeks I have been riding around with the top down. Well, I must depart.*

*Write soon and think of me once in awhile—I love you.*

*Love always,*

*Fran*

*P.S. Maybe I'll get to see you pretty soon—have to go take a look at Lake*

*Erie.*

Fran didn't specify her role in *Ask Any Girl*, but the fact that she was in her class play was a bit remarkable. In January I had told her that I was trying out for the male lead role in our senior class play. Later I learned I had won the part and would become Captain Fisby in *Teahouse of the August Moon*. Stage acting turned out to be one-shot activities for both of us. But having that shared experience, even though we couldn't see each others' performances, was a fun coincidence.

I wrote her back in fairly short order, congratulating her on her Lake Erie acceptance. I answered many of her questions, but steadfastly ignored the one about "Love, Etc."

ROBERT L. ZIELSDORF

1608 PORT JEFFERSON ROAD

SIDNEY, OHIO

March 10, 1961

Dear Fran,

Well, I finally got my fountain pen out of hiding. If this writing is a little stranger than usual, it is only because of lack of practice.

You have no idea how busy I am. The class play, "The Teahouse of the August Moon," in which I've got the lead, is Wednesday, Thursday and Friday of next week. Since you can't get here to see it, I'll send you the reviews (which I am writing for the school paper). We also finally got our yearbook to the printer. 2 weeks late, but <u>there.</u>

My parents have been in Florida all week. They really needed the vacation. Mom's been ultra-busy trying to get our house in shape and Dad is trying to buck the business slump in our new location.

I'm really glad to hear you are in at Lake Erie. It'll be real nice having you so close. I should have gone to John Carroll in Cleveland. Things are looking up at Notre Dame. On Saturday, I have to go to Dayton for some achievement tests. A good buddy of mine, Ray (Woody) Woodruff, is taking the tests for West Point at Ft. Benjamin Harrison in Indiana this week. He is second alternate from our district.

Now to answer all your questions, one by one:

1. I might have "exhausted" most of the Sidney girls but I am not through yet. 2. As soon as the finger I sprained in basketball goes back to normal size, I'll be wearing your ring again. 3. Of course I still love you. 4. I got your Andover High School emblem but haven't figured out where to put it yet, so it's still sitting on my dresser. 5. I write to Lisa once in awhile, because we are still good friends. How's that?

I feel for my parents. They are sailing from Ft. Lauderdale to Miami on some guy's sailing yacht. After that he's going to race it from Miami to Montego Bay. What a life!

Our director caught us behind stage with cartons and cartons of Coke, Pepsi, pretzels, Fritos, potato chips, candy, crackers, cupcakes, etc., today. We smuggled it in and ate it when we were between acts. Needless to say, she wasn't very happy.

Well doll, got a physics test tomorrow; my grade fell from a B to a C last 6 weeks so I better pull an A tomorrow. I love you more than ever.

Love, etc.,

Bob

April and May were our final two months of high school. As Fran pointed out on March 25, "Just think, only about 10 more weeks of high school. This last year has just flown by." As we worked our way toward our June graduations, however, the time seemed to be crawling. But there was still plenty going on. Fran and her parents were discussing a driving trip to Painesville to see Lake Erie College. She asked if I could drive up to see her—Painesville is about 30 miles east of Cleveland, close to a four-hour trip from Sidney. Eventually, they called off the trip. It was a long drive for them and her father couldn't take time off work to do it. But trying to figure out when and how we would get to see each other next was a recurring theme in nearly every letter. I also learned that Fran and Bob—the other Bob—had stopped dating and her relationship with Donnie was on again/off again. She enjoyed her prom but went with a date that she didn't particularly care for.

In April, Chuck Eisenstein and I drove to South Bend to visit the Notre Dame campus. It was exciting to be accepted and even more exciting to travel there on our own to spend a weekend seeing our future from a student's perspective. The minute I saw the campus I knew I had made the right decision. Notre Dame in the spring is a uniquely beautiful place. The more I saw and the more people we spoke with, the more excited I became about the coming fall.

A bit later in April, I went to Columbus to attend a statewide high school mock United Nations assembly. My civics class was to play the part of the delegation from Ceylon. That was a fine educational experience in the academic sense. But more educational, in a very different sense, was the fraternity party we attended at Ohio State. One of my best Sidney High friends, Steve Huxley, had a brother who was a junior at Ohio State and belonged to the Pi Kappa Alpha fraternity. He invited us to come to the party and stay overnight in the "Pike" house. I felt like a big shot, hanging out with real college frat men. Since I was Notre Dame bound and Notre Dame has no fraternities, it was a part of college life I would only experience as a visitor.

Back in Sidney, I had dates with a couple different girls, went to the prom, got accepted into the National Honor Society, hung out with the guys, and just generally enjoyed the rest of the school term.

Then suddenly, it was over. No more high school. It struck me that if I so chose, I would never have to go to school again! College, unlike high school, was optional. It never occurred to me *not* to go to college. I had been raised to believe that going to university after high school was as natural as going to first grade after kindergarten. I knew that if I chose not to go, my parents would have been crushed and I would have made a poor choice. But just knowing that I didn't have to go was an amazingly liberating feeling, and I luxuriated in that sense of freedom. School from now on would be *my* choice and attendance on *my* terms. Recognizing my own responsibility for making good choices became a big step in growing up.

My main memory of my Sidney High graduation was the fact that my friend, Dan Harrigan, came from Milwaukee to help me celebrate. The ceremony was held in the high school gymnasium and was the typical cap-and-gown, valedictorian-and-salutatorian-speeches kind of ritual. I'm sure someone had a party, but I don't have any firm recollection of it. I was still sore that I wasn't graduating with my old gang at Dominican High but I was past the bitterness stage. Having Dan in Sidney was a great way to bridge that gap.

After graduation in June, Fran and I wrote about our plans for the summer and how in the world could we find a way to see each other. This letter from me is typical.

ROBERT L. ZIELSDORF

1608 PORT JEFFERSON ROAD

SIDNEY, OHIO

June 14, 1961

Dear Fran,

I have been wondering why you haven't written me lately and then it cleverly dawned on me that I owe you a letter. So—here you are.

How were your prom and graduation and everything? Frankly, I'm glad it's all over. Things really started to drag toward the end of the year.

What are you going to do this summer? Get your old job back? Jobs are really scarce around here. I don't have one yet, but I may be working for LeRoi as a sales promotion aide-de-crap or something. If it works out I will be traveling all over Ohio & Indiana, Wisconsin, etc. contacting distributers, etc. Sounds like fun.

Did you hear about the one-legged man who went to Arthur Murray to learn how to cha?

Happy Birthday!? As usual, I forgot the date but I remembered the month at least. How about telling me the date once more, and this time I'll write it down or engrave it on my chest or something.

Our pool is coming along slowly but steadily. It should be ready to go in a couple of weeks. You know—just in time for me to go to work out of town.

We register at Notre Dame on the 16th. I hope your father will come a few days early and swing south to Sidney. It would sure be nice to have you out here and everyone wants to meet you. We can talk about that later.

A couple weeks ago Dan Harrigan came down from Milwaukee to spend a week. Remember me talking about him? He's the guy we "shot" in our gangster prank. Well, we really set the town back on its heels for a while. We really had a blast.

Outside of that nothing spectacular has happened. We forage around town for something to do every night.

My car is still holding up—barely, though. I think I'll trade it in on a Jag XKE (chuckle-chuckle).

Did I tell you Ray Woodruff is going to West Point? He has to report in a few weeks. I'll miss him this summer.

Well, doll, time to go again. Have fun while being a good girl this summer. When you are out with other guys—don't forget that I love you and while I'm not around to fight the mobs for you, I still think about you all the time.

Love, etc.,

Bob

Fran responded by telling me she was working once again for the Cedar Crest Restaurant, but this summer as a cashier. She briefly mentioned the transition from high school to college. "Registration at Lake Erie is Sunday, September 16th...It seems so funny to be all finished high school—never see all the kids together again. Graduation was wonderful—I managed to leave with honors—top 10% of the class so it wasn't too bad. Naturally half the girls were crying."

Soon after, I went to work at LeRoi. Summer jobs were hard to come by, especially for someone new in town. I know my father would have much preferred me to find a job elsewhere, but I couldn't. In the end, he was good enough to hire me. He also hired the son of one of the LeRoi executives who had moved to Sidney at the same time I did. Bob McChain, a year older than I, had already finished his freshman college year. We were hired to conduct a marketing survey to learn how construction companies used LeRoi's portable air compressors and what was good and bad about them.

Bob and I were sent all over the Midwest. We would drive to a city early in the week, cruise around looking for construction sites, track down the on-site supervisors, and proceed to take them through an eight-page questionnaire which had been designed by the company's marketing manager. It turned out to be a great summer job! Bob and I were very compatible, and we were both thrilled not to have to spend every waking moment in Sidney. As I explained to Fran, "Well, I got the job I told you about and I'm making a fortune. $1.75 per hour, $16 per day for expenses, and 7 cents per mile for gas. Last week we worked in Chicago and Milwaukee. This week we are working closer to home. I go to Columbus tomorrow for the next couple of days. Do we have a blast, *working*."

Unfortunately, the job ruled out any hope of a trip to Andover—a remote possibility that I might travel to Boston as part of our work never materialized.

Over the summer I wrote Fran letters on motel stationery from Detroit and Louisville. Bob and I worked hard during the day but enjoyed our freedom to explore new cities at night.

Fran thought it was pretty neat, too, as she said in an August letter: "What a fabulous job you landed. Think you would be interested in something like that when you finish school or do you still want to go into the newspaper business with your grandfather?"

During our long talks in Andover I had told Fran about my grandfather in one of those typical teenage "what do you want to be when you grow up?" conversations. That was a pretty easy question for Fran—she knew she wanted to be a teacher, and in any case careers for women were more limited back then. But it was a difficult question for me because I never had a clear career goal. My vision of the future seemed to change with the seasons.

My maternal grandfather had a story that fascinated me. He had begun work as a printer's devil—basically a lowly assistant in a printing shop—but eventually became the owner and publisher of the Fremont, OH, *News Messenger,* now part of Gannett newspapers. For a time, I had I thought working at the *News Messenger* would be an interesting career. My father soon discouraged me from giving any more thought to working for the family paper; among other challenges, there were already enough grandchildren competing for a role there. Still, thoughts of journalism stayed in the back of my mind a while longer, and admiration for my grandfather and his entrepreneurial spirit always stayed with me, inspiring some of my professional choices even much later in life.

Early in the year I had written Fran that I was hoping to drive out west in August with some friends. "Go where we want, do what we want, etc. No definite itinerary." This turned out to be teenage wishful thinking but it underscored a wanderlust many of my friends shared with me. I was fortunate to find a summer job that satisfied it. Of course, Bob and I did have an itinerary—we couldn't just wander. But much of the time we were free of the constraints of small-town life, and we could enjoy small adventures as we toured the major cities of the Midwest.

The job helped the summer pass quickly. Before I knew it, it was September. Time to leave home and to become at last a real college man!

That was the good news. The bad news was the entire summer had passed by, and I hadn't seen Fran. Though the geographical distance between us wouldn't decrease, we both hoped that college life would somehow afford us more and better opportunities to see each other.

*Bob, high school graduation 1961*

*Fran, high school graduation 1961*

# CHAPTER SEVEN

*I*N SEPTEMBER, 1961, FRAN AND I LEFT OUR HOMES AND FAMILIES TO BEGIN the next chapter of life at our chosen colleges. My last letter to Fran before leaving for South Bend was dated September 13. Seeing each other again was still a high priority and I was not allowed to have a car at school, so I told her I was gong to investigate train and bus routes between South Bend and Painesville, where her college was located. I ended my letter, "I am pretty anxious to go to college. We start classes on the 21st. Starting the 16th my address will be: 312 Keenan Hall, University of Notre Dame, Notre Dame, Indiana. If it changes for any reason (like expulsion, etc.) I'll let you know *tout suite*. Good luck at Lake Erie, honey. Remember that I love you, when those guys from Case invade the place. Love, etc., Bob."

The 36 letters and one post card we exchanged that fall talked about whether and how we were going to get to see each other, chronicled our mixed emotions as we dated others, and of course, described our life at college, both academic and social. Although my letters seemed to indicate I adjusted better and more quickly than Fran, I really didn't. I just put on a braver face.

We both wrote to each other during our first week at school. My letter talked about how fortunate I was to be able to benefit from the newly liberalized regulations Notre Dame had made for the 1961-62 school year—definitely a sign of the changing times. The thick rule book still in use when I applied mandated Mass attendance three times a week and lights out every night at 10:30 except Saturday, when they needed to be out by midnight. I knew that a Notre Dame education would be worth the sacrifice of my freedom, but I can't say I was sorry when I got a letter from Father Theodore Hesburgh, the university President, announcing the new thinking.

Starting in September, the overriding rule essentially said that no student could do anything to harm or interfere with another student. Mass attendance was no longer mandatory. There would be no lights out, although with only a few exceptions, students were to be back in the dormitory by midnight. All freshmen were required to live in one of the campus dormitories, and no one was allowed to have a car. There were a few other regulations, but those were the "biggies." Clearly, college life was going to be more relaxed than I had expected.

At that time Notre Dame was an all-male school. As my first letter of the semester explained to Fran, its sister college, St. Mary's, was a smaller all-girls school about a mile or so away. There were frequent social mixers between the two schools, but in those days there was no sharing of classes; academically, the two institutions were entirely separate.

I told Fran that my roommate was a Notre Dame football player, recruited from a Catholic boys' school in South Chicago. Notre Dame challenged my preconceived notions about football players. Required to perform academically, its players were not universally of the "dumb jock" mold. In that first letter, I described my roommate as a "nice guy," an assessment I began to question as the semester went on. When I returned to the room and found him lying on his bed reading or napping, I'd usually give him a bright, cheery "Hi, Bud! Whattaya say?" His usual response was "Words." That generally squelched any possibility of real conversation. But while I'm sure I wasn't his idea of the ideal roommate either, I did manage to stick out the year with him, and he with me.

Though the rules were gone, evidence of the old days was not. The bed frames in Keenan Hall were made of square tubular steel with steel end caps on the upright supports. If you removed the end cap from practically any bed in the building you would find it full of hardened candle wax. The end caps had clearly become improvised candle holders, no doubt to facilitate some late-night cramming before tests and exams.

"I really should like this place by the end of the semester, exclusive of studying, naturally. There is so much here on campus that I could never tell you about in a letter," I concluded in that first letter from Notre Dame. In truth, I was finding myself distracted and confused by all of the different events, activities and demands of college. Setting priorities seemed impossible, and by the end of the semester I was very frustrated.

Fran wrote the day before classes began at Lake Erie College. Her first day was September 21, the same as Notre Dame's. She said her parents had driven her out in 11 ½ hours, "not a bad ride considering we came over big highways all the way from Mass." With the interstate highway system still under development, it was rare to be able to make a long-distance drive only on four-lane limited access roads.

Lake Erie College for Women (or as we men liked to call it, the Lake College for Eerie Women) was a liberal arts college of about 500 students, located 30 miles east of Cleveland. In the 1960s it was a highly regarded academic institution, perhaps the only one in the country that offered a degree in equestrianism. As I've said, its most distinguishing offering was the Winter Term Abroad program, the school's main draw for Fran.

In the same way Notre Dame had a "sister" school nearby in all-women St. Mary's College, Lake Erie's "brother" schools were Case Western Reserve and John Carroll University. Both were in Cleveland, 30 or more miles away from Lake Erie, which complicated the dating scene for Lake Erie girls. They compensated by holding lots of events just for their own women. Fran described an "all college 'bat' which was a day of swimming, boating and a lakeside cookout." In the same letter she admitted that "Stupid me asked what lake we were going to. I felt like a nut when they said Lake Erie. It just never dawned on me that it was so close." I had to laugh at that.

She wrote that her classes were to include Biology, Sociology, Psychology, and General Studies (a four-year course required of all students) and that her roommate from Oswego, New York, made fun of Fran's Boston accent. She even sent me notes from three of her new Lake Erie friends.

To me, the most important thing she wrote was this: "I can come for Thanksgiving—'sur-aah' you want me?" Now that was great news, which gave us something to look forward to as we slowly adapted to college life.

A letter from Fran in late September touched on the upcoming visit and shared the others kinds of news common to our letters at this time. Here is an excerpt:

## LAKE ERIE COLLEGE

*Thursday*

*September 28, 1961*

*Dear Bob:*

*....My mom and dad are coming out here the 14th & 15th for Parents Weekend. I can hardly wait; miss them all so much. Are you a little homesick sometimes?*

*How was freshman initiation? Whatever did they do to you? We have freshman-sophomore days here and we're all dreading them. They make you do anything from getting up at 4 a.m. to running through town with your clothes on backwards. Then they have a "Kangaroo Kourt," of which I know nothing. Should be fun anyway, for a while at least.*

*I got a new silver charm for my bracelet. It's a Lake Erie pennant and is green and white. I just love it. Now it has six charms on it.*

*Are you sure your parents wouldn't mind if I came for Thanksgiving? Will your grandparents or any relatives be there?*

*Is Lisa writing to you—or vice-versa?*

*Please take the time to answer all my questions.*

*Write soon, be good, study hard and think of me once in a while. Never forget that I love you.*

*Love always,*

*Fran*

I did answer her questions. "Too bad you have freshman initiation," I began. "We don't—freshman start out on equal terms with upperclassmen except they get two 12:30's per week and we don't get any.

"Aha! I see more questions before me. Well, as far as I know you are still welcome for Thanksgiving but I had better check again before we make any plans. I think my grandparents will be there. I hope so—'cause I want them to meet you.

"Let's see—next question. Oh! Yes. Lisa and I still write once in a while. In fact—just to make you jealous I might see her this weekend. I'm going up to Milwaukee Saturday. Dominican High is having its homecoming and I want to see the annual slaughter."

I also mentioned that Notre Dame had just beaten Oklahoma in its season football opener, that I had joined the Ski and the Young Republicans Clubs, and that I was thinking about joining the Sailing Club the following semester. Though Notre Dame didn't sanction "Greek" fraternities, it offered lots of activity-based clubs designed to provide similar fraternal relationships without the fraternity trappings.

I had invited Fran to come to our Homecoming weekend in South Bend. I was anxious to get her phone number, which I had lost, so that I could call and talk to her about it. I asked her to send it immediately "or, if you're feeling lucrative, call me. My number is CE 4-9011, extension 615 or CE 30381. When one of the vultures answers, just cool him off quick and ask for me in Rm. 312."

Calling each other was always a bit of an ordeal, and an expensive one to boot. There were no phones in the dorm rooms, and of course the convenience of cell phones was decades in the future. Keenan Hall had two pay phones at the end of the corridor on each floor. If Fran called me, she had to let the phone ring until someone passed by and picked it up. That sometimes took a while—often, the phone rang until the noise became so obnoxious that someone begrudgingly left his room and answered just to make the ringing stop. You could only hope that he would have the decency to yell or knock on your door to let you know it was for you. If you actually expected a call, you raced out of your room and down the hall to answer it before someone else did. To make matters worse, you would sometimes hurry to the phone to find the earpiece coated with shaving foam, which of course you wouldn't notice until you slammed the earpiece into your ear.

Making a call was just as complicated. You went to the Huddle, a snack shop in the student union, to change your dollar bills into the dimes needed to feed the pay phone back at the dorm. You had to wait until a phone was free. After you deposited your dime, you either dialed the number or, if it was to be a person-to-person call (more expensive but safer if you weren't sure the person you were calling would be available) you gave the operator the number and name. You were told how many dimes it would take for the first three minutes of calling time; once enough money had been deposited, the call finally went through. As your three minutes wound down you got a message that you had to deposit more dimes to continue the call. If you didn't, the connection would be broken and you'd abruptly be left high and dry. Many a call ended prematurely for lack of dimes to continue.

Fran turned down my invitation to Homecoming but invited me to Lake Erie College's Founder's Day weekend, which I declined in turn. Transportation was always a critical issue. Our only dependable options were trains and buses. For convenience and safety, trains were a far better choice, and—unlike today—they weren't particularly expensive. Dad was providing me a generous allowance:

$200 a month–to cover books, clothes, local transportation and social activities. With careful management, I could handle a train ticket once in a while.

Unfortunately, Fran's father was not nearly so generous with her. She got five dollars a week for whatever she needed. Even in 1961, that didn't go very far. For her, saving enough for a train ticket was nearly impossible no matter how careful she was.

Even as early as October, our letters often discussed the logistics of getting together. My mother had given the green light to Fran's Thanksgiving visit, setting off almost two months of back-and-forth discussions about how Fran would get from Painesville to Sidney. Coincidentally, there was a sophomore at Lake Erie who lived across the street from my family in Sidney. I had never met Jill Amos—she was in college by the time we moved to town—but we hoped she might be able to give Fran a ride. When we learned she wasn't going home for Thanksgiving, we explored many other alternatives. Working it all out involved lots and lots of ink.

In the meantime, fall at Notre Dame excited me no end. The dating scene was non-existent, at least for me, but there was Notre Dame football. That year Joe Kuharich was coach. Notre Dame hadn't been doing well but in 1961, under coach Kuharich, they got off to a 3-0 start, good enough for a national ranking in the top ten.

Then and now, there is nothing quite like a football weekend at Notre Dame. The Friday night pep rallies were pure energy, in the sense of nuclear fission. I wrote enthusiastically to Fran, "Did you see the article about us in *Sports Illustrated*? They had a picture of a student riot (commonly disguised as a pep rally) and a big story. The pep rally this Friday night will be such a brawl after us winning 2 straight games that I think I'll wear spiked armor to stay alive. Sure would like to get you down here for a football weekend—it'd be something you would never forget."

I loved those campus football weekends. Football Saturdays meant huge crowds on campus; student clubs cooking hamburgers, hot dogs, and brats on the main quad to raise money; the parade of the Notre Dame band to the stadium; painted bed sheet signs hung from dorm windows; and an electricity in the air that was—and is—unique in the world of college football. As a student, I could buy season tickets at a deep discount from fan and alumni pricing. To be in the student section of Notre Dame Stadium was to experience non-stop noise, constant jostling, and so much excitement we rarely ever sat down.

Besides football, I wrote to Fran that "the fall social events around here are pretty good. Things get pretty dull between semester break and Easter I hear, so I'm taking advantage now. Friday Skitch Henderson will be here for a big dance, the 20th the Limeliters will be here for a concert, the 27th Jimmy Dorsey's band with Lee Castle will be around for the Homecoming Dance. The Brothers Four are coming sometime this winter." I didn't actually make it to see all of those big names, but it was exciting to know they were performing right there at my school.

By mid-October I was running low on funds. Maybe I wasn't such a good financial manager after all. I wrote Fran that I was going to call her, then found myself down to eight cents and couldn't afford to. Instead, we continued our much more affordable correspondence.

No doubt in an effort to get even for the one I had once sent her, Fran sent me another version of a "Date Questionnaire Form." With tongue solidly lodged in cheek I completed it and sent it back.

*Don't wise around, dear – just be completely honest*

# DATE QUESTIONNAIRE FORM

sent by (Name of Girl) *Fran Jordan*

Name *Nielsdorf* *Robert* *Lynn* .......... Nickname *Bob*
Last          First          Middle

Home Address *1605 Pt. Jefferson Rd.* City *Sidney* State *Ohio* Phone No. *KY 2-4495*

School Address *312 Keenan Hall* City *Notre Dame* State *Ind.* Phone No. *CE-3-2XX1*

Business Address *Russell Rd.* City *Sidney* State *Ohio* Phone No. *YY 2-2291*

**Statistical Data: (All to be answered)**

Height *6'1* .......... Color of Hair *Brown* .......... Birthday *Sept. 4, 1943*

Weight *155* .......... Complexion *Ceddish* .......... Draft Status *Deferred*

Age *18* .......... Color of eyes (l) *Blue* .......... (r) *Blue*

**What type woman do you like?** (Check yours; if schizophrenic, check each)

Dominating.................... Beautiful but dumb.............. Mother type..............

Satisfying.................... Eager to please. ✓ .......... Sexy..............

Home type.................... Sophisticated.............. Worldly..............

Other: *Beautiful – All 'Round Girl ( No Pun Intended)*

**What do you expect on a date?** (answer yes or no and briefly explain)

Sex *Depends on who I date on* .......... Mental companionship *No*

Attention *Yes* .......... Intellectual satisfaction *No*

Affection *Yes – this depends of girl* Physical retribution *No*

Payment *No* .......... Other: ..............

**Please state the one question, above all others, you have often had an urge to ask of your dates** (Be honest): *"Would you like to do something different for a change?"*

**Are you?** (answer yes or no)

Brave *Yes (to a certain extent)* Friendly *Yes* .......... Talkative *No*

Kind *Yes* .......... Too Friendly *Yes (to certain people)* Self-centered *No*

Obedient *No (only to certain people)* Dogmatic *No* .......... Heartbreaker *Yes (to certain people)*

Were you ever a boy scout? *Yes*

If so, are you prepared? *Yes* .......... For what? *For near anything*

Copyright 1959 by Gimmix Novelties, White Plains, N. Y.

GIMMIX

Novelty — G

2

**General Questions:** (All to be answered. Be at least semi-honest.)

When a girl says "no", do you think:

She means NO ......*✓*................ She's just stalling ................................

She means YES ........................ She doesn't know what she's saying ......*✓*

Do you believe in the supremacy of women? *No* .... Can you be educated? *No*

Do you feel experience is the best teacher? *Yes* .... What has it taught you? *Too much*

How much do you tell your friends after a date? *Only a little* .. Do you exaggerate? *Yes*

What is your favorite topic of conversation (besides yourself)? *The weather*

Do you have a line? *Yes* ........................ Has it been effective? *Yes*

Do you expect your dates to fall for it? *Not all* .. Whom do you quote the most? *Myself*

Do you object to in-laws? *No* ........................ Relatives? *No*

How are you fixed for blades? *Plenty* .. Socks? *Plenty* .. Shirts? *Too many* .. Handkerchiefs? *Plenty*

Would you admit if your intentions weren't honorable? *No* ........ Are they? *Yes*

Do you like to travel? *Very much* .... If yes, will you take me with you? *Certainly*

What's your ambition? *Notalive Island* .. How often? *Every night*

Are you a dreamer? *Yes* .. About food? *Yes* .. Faraway places? *Yes* .. Anything else? *Yes*

Do you object to Bermuda shorts? *No* .... Jeans? *Yes* .... Crinolines? *No*

Do you like argyles? *Sweaters* .. Size: *44* ........ Design: *crew neck* | *long sleeve*

Are you in the know? *Yes* .... Are you in the know that we're in the know? *Yes*

What was your last blind date like? *Not bad* .. Who fixed you up? *A buddy*

Do you scratch like a chicken? *No* ........ Or ask like a man? *Yes*

Do you: Dance? *Yes* .... How well? *Like Fred Astaire* (*check* the dances you prefer:

| | | | |
|---|---|---|---|
| Flamingo .......... | Fox Trot *✓* | Charleston .......... | Rhumba .......... |
| Samba .......... | Jitterbug *✓* | Waltz .......... | Meringue .......... |
| Bunny Hop .......... | Kasatsky .......... | Mambo .......... | Cha-Cha-Cha *✓* |

How far in advance do you call to make a date? *One night* .. How much later than that? *One hour*

Are you ever late for a date? *Yes* ........ Have you ever been on time? *Yes*

Do you have a car? *Yes* .. Year: *1953* .. Make: *Ford* .. Model: *Skyliner*

Color: *Orange & cream* .. Dented fenders? *Yes* .. Big back seat? *No* .. Can I drive it? *Yes*

Have you ever broken a date to go out with someone else? *Yes*

Would you expect me to break a date to go out with you? *Yes*

Do you expect your date to use Lip-stay? *No* ........ If not, do you carry Kleenex? *No*

Would you mind:

General dusting *Yes* ........ Washing dishes *Yes*

Ironing *Yes* ........ Getting up to feed the baby *Yes*

Earning a living? *No* .. For two people? *No* ........ For a family? *No*

3

Would you vote for a woman President? *No.* Why not? *Would waste too much time*

Are you in a position to get serious? *Yes* How serious? *Not for marriage*

Would you marry for money? *No* How much money? *None*

How many kids do you want? *5* Boys: *3* Girls: *2*

Do you work? *Yes* Is it a steady job? *Yes* Salary: *18 credit hrs.*

    Does it show promises for advancement? *Yes* How soon? *1965*

Do you drink? *Yes* Seldom? *No* Frequently? *Yes* AA? *No*

Do you keep secrets from your dates? *Yes* Such as: *Jockey shorts too tight*

Are you impatient? *Yes* Frustrated? *No* About what? _____

    Is there anything I can do? *Probably* Do you think I'd do it? *Sometime* When: *when pictured or married*

Why do you date? (other than sex) *For something to do and to get to know girls I'd like to get to know* (Do not leave blank)

Do you date women older than yourself? *Yes* Why? *I like them* How much older? *1-3 yrs.*

Do you indulge? *Yes* In what? *"Wine, women, and orgies."* How often? *Once in a while*

Do you ever insist your date go dutch treat? *No*

    What type dresser are you:

      Tweedy .................. Collegiate ✓ Very dressy ..............

      Sharp .................. All shoes .............. Plain sloppy ..............

      Hoody .................. Ivy .............. Just lazy ..............

What brand lipstick do you prefer? *Revlon* What type perfume do you like? *Hypnotique*

Is your chest measurement expanded over "36"? *When I'm in shape* If so, are you dangerous? *No*

What do you want from a date? *Everything* What do you expect? *Not much*

    What will you settle for? *More than I expect* What do you usually get? *What I want*

When bringing a date home, do you:

      Raid the ice box *Yes* Ask for a good book *No*

      Slouch on the couch *Yes* Check to see if anyone else is home *Yes*

Are you opposed to chaperones? *Yes* Do you need a chaperone? *No*

Do you have an address book? *Yes* How many girls are listed? *14*

Do you expect a kiss on a first date? *Yes* Do you discourage easily? *Yes*

Where do you take a girl on a first date? *Home* Second date? *Home* After that? *Home (made a her home)*

## Essay Questions:

What is your conception of the ideal girl? *My conception of the ideal girl is difficult to say. She must be good looking, have a good figure, vivacious personality, must like to do the things I like to do, or at least want to learn.*

**4**

Please write a brief but comprehensive story of your life and loves: _I was born when I was_ _very young... and I don't remember much until I was about 15. Not til when I met Fran Jordan while I was in high school I had two great loves, Barbara [illegible] and Lois [illegible], respectively. This excepts Fran Jordan, of course, because I still love her._

I swear that I have never been affiliated with any Communis[t] have I at any time ever attempted to demoralize or unduly influence

I further attest that all the above information is correct to th errors or misleading statements of facts are wholly mine.

Signature _Robert L. Zielsdorf_

**List Two References:**

1. Female: Name _Lois [illegible]_
2. Male: Name _Tony Beck_     Address _1 [illegible] Ave_

    Age _18_     Height _5'9"_     Weight _140_

    Build _?_     Appearance _Extremely handsome_

    Would you mind if I went out with him? _[illegible]_

This Questionnaire to be returned to:

(Name of Girl): _Fran Jordan_      _as soon_

(Address): _Box 112_      _as possible!_

     _Lake Erie College_

     _Painesville, Ohio_

I did wise around, but who could blame me? I knew she wasn't taking the whole thing very seriously. The photo attached was my high school graduation picture, highlighting my spiffy modified "Hollywood" haircut. Pretty normal in Milwaukee, that haircut had been quite *avant-garde* for Sidney. Even though the kids there didn't hold it against me, I eventually lost interest in it, changing it to something more normal before going off to college.

I'm not sure what I was thinking to list my "other" girlfriend, Lisa, as a reference on the questionnaire. I'm sure it was more an attempt to be funny than it was some sadistic poke in the eye, and luckily Fran was her usual good sport about it.

Letters flew back and forth that fall. We talked mostly about how Fran was going to get from Painesville to Sidney for Thanksgiving, but shared other bits of college news as well. I suffered through mid-term exams, something Fran avoided because Lake Erie was on the trimester schedule. Fran got to see the Kingston Trio at the Cleveland Music Hall. "Man, were they ever fabulous," she wrote. "I was so excited I could hardly control myself. After the performance we went to the Kon Tiki room at the Sheraton—what atmosphere. I had the coolest cocktail; it's called a Bolo and is made of rum, pineapple and papaya juice, etc., and it was served in a <u>real</u> whole pineapple with the middle scooped out. Have to have one again sometime."

The Thanksgiving transportation issue was finally resolved when my mother wrote directly to Fran.

*November 14th*

*Dear Fran,*

*For some time I have wanted to write to you to tell you that all the Zielsdorfs are looking forward to having you with us for*

*Thanksgiving. As Bob has probably told you, my parents will be with us also. Their name is Daubel and they live in Fremont.*

*The transportation problems have been the reason for the delay in writing. We had hoped that something would turn up in the way of a ride with friends. But Jill Amos's mother reports that Jill is not coming home because she has classes on Friday and Saturday. So after considering every other form of transportation (and believe me, they are meager), Bob's dad and I feel that the best would be the direct New York Central train into Sidney.*

*This leaves Cleveland at 10:10 p.m. and is due here at 1:54 a.m. This is pretty dismal sounding, I know—and there is not even an attendant at the station here at that hour (although the waiting room is open). But the only other alternative is a train to Findlay on Thanksgiving Day. Findlay is about two hours from here, and if the train should be delayed it might ruin the day for all of us.*

*We feel that if you don't mind not being welcomed until the next morning, you would personally prefer getting in here at night. Sleep as late as you can—and it should work out "jes' fine!"*

*The return train leaves here every afternoon at 5:20 or thereabouts and is no problem. Perhaps a better solution will still turn up.*

*We are leaving for New York tomorrow, returning Saturday— so I have much to do.*

*We are looking forward to meeting you—*

*Sincerely,*

*Mary W. Zielsdorf*

She and Dad had also studied the alternatives, coming up with the only practical one. Somehow Fran found the money for a ticket. The train was delayed many hours, but I met her when the train finally rolled into Sidney about 6:30 a.m.

Fran was a big hit with my family. Even my nine-year-old sister Lissa liked her, despite being jealous that my attention was diverted from her. At one point she said to Fran "Why are you here? You can't even say his name right. It's "Bob," not "Bawb." My grandfather, known far and wide as a practical jokester, unleashed a wind-up tarantula on her at Thanksgiving dinner. Known far and wide as an arachnophobe, Fran wasn't nearly as amused as the rest of the family.

My mother's Thanksgiving dinner menu was always the same. Roast turkey, stuffing, mashed potatoes, escalloped corn, broccoli casserole, and her signature Jell-o salad. A stylish dish at that time, improbably enough it featured cream cheese and chopped carrots in the center. Dinner was served in the evening, usually around 7:00, after the adult cocktail hour. Wisely, Mom always hired someone to help serve the dinner and clean up afterwards. That way we could all collapse together in a food coma when dinner was finished.

Fran was given my sister's room. Each morning I went in and gently woke her. Since the house was full of people, our bedside encounters were all on the up-and-up, but they were still a nice touch of innocent intimacy. In a letter afterwards, Fran remarked, "How can I possibly wake up with an alarm clock after this weekend? I told you you'd spoil me."

Driving around town or sitting together in the family room after everyone else had gone to bed, we found time for some serious talking that Thanksgiving. Our ongoing relationships with Lisa and Donnie were major topics of conversation. Even though we were still primarily pen pals, we had fallen in love with each other. But how could we truly love each other, we wondered, yet have such strong feelings for others as well? As we talked, we realized that we shared the same questions *and* the same lack of answers. In our different ways, we were both confused.

Much of the content of our letters for the balance of the year was lighthearted. For example, Fran wrote to ask me what I wanted from her for Christmas. "I feel that we know each other well enough now that it would be perfectly proper for you to get me that sports car," I responded. "Make sure it is a Jaguar XK-E with wire wheels, 4 on the floor, and full race cam." Her reply? "Sorry, Bob, but the Jaguar I wanted to get you for Christmas was already sold and none of the others particularly appealed to me—wrong color, etc. Will you wait a few years?"

Still, almost every letter voiced some concern about our friendships with Lisa and Donnie. With no formal commitment to each other, we had no real reason to be jealous of the other's relationships. Yet there was an undercurrent of insecurity in our letters, partially masked in my case by some youthful bravado. We both feared that someone might come along and undo our special friendship.

For example, I wrote about our Thanksgiving visit, "It was wonderful being with you this weekend—especially falling in love with you again. I'd love to know how this triangle will end. Be sure to let me know what Donnie has to say—you know I'll be interested. I love you, honey. Please protect my interests. Love, etc., Bob."

She wrote back promptly, referring to a trip to Milwaukee I was planning. "Is Lisa going to keep your pin indefinitely or are you unpinning it on the 9th? Hmmm! Don't forget to think of me that weekend—you promised."

"I took Lisa to the [party] and we managed to have a great time," I replied. "Somehow, things weren't the same, but I did decide to let her keep the pin. Did I tell you I talked you over with a priest friend of mine? He says our situation is not at all unusual and to just hang on and see what happens. Sounds like sound advice."

"I'm sorta anxious to see how the Donnie-Fran relationship stands—think right now it's falling apart," Fran wrote on another occasion. And in another of her letters: "How's Lisa? Still get that old feeling? Saw Donnie Friday and Saturday & Sunday nights—something different—can't figure out what but it's certainly not the way it was when I left for school. Think we're sort of friends now. Hope to tell you I'm not really shook up about it—maybe it's all for the best. Let's wait and see."

"Have you figured out what's with you and Don yet?" I wrote later.

Fran explained that "things between us are the same as usual—we still like each other. Maybe your priest friend was absolutely right—let's wait and see how everything works out. Actually it's much too soon to make any definite move either way—you know as well as I do. I just ask God every night to help me and keep me on the right path—and not let me go astray."

Time and distance were working against us that year and leaving us full of questions. In retrospect, I think the waiting served us well, giving us time to mature, explore life on our own, and get to know each other thoroughly. At the time, though, I wasn't always that philosophical. When and how would we see each other? What would I do about Lisa? What would Fran do about Donnie? How would it all come out? I was impatient to know.

# CHAPTER EIGHT

*A*S 1962 BEGAN, BOTH FRAN AND I WERE GETTING USED TO OUR NEW lives as college students and making the best of being apart from each other.

The year began with a dramatic announcement. I wrote to Fran that I was going to leave Notre Dame after my first year to enroll at Ohio State. "I like ND but don't think I want to stay here for 4 years so Ohio State looks pretty good," I explained. "Say boy, what's this about leaving Notre Dame?" Fran wrote back. "Are you absolutely sure that's what you want to do? You most certainly have the ability to do the work so why do you want to go to Ohio State? It never seemed to carry with it the same prestige etc. as N.D. does. Oh well, I imagine this is really none of my business but it just doesn't seem like you to want to make this change."

I was a bit surprised by her reaction. This may have been the first time Fran had offered advice or a contrary opinion on something I planned to do. As I reflected over time, I found it to be wise advice, and it definitely influenced my eventual decision to stay at Notre Dame. In the short run, though, I didn't change my mind. "About leaving Notre Dame, at the present time it is what I want to do. The lack of things around here is very depressing. For a university 'committed to excellence' there is a definite lack of university atmosphere. Sometimes I feel like I'm in a prep school. The lack of co-ed life gets me down once in a while. Maybe I'll change my mind by the end of the semester." Then I carped about studying and having seen a couple lousy movies the night before. Today it's clear that my frustration was simply part of the growing-up process, but naturally, I didn't see it that way yet.

In early January, Fran invited me to come to Lake Erie for the Freshman-Sophomore Weekend in mid-February—a major winter social event on campus. "I would like to come for the Frosh-Soph Weekend. How 'bout some details on where to stay, how much, what is going on Fri (might have trouble getting there that day) and stuff like that," I answered. I continued, "I am getting to like ND better now. It is at its worst on weekends because there is little to be said for the belles of St. Mary's that I have seen so far....Well, doll, I've got a Theology test and a History test tomorrow so I'd better get busy. I love you very much and I know that's influencing things in Milwaukee. Miss me and write soon."

The comment about "things in Milwaukee" referred, of course, to my relationship with Lisa. While I continued to see her from time to time, my strong feelings for her had been fading in the face of even stronger feelings for Fran. As a college man, I became very aware that Lisa was a high school *girl* while Fran was a college *woman.* Fran and I were maturing in ways that Lisa wasn't—and Fran had a certain sophistication that I sensed even though I couldn't express it. I was starting to realize that Lisa and I just weren't meant to have a long-term relationship.

Fran wrote back saying I could get a room at a local hotel for $3.50 per night. How could I turn down a deal like that? In a subsequent letter she asked if I could find a date for her friend Kit. Scrambling around, I was able to recruit a buddy to make the trip with me. But shortly after sending her this good news, I began to weasel out of the deal. I had discovered during registration that I would have Saturday morning classes that term. As a freshman, I found that trying to understand the Notre Dame class registration process—not to mention getting the professors and class times I wanted—was as difficult as, say, understanding the theory of relativity.

With Saturday classes on my schedule, trying to get to Lake Erie for the weekend just wasn't going to work. In addition, Notre Dame's own famous Mardi Gras weekend was scheduled shortly afterward. I had invited Lisa and laid out most of my funds to buy a tuxedo and pay for the other costs. Even if I had the time for Lake Erie College, I didn't have the money. Fran wrote more letters coaxing me to find a way to get to there, but that time around I never made it happen.

At Notre Dame, students enrolled in one of the University's several colleges: Commerce, Arts & Letters, Engineering and so on. I was enrolled at what was then called Notre Dame's College of Commerce (now Business Administration). In addition to some other freshman courses, I was taking basic marketing and accounting. In mid-February we received our report cards and I shared my results with Fran. "Got my first semester grades this morning and while I am not overjoyed, they are not too bad—average of 2.333 out of 6. That amounts to a C. It means that I am also in the 50th percentile of the College of Commerce— which means that half the guys in my college did worse than I did which means that I had better get at least a 3.0 or 3.5 average this semester." (My high school friend Steve Huxley, now a college professor, tells me in the years since I went to college, grade inflation has added about seven-tenths of a point to grade point averages generally. That makes my performance more respectable by today's standards, and gives me that 3.0 or better that I wanted!)

The only reason I was happy with a C average was the realization it could have been so much worse. Struggling mightily with math and accounting, I felt fortunate to have passed, even by the skin of my teeth. I had taken all of the necessary college prep courses in high school, but math concepts still didn't come easily. Making matters worse, my math teacher was a graduate assistant. All brains and no communication skills, he was hard-pressed to explain freshman math in a way that someone like me could grasp. As for Accounting, what sadist ever came up with the idea that all those numbers had to balance out, and what the heck did "debit" mean, anyway? Those were the days before hand-held calculators. Making the columns do the right thing required the meticulous manual addition of row after row of figures: pure torture for the detail-challenged.

Fran's academic results were similar. "Your average is the same as mine—it (mine, that is) is 2.33 out of a possible 4. That gives me a C average for last term." She went on to say she was currently averaging an A, so we both saw hope for future success.

Most of our correspondence that term described social events and concerts, complained about studying and tests, and discussed plans for upcoming breaks and summer vacation. But there were a few exceptions, like this letter from Fran.

*Wednesday*

*February 28, 1962*

*Dear Bob,*

*Hello there! How are you today? Imagine by now you're approaching*

*that mid-term slump where little of anything goes right. O well, after your weekend you'll be able to face the world again with new courage and foresight. Please don't think me presumptuous for saying the preceding but I sort of thought that maybe you felt like I did around the middle of the semester.*

*Things here in eastern Ohio are busy to say the least. Last weekend was by far the most never-wracking I have ever lived though. I had a blind date with a grad student at Western Reserve. We went to Cleveland and got snow-bound. He had a Sprite and its insides got all frozen. Ex-brownie Fran couldn't remember the college phone number and on trying the pay phone on fourth floor, found it to be out of order. It's a very well-enforced law that if you're late or can't get back to school, you telephone your house mother. I couldn't and didn't.*

*Decided I wasn't going to spend the night with a complete stranger hiking through the snow in high heels, so about 2:30 a.m. I called Paul, the boy I told you about from John Carroll, who also lives in Cleveland. He got out of bed and drove 10 miles to get us, took my blind date to his apartment, and brought me back to his house for the night. Unknown to me was the minor detail that the girl he has been dating for a year and a half was also sleeping at his house as a result of the freak blizzard. I woke up in the morning to Ann's crying and weeping on seeing me asleep on the living room couch. This may sound extremely funny but although the situation was odd the whole thing was really bad news.*

*Paul brought me back to college Saturday after lunch—no one still knew where I was or had been. It was awful—people screaming she's here, she's back!! I felt awful—nervous as anything. Told my story to the house mother and the Dean, and now I'm scheduled to appear before judicial board Sunday night.*

*You couldn't believe how nervous I am. I could get put on Social Probation (maximum punishment) or campused (minimum punishment). Please say a little prayer. My parents know nothing of this as yet. I've decided to wait 'till I see them in two weeks. To add to the crime, I was signed out with my roomie, but neither left nor returned with her. Guess people were up until 4 a.m. waiting for news or calling hospitals, etc. Oh me, God help me. Enough crying on your shoulder—I wish you could be here and lend a little moral support.*

*Thank you for answering all my nosy inquiries, and congratulations on overcoming your mental block! Seriously, Bob, best of luck in whatever you decide to finally do about Lisa. When did the great revelation concerning your feelings finally take form? How does she feel on this subject? Now for the bad one—does she still have your pin? I'll wait 'till after the weekend and its festivities for the answer or explanation for that question.*

*You asked about Donnie—I don't know what to say. I really enjoy dating him but for some weird reason I like him more when I'm here and he's in Boston than when we're together. As for you, young man, someday I'd love to see all the things we talked about over Thanksgiving take form and grow into something very dear and lasting. I love you and there's no denying it, no matter what evidence goes against us. We have many (4) years to live through before anything has to be finally settled and presently I feel too young to be tied down by word, symbol, etc. Don't hate me, please, but I'm still a teenager and still very confused. Besides, at times it's very difficult to express myself on paper and with every word now it's getting harder. Just remember—some strange force has kept us sort of together*

*for 5 years—this must mean something, if not to you, to me. Now may I*

*return the question and ask for the gory details?*

*I'm exhausted so I think I'll go to bed. Sorry to cut this letter off so short*

*but hope you understand.*

*Write soon, you Rockne prodigy, and be good. No holds barred—*

*I love you.*

*As always,*

*Fran*

*P.S. Tell Tim he owes this kid a letter!*

*P.S.S. How are your summer plans coming along?*

*P.S.S.S. Did your dad sell your car and get you a sailboat?  I know, you'll*

*have both—lucky. Still want to take me for a ride?*

*P.P.S.S.S  Love to come to Notre Dame in April but can't say definitely*

*until later. Keep the date free for a while?*


Rereading this letter a half century later, I'm awed and touched by Fran's openness. It took real trust for her to confide in me about her Cleveland misadventure—and it would have been easy for her never to mention it, given how unlikely it was that I would ever find out. Clearly, Fran felt secure enough in our friendship to share what happened without worrying that I would think less of her. The only thing she did wrong was to not figure out some way to call the College—and as she explained, she thought the switchboard closed at 11:00, so she wouldn't have been able to get through. I certainly didn't hold the incident against her in any way. However, the disciplinary committee did, and she was confined to campus for a couple of weeks.

While Fran was dealing with her punishment, the bad Cleveland weather and a boorish date, I was celebrating Notre Dame's Mardi Gras with Lisa. She had clearly come hoping that things would return to the way they had once been between us. But when we talked she was able to accept the change and agree that letting things ease off was for the best. Hurt and disappointed as she probably was, I think she knew that she was no more ready for a serious, long-term commitment than I was.

I wrote to Fran with an update on that relationship and some developing thoughts about our own.

UNIVERSITY OF NOTRE DAME

NOTRE DAME, INDIANA

March 4, 1962

Dear Fran,

Well, the Mardi Gras weekend is pretty much over, for me anyway. The Carnival is tomorrow and Tuesday, but since I only have 10 cents to my name, I won't be able to do too much gambling. I had a real good time, but I honestly think I could have had a better time with you.

Here it is—Lisa and I have finally admitted that we are no longer in love with each other. We are still good friends and I will still continue to go to Milwaukee on occasion to see her. She is keeping the pin as a memento of what we used to have between us, and as a sign of our good judgment in regard to our relationship.

(This letter was just interrupted with some news which I will get to later.)

As for you, Fran, I love you and I'm sure it is the same way you love me. I don't want to be tied down now either, in fact I'm free for the first time in two years. Someday, when I start to think seriously about settling down, I would like to think about you and see ourselves happy together.

I don't know if that covers the subject or not, but that is all I feel like saying about it right now.

Now for the late news…While I was writing this letter I received word that Lisa rolled her car on the highway on the way home. It happened on an icy spot somewhere in Wisconsin. Everyone is alright except that she is extremely shook. I really feel sorry for her—the poor kid has enough troubles without that. I'm sure you understand a little how she feels.

Hope your experience with Ohio weather hasn't soured you on humanity. Let me know how you make out with the Board. Good luck, honey.

Write soon and I'll be in a better mood in my next letter.

Love, etc.,

Bob

P.S. Please don't disappoint me like I did you on this April weekend. RLZ

Fran replied immediately, with a level of clarity and compassion I admired.

*Tuesday*

*March 6, 1962*

*Dear Bob,*

*Hello there! How are you today? Received your letter this morning and am answering right away like I promised. Goodness, I was so surprised and delighted to get your call last night. How long did we talk anyway—*

*half an hour? Somehow a phone call always makes you seem closer than a letter but keep writing—I don't feel that far away!*

*I was really upset to hear about Lisa's accident. You may find this difficult to understand, but through you, I sort of felt that I knew her. After having been in an accident myself, when it happens to someone you know, you really feel it for them. I know I'm very confusing but forgive me. I said a few little prayers for her; hope she won't mind. Well,* bastante.

*Thank you for explaining your present feelings towards me and others—you certainly did it well. It is a nice feeling to be free and still young enough not to have to be serious about your future position in society or something like that. I hate to say marital status because it sounds so final and somewhat frightening, to me anyway. Already I've said too much—you must be having difficulty following my train of thought. Come to think of it, I am too.*

*The excitement of flying home has finally struck me. Tomorrow I make my plane reservations. My parents know nothing of these plans; I'll be home Thursday night instead of Saturday when they're expecting me. Quite a surprise, hmm?*

*It's after ten now and I still have a 2000-word paper to write for General Studies. Once that is finished there will only be three to go this whole school year. Thank goodness.*

*How was the last night of Mardi Gras? Sure hope you won that Corvette! Then you'd have no problem about getting to see me.*

*Tonight we had a Mardi Gras dinner—the whole commons was decorated and there were long black candles on each table. Someone played the piano all during dinner and after that we had entertainment. The menu was even French! It was much fun. Slater certainly goes out of his way to keep the girls here fat and happy. Suppose you could say I fit into both categories.*

*Sure you want a straight-laced Bostonian on the campus of Notre Dame for Jazz Festival? I'd really love to come and will do my best to be there Friday the 6th, but it seems as though I'm the one who has been doing the traveling (or pursing!) lately. I'll let you know more about it after I see my parents. Would you mind if one of my friends comes along with me?*

*Exams start in six days—my nerves are really frazzled. Wish they didn't count so much. Please write often next week—it would really be a help.*

*We're now trying to decide how we can make meals, classes and church tomorrow—looks like I don't eat all day!*

*The big hand on the clock is still moving and the hour of eleven is just about here. I best start my homework for tomorrow.*

*Write again soon. I miss you still. Be good, study hard and you behave yourself, too. I love you and hope to see you fairly soon. Do you know when your friends will be driving to Cleveland?*

*Love as always,*

*Fran*

As this exchange shows, we wisely decided that for now we would get on with our separate lives. Yet we also agreed, at least for the time being, that when the time came to think about settling down, we would think seriously about each other.

In early April, Fran somehow found the money to take the train to South Bend for the Notre Dame Jazz Festival. This annual campus event drew some national big names in jazz. We had a great time together, but when she got back to school I wrote, "You know, I did get to know you better but somehow I don't feel that we got as close as we did the last time we saw each other. Do you agree? Or otherwise? I love you, Fran, but you have to admit that we have the strangest relationship known to mankind. (And I like it.)" I'm not sure any more why I made that comment. It probably just acknowledged that though we had enjoyed a nice weekend in each other's company, there had been no real memorable or dramatic moments.

"Disagreement," she responded. "I got to know you quite a bit better and felt very close to you in many strong but wonderful ways. Agreed, it was very different from Thanksgiving but still I feel that more was said and thought about last weekend. I do love you and our relationship is strange but I, too, like it. Can't forget about what your priest friend said about it either." We had gotten to know each other well enough to share differences of opinion, and the letters allowed us to talk candidly about those differences and everything else.

Spring brought a new tradition for me to savor: spring break. Tom Franck and Chuck Watson, who lived in the room next to mine at Keenan Hall, had gone to high school together in Ft. Lauderdale, FL, then America's spring break mecca. (You can get a glimpse of it in the 1960 film *Where the Boys Are.*) Tom was becoming my closest friend; Chuck was a good friend, too, though not as close. I was thrilled when my parents gave me their permission and their car to drive to "Lauderdale" for our Easter vacation. The 1960 Pontiac Bonneville convertible would be the perfect car for the scene. Tom and two other Notre Dame friends would brave the 24-hour road trip with me, and I would stay for free at Tom's home. As I explained to Fran, "We've got some fantastic beach parties cooked up—Chuck has a boat so we can go where the crowds don't go.

I also am going to learn to water ski all over again. I didn't get a chance all last summer so I must be pretty rusty."

Toward the end of February, I had invited Fran and her parents to come to Sidney after they picked Fran up in June. Now the plans for that visit were beginning to take shape. "Mom would love to go to your house and meet your family after picking me up in June," Fran wrote. "Said she would talk it over with dad so if anything is decided upon I'll definitely let you know."

Many of our letters in May discussed another plan, for her to join me later in the month for Notre Dame's prom. The details provide a sense of her budget. She planned to bring a couple of friends with her so she could get a group-rate train fare and emphatically ruled out staying at the on-campus Morris Inn because it was far too expensive at $14.00 a night. Instead, I booked Fran and her friends into the downtown LaSalle Hotel, which offered double accommodations and a rollaway bed for $8.00.

Attending a college prom was a much bigger event than anything we had experienced in high school. The band was famous—maybe Jimmy Dorsey—and the decorations were elaborate and elegant, from the floral entry arch to the huge centerpieces on the tables. Adding to the impression of sophistication, we were just freshmen amid a sea of older and presumably worldlier upperclassmen. In addition to the prom, we went to a beach party on Lake Michigan with a hundred other students and their dates, all enjoying the unusually warm spring weekend together. There was nowhere Fran and I could go to be alone—women were absolutely verboten in my dormitory and Fran was sharing her hotel room with her friends. But we didn't need to be alone to enjoy being with each other; the weekend was another building block in the increasingly solid structure of our relationship.

That prom visit was the perfect grand finale for my freshman year in college. I endured my final exams the following week and by May 25 was back home in Sidney. Fran had another two and a half weeks of school to go. Her mom and dad had agreed to make the trip to Sidney—an extra eight hours of driving all told—once they picked her up at Lake Erie College. I was excited. Three visits together in a single academic year: that was a real luxury for us.

Back in "Sadney," as I had begun calling my hometown, I dreaded the inevitable boredom that lay ahead. Knowing that it would be a long summer in Sidney without a girlfriend, I started going out with a new girl. Sharon, who had moved to town a year or so earlier, was tall, blond and curvaceous. She represented my best hope for a social summer: someone with whom to go out with at night, share a beer and a few kisses, cruise the town, and enjoy movies and parties. I never contemplated anything beyond some summer dates with her, and probably never thought to even tell Fran that she was in the picture. But a date with her led to a huge lapse of judgment that caused a major rift in my relationship with Fran.

After Fran told me when she and her parents would depart for Sidney, I carefully calculated their arrival time. Or so I thought. Not expecting them until mid-afternoon, I decided to take Sharon to a nearby lake for a picnic, sure that I would get home in plenty of time to welcome Fran and her parents. Except that I didn't. In fact, they beat me by a whole hour.

Very excited about seeing Fran, I had never intended to make light of her arrival. I also really liked her mom and dad, and wouldn't have wanted to be disrespectful in any way. Still, there was no doubt that I screwed up.

Although her folks seemed happy to see me, I could tell from Fran's demeanor that she knew the truth about my lateness. My family hadn't covered for me. The cat was out of the proverbial bag, and everyone knew why I was late. In spite of that, we had what I thought was a good time while the Jordans were there. I harbored the hope that somehow the whole thing would blow over. To me it was a terribly embarrassing mistake, but to Fran it meant significantly more. As her commentary at the end of this book explains, my boorishness made her question my character and wonder if she really knew me after all.

No sooner had the Jordan family left our driveway for their long drive back to Andover than Mom cornered me in the kitchen. Always both sensitive and intuitive, she had really felt the hurt and anger I had caused Fran and her parents—not only for being missing when they arrived, but for being out with another girl. Of course, my behavior had also been embarrassing for Mom and Dad as well. Mom knew that I didn't really understand all of this, and she wanted to send me a very clear message. That conversation in the kitchen wasn't long, but it didn't have to be. I got the wake-up call loud and clear.

I wrote to Fran promptly after the Jordans' departure.

ROBERT L. ZIELSDORF

1608 PORT JEFFERSON ROAD

SIDNEY, OHIO

June 12, 1962

Dear Fran,

Before I get your letter, I want to apologize for the way I treated you last weekend. I didn't realize how hurt you were (or must have been) until I talked to my mother. She said you really were disappointed when I wasn't home to meet you Saturday. I won't excuse myself, but just say I'm sorry it happened that way.

I am going through a "thought process" at the present time, in which I am trying to decide whether I really love you or not. My feelings for you have not changed however, and that is the important thing which you must understand. That is why I couldn't bring myself to say "I love you" and why I still can't. Perhaps we should have talked it out, but you were so quiet I hated to bring it up.

Woody and I are leaving Thurs. afternoon for Notre Dame. Friday we'll be in Chicago, Sat in Milwaukee and Sun – the long ride back to Sidney. I start work on Mon (boo, hiss…).

Sorry this is short, but I want to hear from you before I write much.

Hope your parents enjoyed their stay in Sidney. Mine really enjoyed having them. I promise not to be so busy the next time you come down, and I also promise to try to get to Andover this summer.

Love, etc.,

Bob

Fran was soon into the swing of summer in Andover and her new job as a nurse's aide at Danvers Mental Hospital. I got on with my summer, still dating Sharon and working for the State of Ohio, cutting grass and painting guard rails along Interstate 75.

In mid-June, Fran wrote a candid letter about her feelings. Considering how angry and hurt she was, her letter was not only beautiful but also very fair.

*Tuesday*

*June 19, 1962*

*Dear Bob,*

*Hello—how are you? Did you have fun last weekend? Suppose your new car is all broken in by now. My father's isn't. He just got it last night. It's a '62 Oldsmobile Super 88, about 330 hp. I think. It's metallic-blue with a white top—really neat. I was getting tired of his funeral car and this new one is quite a change.*

*Are you as tired as I am after two days of work? I love my job—no dull routine—every day promises to be different and more interesting than the last. I'm in the women's ward B-1 which is pretty good, only two away from the one that has the least ill patients. B-1 is an admission ward of about 60 women ranging from 20 to 90; mostly they fall nearer 90 than 20, though. The real young ones are the sad cases. These patients aren't violent; they are psychotic, neurotic or depressed people. We have about twelve suicide patients, and about 8 who think they are someone they're not. The funniest one is an old lady who believes she's the superintendent of the entire hospital. She is continuously ordering everyone around and vowing to either report or dismiss them if they fail to obey her orders. She also has a big baby doll she keeps on her bed. Of course to her it's alive, and she screams and yells if anyone goes near it. Today she was chasing another old lady all around the ward because the latter had taken her baby's blanket. Never a dull moment....*

*The worst thing is to be listening to one of them when all of a sudden they say, "You think I'm nuts, don't you?" That's one question that is pretty difficult to answer tactfully. So far I've only had that little phrase thrown at me three times. What does your job involve?*

*Vacation is already flying by—I wish the days would go a bit more slowly. Last Sunday we went to Ogunquit beach in Maine—it was beautiful. This weekend my parents are going to Winnipesaukee. I'm going to try to get up on Saturday since I don't have to work. I'd sort of like to get some serious water-skiing in before the 4th of July. Have you been able to do any sailing?*

*Again, it was wonderful to see you before coming home. Your apology accepted—I suppose it was just one of those things you can't explain too easily in words. Despite everything it was fun being with you and I seriously hope we can do it again sometime. About your "thought process"—keep it up. Like you, I am also happy and excited with my present state of freedom—it's something comparatively new and I love it, to be truthful. I don't want, nor do I knowingly intend, to become tied down again for a long time. Perhaps you share my feelings on this matter and when you tell someone you love them it often times includes and/or implies this binding feeling. Please don't associate this with me—agreed, I do love you but as yet I couldn't honestly say that I am or will someday be _in_ love with you. Again, this is something that I'm not the least bit worried about. I'm only 19 and have many years to fully develop, arrange and straighten out my feelings and emotions. And not meaning to be fatalistic, I still believe that "what will be will be," and I'm more than willing to wait.*

*Perhaps I've said too much. I know my control and usage of English vocabulary and grammar isn't very proficient but anyway, I hope you can understand what I've been trying to say. I think an awful lot of you—*

*please remember this. Also, be good, don't work so hard and think of me*
*once in a while.*

*Don't forget you promised to try and get to Andover this summer—I'm*
*hoping you can make it. Until then, write. I miss your weekly letters that*
*were so great during school.*

*Love as ever,*

*Fran*

*P.S. Guess what? We have to wear a chain with about 50 keys on it*
*around our waist and work and unlock and relock everyone's door as we go*
*through!!*

Although she claimed to not express herself well in writing, Fran did a remarkable job. I couldn't argue with her logic—everything she said was both correct
and wise. And even as a largely clueless teenage guy, I could tell I had a lot of
work to do to get back in her good graces. Did I want her to be "*in love*" with
me again? Yes. How would I accomplish that? I just didn't know.

The coolness between us lasted well into our sophomore year. My final letter
of the summer 1962 attempted to square things. On September 10, I wrote:
"I've been doing a lot of thinking about you lately, and I guess I really haven't
been taking your feelings into consideration in many instances. I'm very sorry
about that and I guess I should do something to make up for it. We can talk it
over when I see you. OK?!"

Sharon and her family moved away in August, bringing our summer romance
to an end. I missed her for a while, mostly because I was suddenly dateless
again. We had never grown really close, so her departure wasn't much of a disappointment. I called a girl named Carolyn. I had known her for a long time

and we had always gotten along well in a platonic way. We seemed to have a lot in common, given that we both called Sidney home and that our parents were good friends. Slender and dark haired, Carolyn was fairly tall, about 5'7", and pretty in a girl-next-door kind of way. She had a good sense of humor and a sociable personality, both of which I enjoyed.

Much more important to me, my second year in college was about to begin.

## CHAPTER NINE

*F*RAN AND I RETURNED TO SCHOOL FOR OUR SOPHOMORE YEAR IN September, 1962. A particularly newsy letter from me to Fran talked about my new dorm room and my hopes for the year ahead. I told her that "I'm really going for the grades this semester—I've only got 16 credits with 18 class hours compared to my 20 and 23 last semester. I've got Geology, Philosophy of Nature, Great Books Seminar, French, and Historical Orientation for the seminar. I've got a pretty poor schedule for sailing but as far as study goes I'm ok. Friday is my worst day with six class hours (got a lab that day) and I've got an 11:30 on Saturday."

Tom Franck, Chuck Watson, and I now shared a large triple dorm room in St. Edward's Hall. Since Notre Dame's dorm rooms were assigned on the basis of GPA and none of us was a great scholar, we had gotten last choice of dorms. One of the oldest buildings on campus, St. Ed's offered less-than-desirable accommodations. At least our room was large enough for three beds, three desks and chairs, and some elbow room left over. By mooching resourcefully from our parents and their friends, we were able to add carpet, bed spreads, and curtains—all acceptable to the University and helpful in making our humble room reasonably habitable.

Though I had decided not to transfer to Ohio State, thanks in part to Fran's wise counsel, I had made a change at Notre Dame. I was excited about my fresh start in the College of Arts and Letters and the General Program of Liberal Studies. My curriculum would now be math- and accounting free, and I could fulfill the science requirement by taking Geology, which was reasonably manageable.

Contact lenses were another change for me that term. Just coming into their own as a reliable substitute for glasses in 1962, the only ones available were a hard plastic that largely covered the cornea. They took some getting used to and not everybody could adapt to them, but to me they were preferable to wearing my glasses all the time. I was understandably a bit anxious to see how they would work for me. "I may have them by the next time I see you," I wrote to Fran. "I wish I could say when that will be, but I'm not going to extend any invitations or promises until I see how my grades are going. I want to see you again and be with you again very much, Fran. Let's hope we can work it out even better than last year."

Given the new coolness between us, my letters that fall omitted any profession of love other than my ubiquitous line, "Love, Etc." Fran's letters to me, while regular, were limited to impersonal news. She signed them simply "As ever" and sometimes tucked in a not-so-subtle dig. "Hello—I guess I should throw my hat in first to see if you still care to acknowledge my presence," she wrote in one letter, "but I'll take it for granted that we are still on verbal terms and just say I'm sorry not to have written sooner." There was a new edge in such comments, a tension that had never before factored into our relationship.

What we've come to call the "big chill" in our relationship troubled us both, but in somewhat different ways. Fran was still more upset than I realized at the time. Deeply hurt by what had happened, she was nursing reservations about me and unsure about where she stood. Luckily, she was at least willing to keep our correspondence alive.

Having been the offender rather than the victim, I had to struggle with neither hurt nor distrust. I just hoped that I could earn back her trust and prove that I wasn't really the jerk that I had acted—and felt—like. Still, I was happy not being tied down to Fran or to anyone else. As Fran had said in her letter that June, we were only 19 and had three more years of college ahead. It was far too early to be thinking seriously about a permanent commitment.

My college life that fall was marked by more study and less fooling around than the previous year. Weekends revolved around football games and all the on-campus hoopla they entailed.

Carolyn and I went out a number of times. She had a habit of patting me on the back in a fraternal sort of way when we kissed goodnight. After a while, it started to irritate me enough that I asked her to stop doing it. Aside from that, we got along well and enjoyed each other's company. A year older than I, she had already spent two years in college. Rather than returning to school, she had moved to Chicago, where she planned to get a job and share an apartment with a friend. Chicago was an easy 90-minute ride on the South Shore Railroad, and I would occasionally see her when I went to the city. I was happy to have a new friend to help take up the slack in my social life—the emptiness caused by the fact that I had inadvertently pushed Fran into the background at the same time I was purposefully easing away from Lisa.

Fran's life at Lake Erie College involved mostly academics with an occasional social break. That fall, she wrote about her new dorm room and life as a sophomore. It was now her turn to enslave the freshman girls, as had been done to her the year before. About another event, she wrote: "Saturday about 50 freshmen from Kenyon arrived to see our 'new faces.' There was a very large mixer that night and I took Kit's reception duty at the Commons so I could see what was going on. Met a real interesting junior from Kenyon while I was working. He was born in China but is now a naturalized citizen of the US. He talked about so many interesting things about life in China, his family, etc. I wish I had had more time to listen to him."

I didn't leave campus much that fall, but once in November I announced that I was going to hitchhike home to Sidney for the weekend. Hitching the nearly 200 miles from South Bend was very different from the short trips I used to do along Lake Drive in Milwaukee. But it was still relatively safe, not to mention cheap, and thus a common way for Notre Dame students to get home for visits. Like my fellow students, I began by writing my destination in large block letters on a large piece of cardboard, then stood next to a busy highway and hoped someone would offer me a ride. It was rarely possible to get a ride all the way home; you had to take what you could get and hope to make it home with relatively few different drivers. It wasn't always fast or convenient, but in all the times I hitched from or around Notre Dame, I never had a negative incident.

By November, Fran and I were both feeling the stress of academics and the tensions in our strained relationship. Though I knew very little about it—I was never on Fran's "need to know" list when it came to him—Fran was on again with Donnie, their bond stronger than ever in the vacuum created by her coolness with me. My new friendship with Carolyn was serving the same purpose. Finally, a crucial exchange of letters brought matters to a head.

It started with a letter from Fran. On its surface, it contained just casual news. But it also directed a rapier thrust squarely at me—the reference to pictures from her visit to Sidney where everyone "looked" happy.

*Sunday*

*November 4, 1962*

*Dear Bob:*

*For once all my work is caught up and I have a few hours completely free. Today I wrote a research paper on Cubism and yesterday did all my regular assignments.*

*Tomorrow marks the beginning of freshman initiation. You may get several letters glorifying Lake Erie and exalting yours truly. This is just one of the little chores the freshmen must graciously perform. We sophomores are waking the naïve ones up at 5:30 a.m. and taking them for a walk. On the way to an unknown destination they must walk in pairs holding hands, with their free hand held up with one finger in their ear. When we arrive at the site they must all bow to us upperclassmen and then stand at attention while they receive their instructions for the two-day period. After they listen and salute, they march back to school and memorize a twelve line poem which they will recite verbatim when asked, "How are you animals?" They also have to wear some type of derogatory sign and be at our beck and call. We each have a "little sister" who does extra work and entertains us and our friends. Should prove quite interesting, but thought I'd warn you before you received any strange letters.*

How come you're looking for an apartment off campus? I mean, I thought only those academically below average didn't live in the dorms. Maybe you'll be able to find one as nice as your girlfriend's if you're fortunate.

Many thanks for your Thanksgiving invitation. Jill Amos offered me a ride right down to your door but I won't be able to come because I'm going home the twenty-first. It was very thoughtful of you to ask and I'm sorry that my plans won't let me come. Perhaps some other time before the school year is over we'll be able to get together.

When you do go home, give my best to your family for me—they have been so nice to both me and my parents. Sometime I'll show you the pictures dad took in June—they really turned out well—everyone looked happy.

It was Fall Dance Weekend here this weekend and for three days the campus was crawling with beautiful men. They had a fun schedule of events most of which took place at the president's home, Morley Farm. That is a beautiful place and is big and impressive. I was out there last year for a few combo parties—elegant.

Have run into a small problem. It seems our little group has to appear before dorm council tomorrow night to answer the charges of being in Painseville after hours. Seems we can be out until 1:30 a.m. anywhere except in this little town. I will literally break down if we get campused and have to stay here over Thanksgiving. My roommate better do some fast talking, seeing as how she started this little snowball on its way—she reported herself and we were all there together! Sometimes I could—never mind, at least she's honest.

*Think I should go to bed and try to get some sleep. 5 a.m. will come*

*awfully fast. Be good and study much.*

*As ever,*

*Fran*


Well, that did it.

I didn't blame her for her feelings. Still, since June her letters had been cool at best and sharp with barbs at worst. I had been ignoring the digs, hoping she'd let up. Now I decided it was time to clear the air.

I wrote back, hitting the issue head-on. Even after signing off, I kept going in a lengthy P.S.


### UNIVERSITY OF NOTRE DAME

### NOTRE DAME, INDIANA


Nov. 8, 1962

Dear Fran,

Nice to get your letter—and the letters from your freshman friends.
You know, I never had any idea that you were so thoughtful and kind.
Seriously, I really got a kick out of it, especially the one in French, which
I didn't have much trouble in translating. Hope you weren't too hard
on the poor girls...

As for an off-campus room (undergrads can't have apartments),
dorm life is a real pain because of all the interruptions and noise, and a
room in a real live house would be much quieter. I don't know, though,

I'll probably wind up on campus next year. As for academic average—you <u>have</u> to live off campus if you are substandard, but you <u>can</u> by choice if your grades are good enough.

I really wish you could make it down for Thanksgiving, but I imagine there are things you would rather do at home. How about Christmas? If you are still planning to go to Milwaukee, I am, although I hope we can get together before then. Let me know.

How did you come out with the disciplinary action? Seems you average this pretty regularly of late, but at least you will get to know the "Board" pretty well. Seriously, I hope you don't get into trouble, especially with a vacation coming up.

Fran, let's cut out the snide remarks in the letters—OK? I realize I have been twisting the knife lately, but it has been unintentional. We were in love once, and maybe we still are (I know I sure as hell haven't been showing it lately), but we've got a long time to go before we can start thinking seriously about anything permanent—right? Right. So the "catty" remarks are doing no one any good and a more direct approach is definitely in order.

For the last few months now your letters have been very impersonal and a little too newsy. What am I supposed to think? Now if you and Don are going so strong that you have no more feeling for me at all, then please let me know where I stand.

Where do you stand? Fair question. There is a girl at home (in Chicago now) whom I date when I can. The reasoning follows your same lines when talking about Don—someone to date and someone to come home to. There is no one that I feel the same way as I do about you—and I'd rather talk about that in person.

Love ya,

Bob

P.S. I was going to quit there, but now that I am going, I might as well stay on the tracks.

You keep asking about Lisa—as far as she is concerned it is all over. To be honest, I still feel something, but it's only normal and I will eventually forget about it—it's a matter of time.

We have known each other for more than five years now and to me, that is plenty of time to know something I like. I honestly feel that when the time comes to think about marriage that I would think of you. You said that you always wanted to be special to me and you have succeeded. You are.

I do want to see those pictures your father took—you know, most of us <u>were</u> happy.

Love, etc.

Bob

What irony! Though I began by demanding an end to the digs, I closed with a barb of my own. Despite that, Fran had the good grace to send an honest reply *and* a heartfelt apology.

*Sunday*

*November 18, 1962*

*Dear Bob,*

*The tension is finally passed—I can once again live the normal rat race life of a co-ed in her sophomore year at an all-girls school. This afternoon after weeks of note taking, days of semi-organization and about twelve solid hours of writing, I finished my first sophomore General Studies paper. One of the naïve little freshmen from Hawaii has offered to type it (for a small fee) so until it has to be passed in, I hope I don't set eyes on it. If my calculations are anywhere near accurate it should develop into a twenty-two to twenty-five page typed paper, which should rate a passing grade. The thought of this paper has been like an ax over my neck since September, so I hope you can appreciate what a personal relief it is to have it finally completed.*

*A week ago my Fine Arts class was assigned to write individual plays and this past Friday, five out of the forty-plus were produced. Right agai— one was mine. It was truly a traumatic experience seeing your own work produced on stage—hope it never happens again.*

*Are you about ready to go home for Thanksgiving? Only have two and a half days left before I leave, that is if it doesn't decide to snow. We are leaving about 2:30 which means I should arrive in Andover in the wee hours of the morning. Certainly hope my mother doesn't have me locked out.*

*I am really pleased we have the opportunity to go home; you see, my grandmother has been quite sick since the middle of June—she has had three strokes and is now almost completely paralyzed on her left side. Now that she is 76, there doesn't seem to be too much fight left in her. It is very* upsetting to watch her consistently go downhill. We actually didn't expect her to last during the summer and although she did, there is no hope of any noticeable improvement. I love her dearly, she's always lived with us, and every extra chance I have to see her could possibly be the last. So this is my primary reason for going East this November and negatively answering your invitation. Please forgive me if my reply sounded nasty but yes, I do have "important things to do at home."

I also realize that my letters have been satirical, snide and catty. Admittedly, part of this was done intentionally, but it was also an outlet for many pent up emotions. The situation at home is anything but relaxed and compatible. There are many brooding problems that always seem to grow rather than diminish in size and importance. Don't misunderstand, my family is still as close as ever, but the constant tension is a strain and basis for much worry. In some attempt to parallel all these weird pictures I have drawn, let me say that being unkind to you was an outlet for my own mixed feelings. In my letters I could be very nasty with relatively little worry that you would meet me face to face and call my bluff—but mistaken I was, as your last letter undoubtedly proved. Again I'm sorry that I singled you out as my personal scapegoat—it won't happen again. I'll be mean to my roommate Pidgeon instead.

To continue, I fully agree with you that it is much too soon to think seriously about future plans. As yet, I am not in a position to commit myself to you in any way, nor do I honestly want to. This may sound crude but this is my personal attitude. Agreed, we were once in love, but so many upsetting and conflicting things have happened since then that at the moment my *feelings are in a turmoil. I'm not at all sure how I feel about many things,*

*but please try to understand while I fight things out with myself.*

*This has been an exceedingly difficult letter to write, and my doubts*

*as to whether I've partially succeeded in saying just what I wanted to are*

*great. Little of importance has happened in the realm of college life except*

*the presence of a cold war of 2 roommates against 1. The third has been*

*very difficult to live with recently, and we are almost glad she won't be here*

*next term.*

*Please write soon; I think of you often although I haven't admitted it*

*lately. Hope you have as nice a Thanksgiving at home this year as I had*

*with you a year ago. Be good.*

*Love, Fran*

I was beginning to learn that there is often more going on in a relationship than meets the eye. The insight into her family's tensions was news to me; now that I knew about it, I felt I better understood her life and feelings.

Though she was almost brutally honest about not wanting our relationship to develop any further right then, this exchange turned out to be one of the first steps in our reconciliation. It immediately cleared the air a bit between us; at least we both knew where we stood.

Not long afterward, we both went home for Thanksgiving break. I had a lousy time in Sidney while Fran had a big family gathering in Andover. She got to Boston for some shopping and went to see "Whatever Happened to Baby Jane," although I never learned who she went with.

Back at school after Thanksgiving, things were quiet. We continued to write, both glad to be free of any pressure to make our unusual relationship anything more than it was. December passed uneventfully. We each spent our Christmas breaks at home, sending each other a small gift. I bought Fran a string of crystal beads, while she gave me an Ahmad Jamal album. For now at least, the urgent need to see each other had passed; we rarely mentioned the possibility in any serious context.

Then the ball in Times Square dropped. Suddenly, it was 1963.

## CHAPTER TEN

*N*OW MIDWAY THROUGH MY SOPHOMORE YEAR OF COLLEGE, I WAS STILL
enjoying the freedom of not being strongly committed to any one girlfriend. At
the same time, in spite of our outward attempts at normalcy, there was still frost
on my relationship with Fran. To me that was uncomfortable and unsatisfying.

As we returned to our collegiate lives after New Year's, I was trying to figure
out how I might patch things up with her. Our exchange of letters in November
had helped, but something told me I'd better pay Fran a visit if I was going to
salvage our relationship.

In January, I wrote her to say I'd like to come to LEC. She lost the letter. I was
anxious to see her to tell her face to face that I wanted back in her good graces,
so I wrote again to announce my plans.

**UNIVERSITY OF NOTRE DAME**

**NOTRE DAME, INDIANA**

Jan. 13, 1963

Dear Fran,

I just got your card and thought I'd better write, since my January budget doesn't allow for a collect telephone call.

I'll just make this brief, necessarily, and clue you in on the letter you lost.

As you may have gathered from my follow-up note, I am planning to come to Lake Erie for a weekend over semester break, unless you have something to do, of course. But if you don't, and if you want the pleasure of my company, I'll be there. Jerry Houlihan is also planning to come along, so if you can get him a beautiful date for the weekend he will be very happy. If you get him an ugly date for the weekend, he will be very mad.

Anyway, we plan to be there on Feb. 1st and leave on the 3rd or so. That was the gist of my letter. If it sounds good, let me know.

Love,

Bob

This letter triggered a rapid-fire exchange of four more letters laying plans for the trip. Fran asked me when I was coming, how I was getting there, and how long I was going to stay.

The envelopes to these letters show that first class postage had increased from four cents to five cents—a 25 percent increase that began on January 1, 1963. While the cost of our stamps didn't break the bank, every penny counted in those days—literally.

I had a week between my last exam, on January 30, and registration for the next term. I planned to hitchhike to Sidney with my friend Jerry Houlihan (a Notre Dame classmate from upstate New York), spend a couple of days skiing somewhere in Ohio, and then drive the Corvair to Cleveland on Friday or Saturday.

After explaining all that, my letter went on to say, "Have you got a date for Jerry yet? He has asked me to request somebody who is very good looking—as opposed to someone 'all the girls like, is cute, makes her own clothes, and has a great personality.' I guess you know what I'm getting at. As he says—"I can be made, but I still have my pride!'" Obviously under pressure from Jerry, I added, "Jerry has been talking to Ron Kasprisin and he has asked that you don't fix him up with Kit. I think she is a real nice girl, but not Houlihan's type."

I guess I hadn't gotten all boorishness quite out of my system. Oops....

*Monday*

*January 21, 1963*

*Dear Bob,*

*Are you getting nervous now that your exams are getting so close? That oral exam even sounds scary. We don't have any orals until our senior year, and then only in our field of concentration.*

*You certainly have a long semester break—wish you could spend more time here but unfortunately I have to work in the library Saturday morning (student service) and also have a Spanish class. So it would actually be best for us to meet you in Cleveland Saturday afternoon. We will be staying at the Wade Park Hotel in University Circle, which is about fifteen minutes west of Cleveland proper and right off US Rt. 30. Should*

*we expect you to meet us there around 2 p.m.?*

*As far as Saturday night goes, cocktails (either in our room or*

*elsewhere), dinner and maybe a concert or show would be divine, from our*

*standpoint anyway. How about you? It's not often that we get off campus*

*and doing something exciting is always more fun than just the regular stuff.*

*Your friend Jerry must think he's really something special if he persists*

*in being so darn particular about his date. I will ask whoever I please, and*

*he'd best appreciate it and be on his best behavior. The opinion of Notre*

*Dame isn't high enough around here to make it an easy task to find dates*

*for strange somebodies. Don't truly mean to sound sarcastic, but his, and*

*your, attitude makes it sound as though I'd fix him up with some fourth*

*dimensional witch-type character. Bastante dicho.*

*Let me know how our respective plans correlate and say hi to your*

*parents for me when you see them. Good luck on your exams.*

*As ever,*

*Fran*

The Cleveland weekend was memorable in two major respects. One, it provided Fran a golden opportunity to extract some female revenge. But more importantly, we finally could talk, blow away the smoke that had been obscuring our friendship, and—in the newly clear air—discuss where we might go from there.

Fran and Kit (yes, Kit) were fully prepared for us. Though the main purpose of the weekend was a serious conversation, we had planned a pleasant dinner for four beforehand. The girls proposed Saturday night dinner at the Red Fox, suburban Cleveland's most expensive restaurant. As rubes from Indiana unfamiliar with its prices, we agreed to the suggestion.

It wasn't unusual to dress up for a restaurant dinner, but especially for college kids, we were outfitted in grand style. Jerry and I sported our best suits. The girls were in dresses and heels—Fran wore a simple black Lanz dress with maybe a million satin-covered buttons up the back. Perhaps we didn't have money, but we sure looked like we did.

The meal was great and so was the service—Jerry observed that the waiters did everything for us but wind our watches. The bill was stupefying. Visa and Master Card had not yet been invented. Between us, Jerry and I fortunately found enough cash to pay the bill. That involved me spotting Jerry a loan. Though he felt he had been completely hosed, Jerry and I continued to be good friends. He never held his unbelievably expensive blind date with Kit against me, though I recall that he paid back the loan I had given him for dinner rather grudgingly!

As we men came to grips with the financial terrorism, the ladies enjoyed the satisfaction of knowing they had stuck it to us. Still, Fran and I were enjoying each others' company. Happy and satisfied by our epicurean experience, we returned to the hotel around ten o'clock.

Jerry and I were sharing a room while Fran and Kit shared another. Jerry and Kit let us have one of the rooms for a while so we could talk privately. God knows what they thought went on for the next couple of hours.

The hotel was an elegant older property with rooms that were simple but nicely decorated. Fran sat on one of the room's two beds and I sat on the other. We spoke for a long time, having a serious heart-to-heart. Talking about everything that had happened since June, we agreed that we weren't happy about how our relationship had deteriorated. We not only wanted things to be back to normal between us, we were ready to be "in love" once more. I was more relieved than I could express that Fran felt the same as I did.

We were both still content with our pressure-free college lives. But with trust established between us once again, I told Fran again that when the time came to talk about marriage, I would like to marry her—and she said that someday she would like to marry me too. I even paid her what I meant to be a high compliment—I told her that in many ways she reminded me of my mother. Both were intelligent, capable, socially sophisticated, insightful and caring, among other qualities. From me, this was high praise.

By the time this point in the conversation had been reached, we were both sitting on the same bed. It was a monumental moment. At last the smoke was cleared. We could see a present in which our loving relationship was reborn, and a future that had bright prospects. Fran and I kept talking, we embraced, and we kissed for a while. But good and proper kids that we were, sometime around one a.m. we dutifully rejoined Jerry and Kit, said our good-nights, and retired to our respective rooms.

Crucial as that moment was, things didn't change dramatically right away. Fran continued to sign her letters "As ever" with the occasional "As ever—love..." for some time afterward. But that heart-to-heart in Cleveland did its work, producing a gradual thaw that ultimately led to more letters, more visits, and a deeper bond than ever.

Knowing that we were too young to commit, we gave each other permission to date others. I was seeing less of Carolyn, but I would have an occasional date with someone else. As far as I knew at that time, Fran and Donnie continued to see each other.

In April, Fran came to Sidney for Easter. In June, I saw her again when the Jordans drove to Painesville to collect her for the summer. Notre Dame always ended classes earlier than Lake Erie College, so I had been home for a while by that time. I drove up to Cleveland to see Fran, her mom and dad, and her younger sister, Nancy. I have to admit that I felt a bit awkward when I first saw her parents again—I didn't know if they had forgotten my brilliant performance a year earlier. Fran must have told them that I had atoned, because they acted like nothing had ever happened. I even got the welcome impression they were happy to see me.

Not surprisingly given the dullness of same-sex colleges in cold, gray climates, we both took every chance to get away from our respective campuses. While Fran wasn't nearly as peripatetic as I was, she did score the occasional trip to Cleveland. In March, she drove with her friend Janet to Janet's home in Elmira, NY, for their spring break. After spending a few days there, she flew home to Andover for the rest of her time off.

Most air travel then (and all flights between small towns) was by small, propeller-driven aircraft. Fran travelled to Boston on Mohawk, which served the eastern US and later morphed into US Airways. "Still seems unbelievable that the flight from Elmira took three hours and last spring it only took two hours from Cleveland to Boston. Don't think Mohawk has heard of a four engine plane yet." On today's regional jet aircraft the same trip on US Airways takes three hours and 53 minutes thanks to the modern hub system, which requires a connection in Philadelphia. Maybe there was something to be said for slow propeller planes after all....we just didn't know it at the time.

One of Fran's most enjoyable escapes was a weekend in early March spent babysitting for a former professor. She wrote a long, philosophical letter during her stay.

*Saturday*

*March 2, 1963*

*Dear Bob:*

*If only you could be as happy, content and as free as I am right now. Yesterday at noon Mr. Donovan White, PhD, called and asked me to spend the weekend at his home in Montville, Ohio to babysit for two nights. I accepted and couldn't be happier. He was my philosophy professor last year and is one of the most wonderful people I've ever met. At one time he was a Methodist minister. Now he's a Unitarian, looks like an Amish man, and teaches at the college. I admire and respect him immensely and he is the first professor that I've ever known very well. Strangely enough he reminds me remarkably of my father and possibly this could account for part of my admiration. Someday I hope that you will have the pleasure and opportunity of meeting him, for he's heard all about you and calls you one of my "Charleys."*

*So here I sit, alone except for Sammy, eleven (who's in bed, in a sleeping bag on the floor next to my bed) and two dogs. The refrigerator is full of ice-cold beer. The stereo works beautifully and there are a hundred intriguing books lying around. This is the first time I've felt so completely relaxed and free. Completed the second third of my General Studies paper before leaving yesterday and have only nominal assignments to complete before taking exams. Entirely disregarded and ignored my student service* work this morning, along with my Spanish class. The librarian will undoubtedly lash me verbally and very soundly on Monday but at the present I couldn't care less.

This afternoon Mr. White and I walked for about five miles and just chatted. It snowed yesterday and last night. The snow banks at the road's edge are about four feet high and everything looks as pure and white and uncivilized. The town has a population of about 300 and although the house is on the main road, only about one car passes every three hours. I could go on all night telling you what it's like and how I feel, but it would probably bore you to death so I won't.

Still don't know if I'll be able to spend part of the vacation in New York—hope to find out definitely next week. When is your next vacation—Easter? We'll be back in session then and going great guns; confusion will prevail, for the juniors will be back and bursting with tales of Europe and their foreign families. I'll be sort of glad to see Pidgeon for I think things will be somewhat easier with her in the room. Kit and I have been getting on each other's nerves so much lately it's like fighting a silent verbal war. Sometimes I find it extremely difficult to be compatible with Kit and although it's probably my own fault, it's still awfully trying, and conducive to tension.

Glad you had a nice weekend with your parents et al and enjoyed the Mardi Gras. Did you win the Corvette? Winning contests isn't one of my good fortunes but hope it's one of yours.

Had another birthday party Thursday night for one of our friends and there's still another coming up next weekend. Have spent more money on gifts this term that I usually do all year.

*Next Sunday the Vienna Choir boys are appearing on campus and I am truly looking forward to seeing and hearing them. The Whites have asked me to join them. The two kids make such a fuss over me, I'm embarrassed at feeling so important and wanted—it must be because they're still so young.*

*Beginning to wonder if spring will ever arrive—love all the snow but it's not the nicest climate to live in for such a long time, especially when the sun shines so infrequently. I sort of envy Kit, packing all her cotton clothes, bathing suits and shorts for her California trip. Suppose New England will be even snowier than here.*

*Well, think I'll take advantage of this solitude and peace and read for awhile before going to bed.*

*Like to quote something Dr. White read to me this morning from* The Prophet—

> *Give your hearts, but not into each other's keeping.*
>
> *And stand together yet not too near together.*
>
> *For the pillars of the temple stand apart,*
>
> *And the oak tree and the cypress grow not in each other's shadow.*
>
> *When love beckons to you, follow him,*
>
> *Though his ways are hard and steep.*
>
> *And when his wings enfold you yield to him,*
>
> *Though the sword hidden among his pinions may wound you.*
>
> *And when he speaks to you believe in him, though his voice may*
>
> > *shatter your dreams.*

*Fran*

I didn't know what to make of some professor type quoting love poetry to Fran, nor what to make of her quoting it back to me. I had never heard of Khalil Gibran and his 1923 book, *The Prophet*. In retrospect I can see that this letter was a window into Fran's heart and soul. Did I take the time then to really look into that window? Probably not. It was more like a passing glance—I glimpsed something for a brief moment and filed it away without dwelling on what I had seen.

Rather than really responding to what she said, my response was simple. "Was glad to hear that you had such a pleasant weekend," I wrote. "I envy your tranquility because everything has been pretty 'rush' around here. Mr. White sounds like a very profound "Prophet," if you'll forgive a pun. I would like to meet him some day."

The same early March letter told her that "Tom and I moved out of St. Ed's. That triple just got to be too much to bear, so we moved over to a nice fire and cockroach-proof double in Keenan. The advantage of being a sophomore in a freshman hall is not having any hours. That is, needless to say, a great deal. For example, Monday night I was sitting around the Scholastic office drinking beer and eating pizza with the campus wheels and strolled in here around 1:00. Could hardly do that before."

Later in March, Fran traveled home for semester break. "Maybe I'll get some extra reading done this vacation after all, for like you, I too am free," she wrote to me. "Don't really know how happy I am about it but the lingering feeling that's here now isn't exactly unpleasant."

That was real news. She had actually ended her relationship with Donnie immediately after our Cleveland visit, but I didn't know that yet. "Why the 'lingering feeling'? Have you and Don called it off? What happened, if I may be so bold as to inquire?" I asked in my next letter.

"I have made two large decisions in the last week," I wrote as well. "#1—to stay at ND and graduate. #2—to transfer from the General Program to a major in Communications Arts. This way I will have a fantastic number of electives so that I can take the GP courses that I want, but I will have courses in Journalism, Mass Media, public relations, etc. Even though I still like GP this is more up the alley of my future and I think it's a sound decision. Hope Dad agrees with me."

Now at the end of my sophomore year, I was learning to make sound choices about important and complicated issues. Another decision came in relation to my unpaid role as copy editor for the *Scholastic*, Notre Dame's well-regarded student publication, which contained news, essays, fiction, and student commentary. My job was fun and I enjoyed the other guys I worked with, but when the Notre Dame administration decided to impose its own view on the publication's content, I resigned out of solidarity with the senior editors. This disagreement with the University's powers-that-be didn't discourage me about Notre Dame. In an odd way, it might have even helped me feel a little more part of things. I was slowly starting to realize the greener grass I saw beckoning from some other institution was likely a mirage. Whether or not I knew it yet, it was another sign of growing maturity.

It was thanks to my roommate Tom that I had learned about Notre Dame's Communication Arts major. Communication Arts focused on written, oral, and visual communication skills. With a CA major under our belts, we were told, we could have our choice of many fields including journalism, advertising, public relations, and radio or TV broadcasting. This was a huge discovery for me. Finally, I had found my center and was ready to roll with a true destination in mind. It was not yet clear to me exactly what career in communications I would pursue, but I knew this was the track for me.

As I began to look for my niche in the field, a friend suggested I get a job at the student radio station. Though they had no open positions, the suggestion sparked what turned out to be a short lived interest in a radio career. While I was in Sidney for spring break I wrote to Fran: "Just for the heck of it, I went down to WPTW [the Piqua, OH, radio station] to see about a summer job. It seems they are opening a new station in Celina in June and so I may have a job. He gave me a tape to take back to school. I have to take it up to WSND and do an audition and send him the tape by next week. 'We'll work from there,' he says. At any rate, you might have to buy a short wave receiver so you can hear the 'Bob Zielsdorf Show.' Maybe I'll have to use an alias on the air. Got any ideas?"

I never found out if "Bob Zielsdorf" would make a worthy radio name because I didn't get the job. Having had no training at that point, I guess my vocal skills weren't adequate. At the end of May I confessed to Fran that "I have really been depressed" about the news.

The manager at WPTW did agree to let me hang out at night with their regular on-air talent that summer, however—strictly a no-pay opportunity to get my toes wet in the field. In August I wrote Fran: "Been playing games at WPTW-FM in Piqua—just picking up experience on my own time. Last night I was on the air from 8-12 p.m. I enjoy it, but I sure wouldn't want to spend the rest of my life at it." So as it turned out, my failure to get the radio job worked out for the best.

As our school year wound down, I wrapped up my studies in the General Program and, with Tom, enjoyed life as sophomores in a freshman dorm. Tom's parents had given him a car—illegal for a student living on campus, but possible to finagle with the right know-how. We often drove to Chicago on weekends, hitting our favorite bar—Figaro's in Old Town—closing it down and driving back to campus in the wee hours of the morning. My friendship with Fran was back on an even keel, my professional future was clearer, and I had lots of freedom. Life was good.

Fran too was making decisions. "Declared my major in Language & Literature, English predominating," she announced in May. "The courses available next fall and spring term look interesting and fun. Maybe after I complete my two writing courses my letters will show some noticeable improvement." For my part, I managed to pass Geology and finish the year with a grade point average of 2.94. Not much to brag about yet, but my average would improve even more the following year as I enthusiastically jumped into my major courses.

As we segued into vacation, both Fran and I were preoccupied with finding summer jobs. Fran learned that she would be rehired by Danvers State Hospital. She liked the job despite its occasional alarming moments and was glad to have the question of summer employment settled. In contrast, I was struggling to find anything. I had fantasized during the year about working somewhere other than Sidney, but by the time term ended I knew that wasn't going to happen. Once the radio station opportunity was off the table, even finding a job in Sidney became a huge problem. Finally taking mercy on me, my father once again arranged a job at Le Roi. They had been thinking about instituting a company newsletter, then called a "house organ," and I was hired to create it. I couldn't complain. Though the job didn't pay much, it kept me busy and provided some excellent experience.

My most exciting project for the summer was an entrepreneurial adventure. My Sidney friend Dick Cotterman's buddy Karl had a rock 'n roll band called the Catatonics that needed a place to play. Just outside of Sidney was a lakeside pavilion, Avon Lake, owned by a local corporation. Dick, Karl, and I pooled our money, leased the use of Avon Lake two nights a week, and started to do all the work necessary before we could open our new dance hall for business in late June.

We had to secure liability insurance, figure out what we were allowed to sell in the way of drinks (no alcohol) and snacks, prepare our advertising and publicity, and handle all the other things involved in a start-up business venture. On June 16 I wrote to Fran, "The dance hall is giving us some more headaches but we are still going to open June 26 if it kills us. We have to go to the Junior Chamber of Commerce board meeting tomorrow night and try to enlist their moral support. Actually, all we need is chaperones but we can't tell them that."

While all this was going on in Sidney, Fran, who had survived a car accident only a couple years earlier, experienced another serious brush with death. On June 16, only days after I had seen the Jordans in Cleveland, Fran and her father took their 18-foot outboard motor boat down the Merrimack River and into the Atlantic Ocean. They were fortunate to get back alive. Here is how she described the event.

> *Thursday*
>
> *June 26, 1963*
>
> *Dear Bob,*
>
> *Well, Dad just left for work and the boat dealers—he's done it again—a new boat, new motor and several new accessories. This is almost becoming a summer ritual. We had a good trip home—I slept most of the way so it went fast. Right after church Sunday, Dad and I took the old boat and went down to the ocean. It was a beautiful day but the water was extremely*

*rough: 10-12' waves and all. About 2:30 we got caught broadside by a*

*wave. For a while I thought it was all over. But then I started to think of*

*September and held on to the prop for dear life, as did my father. Think*

*the enclosed clipping will tell you the rest. Don't think I've ever been quite*

*so bruised and cut in my life. But that's of little worry now. The only thing*

*that really upset me was the awful picture they put in the local paper.*

*And Dad was rather annoyed that they stated his age—no more fooling*

*anyone.*

Her letter didn't really convey the full scope of the accident. The two of them were well off shore in turbulent 55-degree water with no lifejackets on. Luckily, it was the first day of the season that lifeguards were on duty at the beach. After they had attempted and failed to reach Fran and her father (the wave action was too powerful), a Coast Guard boat rescued the pair. They were released fairly soon after they were taken to the hospital for observation, but the more I learned about the accident the better I understood how serious it had been. Without determination and luck Fran could easily have died that day. When her letter says that thinking of September gave her the incentive and strength to hang on, Fran was speaking of our upcoming visit at Lake Winnepesaukee. She still credits the intense desire to be with me for being the driving force that saved her life. She wasn't about to surrender to Mother Nature—our relationship was too important. Later, she told me that my future mother-in-law believed that Fran was being saved for me—and Fran thought she was right!

Back in Sidney, my business venture was also having trouble staying afloat. "The kids really seemed to enjoy it and I'm pretty sure that they will keep coming back and bringing more people," I reported optimistically after our Avon Lake dance hall's opening night in late June, mentioning that we were $75 down from our initial investment. On July 9, I wrote Fran that "Avon Lake is still operating in the red. In fact we are going to drop our D.J. and our Sunday night performance in order to cut overhead. Hope all goes well tomorrow night. Dick and I are going to be hammy M.C.'s."

Fran's responses were always sympathetic. "Sorry to hear that your place at Avon Lake isn't as successful as possible. Hope things pick up very quickly. Do you like being an M.C.?" she wrote. Though her encouragement helped me keep going, in the end we decided to shut down our dance-hall business. The Catatonics would have to fend for themselves. On July 23 I told Fran, "We decided last night to close our dance hall at Avon Lake. It still looks good in theory but the black & white (or rather red) figures don't bear that up. We each lost about $50 but it was fun and a good experience." The latter comment was definitely true; the many lessons about business the venture taught me were worth much more than the $50 it cost.

That summer, Fran learned that her Winter Term Abroad, or WTA, would take her to Valencia, Spain, where she would live with a Spanish family and attend classes at the local university. Around the same time, her beloved grandmother had to be moved to a nursing home due to the effects of a series of strokes. "Gram" had lived with the Jordans all of Fran's life, so it was a painful transition. With things tense at home, Fran was suffering from headaches; she had to return to Boston for x-rays to make sure they were not caused by her earlier neck injury. Luckily, they weren't, but preparing to return to school and get ready for her Spanish WTA was weighing on her heavily.

In July, the post office instituted the use of non-mandatory ZIP (Zone Improvement Program) codes to speed up mail delivery, changing the way we wrote to each other. We always complained about the slowness of the mail but it actually moved pretty efficiently most of the time. Fran and I could usually count on a letter going between South Bend and Painesville in about two days, and sometimes it even happened overnight. Personally, I wasn't too sure America needed Mr. Zippy, as the hokey cartoon character used to hype the use of ZIP codes was called.

Along with ZIP codes came the advent of the two-letter state abbreviations. Postal authorities felt that adding a five-digit ZIP code to a standard state abbreviation like, say, "Mass" would be too much for some labels to accommodate. So "Mass." became "MA," "Ind." became "IN," and so on. In quixotic protest, I refused for a long time to use the two-letter form. I reasoned that the old state abbreviations that I had worked so hard as a kid to memorize were still perfectly good, and no bureaucrat was going to make me change.

On July 10 I addressed a letter to Miss Fran Jordan, 180 Chestnut Street, Andover, Mass. 01810. Hah! No two-letter BS from me. I asked Fran if using the ZIP code actually speeded up delivery. Her return letter, sans ZIP code, noted on the back, "ZIP code takes 3 days rather than usual 2." That did it. Not only no "MA" for me—no playing with Mr. Zippy either. Take that, Mr. Zippy! It was months before I would deign to use a ZIP Code again.

Other than my failed business venture, I got through the summer unscathed. When my job at LeRoi ended in early August, I found work for a few more weeks at a local lumber yard unloading box cars and building pallets. Fran and her parents invited me to spend Labor Day weekend with them at Lake Winnipesaukee; naturally, I accepted. This would be our third visit since Cleveland and the perfect ending to the summer.

Fran loved Lake Winnipesaukee, and I fell in love with it too. (After our marriage, we returned there every summer for more than 25 years.) One of the most beautiful lakes in the country, it's nestled in the foothills of New Hampshire's White Mountains. Each summer, the Jordans rented a small cabin in an old-fashioned cottage resort there. It had two very small bedrooms, an even smaller kitchen, and a Lilliputian sitting room. Somehow we managed comfortably enough, mainly because we were rarely indoors. We spent our time water-skiing, socializing with their cottage neighbors, and exploring the mountains and the other beautiful areas surrounding the lake.

Great hosts, Fran's Mom and Dad had clearly forgotten the unpleasantness of the prior June. They seemed to welcome my company, even in its goofier moments. A fan of the folk music of the day—the Kingston Trio was a favorite—I had bought a used guitar in a pawn shop and taught myself to play it. I was a mediocre player and an even worse singer, but something possessed me to bring the guitar to the lake. One evening Fran and her parents prevailed upon me to entertain them and their fellow cottagers by the communal fire. To my great surprise, they all seemed to enjoy it—and even insisted on my doing it again.

Though there was little private time, Fran and I did steal some moments alone. One night we borrowed the car and went to the local drive-in movie. Of course, we didn't care about the film. We just reveled in the chance to talk privately and indulge in the passionate kissing we loved so much. It was just enough time together to know the magic was back. We were definitely in love with each other once again.

Fran drove me from Lake Winnipesaukee to Boston's Logan Airport so I could catch a flight to Dayton on the first leg of my journey home. After dropping me off, she returned to her car at the airport to find a policeman giving her a parking ticket. That rattled her so much that she drove away going the wrong way on a one-way street. It was a crazy ending to a wonderful time together.

When I got home I wrote, "I'm not sure how to start this letter. After such a wonderful week a letter is a pretty poor substitute as a means of communication....I wanted to talk to you tonight but I couldn't quite swing the price of a call so we had to do without....know that I miss you and that I'm thinking of you with love."

Two more years of college lay ahead. Fran had escaped another near-fatal accident. With the "big chill" replaced by warm affection, we started our junior year with a renewed love for each other and a fresh appreciation for life.

# CHAPTER ELEVEN

*F*RAN'S CLASSES DIDN'T RESUME UNTIL SEPTEMBER 26, BUT SHE WROTE the first letter of our junior year on September 13, 1963. "Can't believe I've got to re-learn all my Spanish (before classes start) plus read 4 novels on Spain," she wrote, glad that she had almost two weeks for the work before classes resumed. She asked a few questions about what I had been doing and closed with a cute P.S.: "My aunt bought Bobby a new story book—"Cinderella"—like my version better…" Fran's Aunt Carolyn lived with the Jordans; Bobby was Fran's seven-year-old brother, who as I've mentioned suffered from Down syndrome. In Fran's mind, her private version of the Cinderella story, with Fran as Cinderella and me as Prince Charming, was far more compelling than Disney's.

Now that we were seeing and phoning each other so often, the nature of our correspondence changed. Our letters now rarely told complete stories, anecdotes or items of news. Instead, they are full of allusions to things we experienced or discussed together. To an outside reader, these references are confusing—but of course, we weren't thinking of that at the time.

A few days after receiving Fran's letter, I returned to South Bend. This year I would be living off-campus, in a University-approved rooming house—Notre Dame's solution to its lack of undergraduate dormitory space. While my grades still weren't the greatest, they would have been sufficient to win me a spot in a dorm that year. Instead, my friends and I decided we would be better suited to the off-campus lifestyle. I wrote Fran as soon as I settled in.

UNIVERSITY OF NOTRE DAME

NOTRE DAME, INDIANA

Sept. 17, 1963

Dear Fran,

We registered today and all my classes are on Monday, Wednesday and Friday. Hope that works out all right.

We couldn't find a nice apartment but our house is real nice. Chuck, Tom, Gary Hosbein, and Lou Esposito are all living here. Lou is a senior and he has lived here for the last couple years, so he knows all the ropes and that comes in right handy.

We each have a car! Tom has a TR-4, Chuck a '63 Tempest, Gary a '53 Olds, Lou a '53 Merc convertible and Dad is letting me use the Corvair. I'm afraid he is going to want it back though when he finds out that everyone else has a car.

I've got 5 three-hour courses; bought 9 books today for only three of the courses. They all look very interesting.

We have a TV, a stereo and radios galore upstairs here, so it's all the comforts of home.

Notre Dame switched to a 4.0 system this year. That brings my cumulative average down to a 1.95. Guess I'll have to get busy this year and prove that I do have some brains. At this rate, it sure doesn't look like it, does it?

I bought your parents a thank-you gift today. When the salesgirl found out what it was for, she tried to sell me a diamond ring, too. Said she'd be glad to take my order for Christmas. I decided it was a nice offer, but to wait for awhile. Ha ha.

We are getting set to go out for dinner now. Wish I could write more but my stomach says no. So good luck at school and write me soon—I miss you.

Love,

Bob

I was truly looking forward to my junior year. I was excited about starting my new Communications Arts major and equally excited about living off-campus with my four friends, away from the bustle and distractions of dormitory life.

Our rooming house was owned by Rae Shaw, who combined the warmth of a grandma with the wise, "I've seen it all" demeanor of a school headmistress. A longtime widow, Mrs. Shaw seemed to enjoy sharing her home with five college students. To maintain their University-approved status, landlords had to enforce a certain amount of decorum. Mrs. Shaw definitely knew just how much nonsense to tolerate.

Her house was an old two-story on a busy north-south highway that ran through the city. Her personal quarters were all completely off limits to her roomers—I never laid eyes on anything past the kitchen door. The first floor held a common living area plus two bedrooms and a bath; upstairs were two more bedrooms, one large and the other smaller. Somehow it was decided that Lou would have the better of the two downstairs rooms and Gary would have the other, while Tom, Chuck and I would live upstairs. We had all the comforts of home, with the exception of a kitchen, as Mrs. Shaw wisely didn't share hers with her five male "roommates."

Meals never seemed to be a big issue. Breakfast, if we ate anything at all, consisted of a donut and a cup of coffee, bought on campus or at our favorite casual restaurant down the road. Lunch came from a campus sandwich shop or inexpensive off-campus diner. Even dinner was easy enough, as there were plenty of inexpensive restaurants nearby. In 1963, McDonald's was just beginning to open franchised restaurants. South Bend was, we thought, fortunate to have one not very far from campus. They sold a good hamburger, fries and shake meal for 45 cents. Even by 1960s standards, that was cheap. We preferred real meals most of the time, so a McDonald's dinner was the exception rather than the rule.

Because we lived off campus, having a car was now completely legal and necessary—it was two miles or so to classes. Since each of us had a car, getting around was never a problem.

Although I had improved my scholastic performance as a sophomore, my grades were still disappointing. As my letter explained, Notre Dame converted its grading system from its unusual six-point scale to a standard four-point system. Finding that I now was the owner of a lowly 1.9 GPA, barely a C, was a rude awakening. I didn't have to be a math genius to know that with only two years to go, the outlook for graduating with a respectable GPA was bleak. By starting junior year with a C average, I would have to get straight As just to finish college averaging a B.

Fran wrote to me as soon as her parents dropped her off in Painesville on September 20.

*Saturday*

*September 21, 1963*

*Dear Bob,*

*It was great to arrive here last night and find a letter in my mailbox—started things off in just the right way. We had a pleasant drive out although it rained the entire eleven hours. Arrived in Painesville and my parents got a motel room and we all had two very potent drinks. When I went to to register about 8:30 I could hardly sign my name. There are only about 80 girls here now. The freshmen all arrive tomorrow, and the rest of the kids on Wednesday. I stayed with Kit last night because it was so lonely in the new dorm. Haven't heard from Janet so don't know when she'll be back. Our room is really great—so much room, and gigantic closets compared to the last two years. We don't have a TV but do have just about everything else, including a radiator that drips incessantly.*

*Not much to do until classes start Thursday—I only have 2 classes that day—only 8 classes per week for fall term. Bought a few books this afternoon—they don't look particularly interesting. Also received our Winter Term Abroad schedule. We have to be in New York on Dec. 27th. The Queen Mary will have us back in the U.S.A. March 16th, giving us a two-week vacation before spring term begins. Still can't believe that we're truly going.*

*Haven't got any stationery yet so please excuse the paper. Did you get my last letter? I sent it to this address not knowing whether or not you'd be there.*

*Are you going to Wisconsin for your opening football game? You'll*

*be able to do a great deal of traveling this year with your car at school.*

*Kit had said that any time Fraser, her pin-mate, was coming here from*

*Michigan, he could pick you up in South Bend. But I guess that would be*

*unnecessary now.*

*Still haven't finished unpacking—I forgot I had left so much junk at*

*school. Are all 5 of you living in one apartment or is it a boarding house or*

*what? Still planning on looking for another place?*

*I'm so tired I hardly know what I'm writing. Must be up for early Mass*

*and start greeting new faces at 8:30 a.m.!! Take care and write when you*

*have a minute.*

*As ever—*

*Fran*

*P.S. Would like to see your pictures of N.H. if you have had them*

*developed. Think you could send them? Dad's sending me a few next*

*week—finished slides of the mountains. Sure that'll only make me think of*

*you even more.*

Taking and sharing photographs has changed so much since then that it's hard for even those of us who lived through it to remember how cumbersome it was. You bought a roll of film which would take, say, 24 images. If you only shot 22 pictures, the film remained in the camera until you got around to using the other two. Since it was practically unheard of to develop a roll that had not been completely used, sometimes film remained in a camera for months. By the time you finally had it processed you often forgot what was on the start of the roll.

I don't remember if I had pictures to send to Fran right away, or waited until I finished the roll of film in my camera.

Back at school, Fran found herself in the school's infirmary with a bronchial infection. Besides getting her well, our primary goal for the term was to see each other as soon as possible. We made plans for her to come to South Bend for the Notre Dame homecoming the last weekend in October. In addition to discussing our homecoming plans, my letter was full of other news.

"The biggest news as far as I'm concerned is that I broke up with Carolyn for good. It's the smartest thing I've done for a long time and that's sayin' somethin', brother," I wrote Fran. Carolyn and I still considered ourselves good friends, but we had been drifting apart for months as our lives went in different directions. More than ever, mine was going toward Fran. Cutting things off with Carolyn just made sense.

But the really big news was that one of my friends had suddenly gotten married. My letter didn't state what was obvious at the time: my friend and his girlfriend had gotten married because they had to. By the time they were in college, the raging hormones of young adulthood made abstinence extremely difficult for many young couples. Still, the public shame if one "made a mistake" was a prime deterrent to giving in. Out of wedlock pregnancies and even living together without marriage were not taken lightly. The basic rule was "get girl in trouble, get married."

Sadly, my friend's "shotgun" marriage turned out to be unnecessary. His girlfriend's home situation had been intolerable. She had been desperate to get away from her parents, and at a time when few jobs were open to women, marriage had seemed the only way out. She knew that he would do the right thing and marry her if she told him she was pregnant, after which she would have a "miscarriage." Within five years, when it grew clear that things weren't going to work out, they divorced. It was a tough lesson for him, and sobering for his friends as well.

Though Fran was visiting for Homecoming, we would not be going to the actual Homecoming Ball. It was so popular tickets were allocated by lottery and, as I wrote, "my number came up about 400 too late." Of course, Fran wanted to know what to pack for the weekend. I wrote that "You might want to bring along a dress or two and heels, a couple of skirts, sweaters, lots of long underwear, heavy socks, and a tent and bedroll. Actually I do have a motel reservation for you—either at the Bali or the Blue and Gold." Needless to say, even in the relative freedom of off-campus living, having a girl stay with us at a university-approved residence was completely out of the question.

That fall I took a part-time job at WNDU-TV, a campus-based NBC affiliate. I was a production assistant, working on a live morning children's program and the nightly 11:00 news. This afforded me a regular income, and thus the wherewithal to buy my own car. I wrote Fran about this, the first of that fall's two big steps. I found a 1957 Ford in fairly decent shape. Beyond the AM-only radio it had no options, but it was roadworthy. The Green Hornet, so named for its color, cost $700, which I was able to borrow from a bank in Sidney with my father's co-signature. To the bank manager's surprise and delight, I never missed a payment.

The second big step I was keeping as a surprise. I planned to formally "pin" Fran on homecoming weekend—provided, of course, that she would accept. A more serious version of high school's going steady, pinning was tantamount to a pre-engagement. The boy presented the girl with his fraternity pin with the understanding that someday they would be engaged. Though Notre Dame had no fraternities, it did sell university pins which served the same purpose. As Fran and I grew closer, becoming pinned seemed to me to be the logical next step. The pin expressed a stronger commitment, affirming that our love for each other was both special and enduring.

I was confident Fran would accept my pin, but things didn't go quite as smoothly as I envisioned. After she had arrived and settled in her motel room on Friday evening, I went to pick her up for dinner. That's when I took the opportunity to spring the surprise. Standing just inside the door of the cramped room, I told Fran that I loved her and said that I would be very happy if she would accept my Notre Dame pin as a token of that love.

Though Fran was completely surprised, she didn't hesitate for a second before accepting. When she said yes, I believe I pinned the University of Notre Dame symbol to her jacket. (As you'll see from her version of this moment, Fran remembers it a little differently.) I went to give her a big hug and kiss, intending for us to fall onto the motel bed in a passionate embrace. But in true Inspector Clouseau fashion, our aim and our timing were way off the mark. We bounced off the edge of the bed and landed on the floor. At that point we both broke up laughing so hard that any romantic inclination was lost.

My parents had come to Notre Dame that weekend for the football game, something they did two or three times a year. When Fran and I joined them for dinner that evening, we proudly made the announcement over cocktails. It never occurred to me to hold off with the news; I wanted to tell them in person, and there might have been no other opportunity that weekend. I also really liked the friends my parents were with, who were actually midway between Fran and I and Mom and Dad in age. I knew they would be happy for us.

Mom and Dad were clearly more shocked than pleased, but they made a great effort to be congratulatory. They knew that pinning was the first step toward a serious commitment; as much as they liked Fran, they were no doubt afraid I would settle down too early. Like my folks, Fran's were less than thrilled about the news.

*Friday*

*November 8, 1963*

*Dear Bob,*

*This has really been a hellish week and I'm so glad it's over. Believe I've finally learned my lesson regarding the results of procrastination. Had a mid-term Wednesday in Philosophy of Education and a paper due this morning. Remember that book I had with me last weekend? Well, I started to read and outline it simultaneously Wednesday about midnight and worked straight through until 7 p.m. last night, at which time I collapsed and slept for fifteen hours without hearing a sound. Never want to go through that again. Guess I'll start one of the three papers I have due by Thanksgiving tomorrow.*

*Didn't intend to begin this letter on such a sour note but guess I'm still a little tired. Called Mom and Dad last Sunday and they sounded pleased although I've never heard dad talk quite so softly. Had a letter from mom yesterday and she again extended her congratulations and told me not to forget to write home.*

*Had the entire dorm in an uproar when I came back—I've never received so many really sincere congratulations in my life. Got thrown into a freezing cold shower, fully dressed, twice before getting to bed. Guess it's sort of a traditional ritual but I've always been on the other side before.*

*People are still asking me about you and us—I think the whole thing really shocked a few girls—Kit for one. I'm still walking around with that silly grin—I can't quite believe it myself! Have never ever been so completely happy....*

Two weeks later, as we basked in the congratulations of our friends and dealt with our parents' mixed emotions, our joy was overshadowed by national tragedy. President John F. Kennedy was assassinated. On November 22, 1963, the bold-faced banner headline in the *New York Times* read:

KENNEDY IS KILLED BY SNIPER

AS HE RIDES IN CAR IN DALLAS;

JOHNSON SWORN IN ON PLANE

I was in a Friday morning class when the word started to spread. Everyone rushed in silence to the nearest television. Shocked, I watched the coverage for a while in a classroom building, then went home to join my roommates around the TV in our boarding house. In denial at first, we hoped and prayed that Kennedy would survive. We spent the weekend glued to the TV, struggling to come to grips with the reality of the President's death and to make sense of the events that followed.

As the newspapers reported on the President's burial, the nation's mourning and the tributes of leaders from around the world, an almost palpable pall fell over our house, the University, and the land. Americans were seized by the sense that we were no longer invulnerable—that the world we knew, the innocence and bright hope of the 1950s and early '60s, was lost forever. In our letters, Fran and I barely mentioned any of this. We must have spoken about the event by phone, but it was too painful to write about.

Fran's letter of November 23, the day after President Kennedy had been killed, contained the only written reference to that cataclysmic event that either of us made. "Just received your letter this morning and it was great to get some pleasant news after the happenings of the past 24 hours," she said. "Don't even like to think about it—it's so very difficult to accept such a terrible fact."

On a lighter note, she added, "Had a letter from Dad yesterday—first I'd heard from him since I called home the 3rd. He was quite sentimental but did say he was very happy about us." I was glad to hear that Fran's father was beginning to accept the seriousness of our relationship.

Fran would be joining our family once again for Thanksgiving. Knowing my practical-joking grandfather would be there, she wrote, "Do hope your grandfather doesn't bring any of his jumping animal toys—I'm nervous enough without anything like that." The visit was pleasantly uneventful, with a normality we welcomed after the shock of the President's assassination. No trick spiders were unleashed, and my family was warmly welcoming to Fran. It turned out she had nothing to be nervous about after all.

Knowing we would have a long separation while she was in Europe, we lobbied our parents to allow Fran to visit Sidney again when she finished classes on December 13. Surprisingly, they agreed. My parents were still slightly wary about the seriousness of our relationship, most likely worried that it would lead to illicit sexual behavior and, God forbid, early marriage. But they adjusted to the idea over time, and never stood in the way of our seeing each other as frequently as we could.

Fran was able to get a ride to Sidney, visit for a few days and then fly home for Christmas. Afterwards, I received her final letter of 1963.

*Friday*

*December 20, 1963*

*Dear Bob,*

*I miss you —*

*The flight from Dayton to N.Y. was great—will try to take jet flights from now on. Arrived in Boston almost an hour late but Mom was waiting and didn't seem to mind the delay. It's wonderful to be home again but still I hated to leave you and your family.*

*Been trying to write Christmas cards all night but am far from finished. Tomorrow we're going to attempt a final round of shopping. It's so terribly cold I hate to go outside—much more snow here than in Ohio.*

*Have you been skiing yet? Hope that you are able to ski as often as you want. Think you'll be going north at all during the vacation?*

*My family thinks your pin is lovely—Mom was naturally full of questions, all of which I couldn't answer. Dad doesn't say too much, but it seems that fathers never do.*

*As you can probably tell, it's very difficult for me to write this letter. After being able to talk to you, writing seems so inadequate, but unfortunately it will have to do for the next few months. It will undoubtedly get easier to write once I become re-accustomed to it.*

*Nothing exciting has happened since I came home. Andover is its usual dead self. Think most of the kids will be home this weekend so maybe something will happen then.*

*Wish there were more to say, but can't think of a thing. Thank you again for the most wonderful week—I enjoyed every minute. Please write soon. I love you so very much.*

*Love,*

*Fran*

We had been spoiled that fall: two visits in less than a month and much more frequent phone calls than before. Now the hard reality of her WTA was sinking in. Once she set sail from New York, we wouldn't be able to see or talk to each other for nearly three months. From January until April 1964, our contact would be entirely by letter.

My feelings were mixed. I was happy for her, envied her chance for adventure, and felt sorry for myself knowing how much I would miss her. She too was ambivalent, both excited and scared to death.

# CHAPTER TWELVE

*F*RAN SAILED JANUARY 3, 1964, FOR EUROPE ABOARD THE SS *FRANCE*. SHE
would return to New York on March 23 aboard the SS *United States*—a last-min-
ute change from the *Queen Mary,* the ship originally planned for the return
journey. Trans-Atlantic phone calls existed, but were far too expensive for us.
Talking by phone was such a far-out concept that we never even discussed the
possibility. Instead, we simply resigned ourselves to a long separation and relied
on the American and Spanish postal services to keep us connected in writing.

And write we did, especially Fran. In the nearly three months she was gone, she
wrote 34 letters and a couple of post cards. That year, an airmail letter from the
US to Spain cost 15 cents, while one from Spain back cost 10 pesetas, or about
8 cents. Delivery generally took about four days in either direction. If you didn't
specify or pay for air mail, your letter cost less but took much longer to arrive.

Fran's letters were written on lightweight onion skin paper, used for air mail
because it saved weight. From a reader's standpoint, onion skin was awful. Ink
bled through the translucent pages, making reading an arduous task. Sometimes
Fran would write every day for three or four days and then gang-mail the letters

in the same envelope. Her envelopes might contain eight or more sheets with writing on both sides. No matter how hard they were to read, it was a thrill for me every time one came, so I never complained.

Not sharing Fran's scruples about letter weight, I continued to write on my regular stationery. I didn't write as often as she did but managed to get off about a dozen letters in those three months. With the time lag of overseas mail and the fact that most of her letters were actually groups of three or four, our correspondence was no longer the back-and-forth "here's my answer to your last letter" writing we were used to. Instead, our written conversations tended to be somewhat disjointed, filled with gaps and overlaps.

The *France* took almost a week to sail from New York to Le Havre with a stop in Southampton, England. Fran's first few letters were written aboard ship and mailed from Europe on disembarkation. The *France* was a luxurious ship with two classes of passengers. Lake Erie College was obviously not going to spring for first-class accommodations, but the crossing was good even in second class. It wasn't always smooth, however. She wrote on January 7: "Dear Bob—my love, today we land in Southampton—makes me feel a little safer to know that we're close to shore. Already the English fog is evident—vision is good only for about 1/3 of a mile. The sea is extremely calm—hardly a ripple—quite a contrast after yesterday. We went through a storm for almost 20 hours with winds up to 80 mph—it was frightfully beautiful and after a while I wasn't even scared. Now I don't even feel the rolling of the ship."

Her first stop in Paris was at the American Express office to change some money. "Of all places I expected to find somewhat friendly, this was foremost but everyone was cool and almost snobby," her letter told me. But after meeting a friendly English-speaking couple, a couple of friendly waiters, and some welcoming young men in uniform who turned out to be firemen, Fran's feelings for the city warmed. She remained shocked by the high price of coffee, however: two francs (42 cents) was an unheard of price in those days.

I enjoyed Fran's evocations of Paris. Her introduction to the city was remarkably similar to mine four years earlier. It was fun to feel that we shared this magical place in some way.

I'll let Fran's pages in this book describe the European experiences not shared in her letters to me, and spare you the challenge of trying to read the mostly illegible pages. Here, however, is an excerpt from one early letter that helped give me a vivid sense of her life abroad. When she refers to her mother and father, she is of course referring to her WTA family members; Amparano was her Spanish "sister."

*Arrived in Valencia Monday night about 9:30—my mother was there to meet me. Think I'm the third girl they've had from LEC. My father is a real comedian and even though I can't always understand him I have to laugh. He reminds me of Fernandel only much heavier. He is about 70 and works someplace during the morning....My mother is very patient but still talks much too fast for me—she's about 63....[Amparano is] the most fun of all and seems so willing to help me. She is about 5' 1" with silvery blond hair and the biggest brown eyes I've ever seen. Hope we become really good friends.*

*Right now I'm sitting at a little round table that is in the dining room— there are 2 tables....Under the table cover there is a blanket that hangs to the floor. Under it is some kind of heater—when you sit here you put your feet under the blanket and the bottom half of you burns while the rest freezes. There is no central heating at all —did see a portable heater but*

*was told they only use that when it gets cold—am beginning to wonder*

*how cold it gets before they think it's cold! Actually, during the day it is*

*about 50-56 degrees, especially in the sun which supposedly shines every*

*day. The temperature in the building is another story – most are made*

*of some kind of cement and really hold the cold. My bed has five heavy*

*blankets on it so at least I'm fairly warm at night.*

Fernandel, I should explain, was a French vaudeville and movie comedian who performed from the 1930s into the 1960s.

Two weeks later she wrote: "Had some great news today—my sister said I could take a hot shower tomorrow! There's a water container in the bathroom that plugs in and heats and is also connected to a shower. Can hardly wait—feel like a skunge since arriving. If I'm really lucky they'll let me bring the portable heater with me so I won't get pneumonia."

As she got to know her family better, Fran got on well with her Spanish mother and developed a close relationship with Amparano. In contrast, though her father never mistreated her in any way, his behavior was strange. "My father here is very old and the victim of a slight shock—he's extremely set in his ways and evidently makes life very difficult for my mother & sister more than they care to admit. My sister is unable to have friends in when he's home because he thinks it's all foolishness. Think he and my mother are going to Barcelona this weekend and, if so, Amparano and I are going to have a fiesta here on Saturday afternoon."

"....You'd never guess what my father is doing now—reading the dictionary," she wrote another day. "When he reads out loud or begins to explain anything my sister sings real loud so I can't hear him—almost all he says is some form of foolishness."

As her letters all too vividly evoked, Fran's social life more than made up for any rough spots with cold, lack of showers, and Senor Oñate. Attending a daily Spanish grammar class at the University of Valencia with the other Lake Erie College girls in town, Fran and her friends had ample opportunities to meet the local Spanish boys. They took full advantage of it. Fran developed a special friendship with one named Paco, with whom she spent a lot of time.

A typical afternoon might involve a group of eight or ten going to someone's apartment for dancing. After dinner they often went to a cafe for wine and conversation. If Paco wasn't available for some reason, one of his friends would show up to escort Fran around. She learned to thoroughly enjoy most of them. Nights out were dirt cheap—easy to handle even on her meager allowance. One place she went served them two bottles of wine and two dishes of peanuts for about 30 cents.

Despite her busy schedule, Fran wrote to me nearly every day, using her letters both to keep me up to date on her activities and to reflect on her own thoughts and emotions. This is typical, with letters from several days sent together.

*Monday*

*January 20, 1964*

*Dearest Bob,*

*Or maybe I should say dear diary—you seem to be the scapegoat for all my problems and complaints. Forgive me, but there is no one here that I can really talk to. When I write to you it's the closest thing I have to having someone here who is listening and trying to understand. I truly envy people* who have a built-in literary skill—some people are so good and so coherent when they write.

Today was terrible. I stayed in all day except to go to classes this morning and after a few hours I felt like I was in an escape-proof box. Wanted to scream. My mother and sister had to repeat everything that they said to me—how does one explain that there are times when you'd rather be left alone? Realize now that I should have gone for a walk but instead I just sat and felt sorry for myself. Guess I am as moody as my father thinks.

My mother here has a transistor radio, and tonight my sister let me bring it to my room. After much searching I found a local station that is playing nothing but American jazz, blues and dance tunes. If my eyes are closed and I think really hard it's almost possible to feel myself in your arms dancing in some dark cocktail bar. This all probably sounds silly to you but it's true.

I am learning, and I do think many of my ideas have been altered. But generally I'm the same, confused person I was when I left the States.

Tomorrow it's supposed to be sunny and warmer—no more rain like today—perhaps everything will be brighter.

Don't know when or where you'll read this because I've forgotten when you have semester break. Hope your exams aren't too wearing. I miss you so much.

All my love,

Fran

Tuesday

*January 21, 1964*

*Now I can say we've been here over a week—doesn't seem possible. Sometimes I feel like a native and others like the foreigner I am. It's getting a little easier to speak Spanish and my comprehension of what my family is saying is greater. I think they realize this too for they don't talk about me when I'm around. When I first arrived they did all that the time because they knew I was unable to understand.*

*Tomorrow is a local fiesta—the feast of St. Vincent, patron of Valencia. We all are required to hear Mass and all classes have been cancelled. As far as I can figure out it will be just like a Sunday.*

*Had a very novel experience tonight—took what might be called a bath. My mother heated a small pan of water for me and when it was hot, dumped it into the tub. Without exaggerating one bit, I can honestly say that the tub is 2 feet square. You can imagine trying to sit in that. Besides, it was so cold in the bathroom that the water was cold in a matter of minutes. As a matter of fact it's still so cold that my pen will scarcely write. All the girls have colds and I feel quite fortunate that I'm not ill too. It must be continual dampness—everything is always clammy & wet. If this is supposed to be the warmest center, I'm glad I'm not elsewhere.*

*Met some of our Spanish friends tonight and went drinking wine. It's as easy to get smashed on wine here as it is to get high on liquor in the US. A strange thing though: Spanish beer has no alcoholic content at all, so maybe it would be best to switch to that.*

*It's difficult to get to bed before 1 A.M. here because dinner is so late. Every night I'm exhausted—think I'll go to sleep.*

*Remember that I love you very much.*

*Love always,*

*Fran*

*Wednesday*

*January 22, 1964*

*You must be getting tired of hearing me say this, but I love you, I love you. Every day it just means more to me, and the realization of how much you mean to me is greater. I wish I knew more and better ways to tell you how I feel but I don't. Just know that I want you with me all the time, day and night, and that the next six weeks especially, and the next year, are going to be hell. Right now I have no idea how you're thinking but I hope and pray there aren't any great changes during these three months. If we were both in the US it's possible that we'd only see each other a few times, but the thought of having you so very far away is terrible. I never thought it possible that a person as seemingly inhibited as me could be very much in love. Please forgive me if my letters all seem identical. I can't help but write exactly what I think.*

*Tonight we went drinking and dancing. The social life that I've encountered here is so different than that at home. No matter how much I try, I can't understand the reasons behind all the changes and mix-ups. One thing is certain. There's nothing the least bit serious about anything. Only one girl in the entire group has been acting without much reservation and good conduct—suppose that's to be expected but now she's settling down. Hate to think of anyone leaving a poor impression.*

*My sister and I are both sitting here writing letters, she in Spanish and me in English—neither can understand what the other is saying! The radio is playing a very popular American song, an instrumental that was*

*real popular a few months ago. Can't remember the name—I think it's*

*"Sleepwalk"—but the sound of electric guitars certainly creates nostalgia.*

*Please try to understand that this whole trip is marvelous. It's definitely*

*taking me longer than most to adjust but then again, I have more at home*

*than most. I'm sure that after a little while longer my letters won't be quite*

*so complaining, critical or depressing. Think I'll close this letter now—*

*hope you receive it before you start semester break.*

*All my love and thoughts—always.*

*Fran*

Although my social life at Notre Dame wasn't exactly dull, it was nowhere near Fran's level of seemingly non-stop partying. After about a month of reading her almost daily accounts of parties, cafés, Paco and other male friends, I found it hard to suppress my jealous feelings. Her continual declarations of love not-withstanding, I began to imagine that this story would not have a happy ending for me. What if she found some exotic Spaniard who would change the way she felt about me?  I finally let my growing concern surface in February, weaving comments through accounts of my own activities.

"Where do you meet all these charming people that I get so jealous reading about?" I wrote. "I'm curious about where you do all your dancing in Valencia in the middle of the afternoon."  And finally, "I hope that your love for me hasn't been cooling. If I read things into your letters it sometimes sounds that way, but it is probably just my overactive imagination. I love you very much, Fran—and I hope that someday you'll realize just how much. Be good and keep writing—and I really look forward to your mail. Love always, Bob."

Her response came in an onion skin aerogram, a single sheet that folded three times to become a self-mailer. It was a bit hard to read, but worth the effort.

*Thursday, February 13, 1964*

*Dearest Bob,*

*This is going to have to be your valentine—at least it has more color than an ordinary letter. Didn't quite know where to start writing—there are so many places to fold this darn thing.*

*Found out this morning that we don't have to leave Valencia until the night of March 2nd. That means another free Sunday here—when we do leave we have a 48 hr. train ride to Rome.*

*Today it was cloudy and even rained for a while—my cold is getting worse. Spent a large part of the afternoon shopping—there are some of the most intriguing little stores here. Bought a beautiful black mantilla for myself—can hardly wait for Sunday to wear it. Think I already told you that we have to ship one suitcase this Saturday and I'd like to put as much as possible in it.*

*Hope Mardi Gras was much fun—would have loved to have seen Peter, Paul and Mary. Too bad all the tickets were sold out but suppose a motel or hotel would be apt to be a trifle more amusing, etc. Very often during the afternoon we go dancing at someone's apartment—on Sunday it's the University Club and with Ricardo some sort of night club. The latter occurs seldom—the other more often—one of my friends has a huge collection of American records that aren't too old. Actually I have just as much fun going for a walk or sitting in a café drinking wine.*

*Pobrecito—forgive me for being so sarcastic in this little letter—don't really know what is wrong except that your letter this afternoon made me feel quite uncomfortable and rather upset. I realize that I am very poor at expressing myself in writing and it is possible that you could "read into" what I say—however, if you feel that my love for you is any less than in December, something is wrong. I only tell you everything I do because I thought you'd want to know. Surely you know as well as I that once I leave here I'll never again see any of the boys I have dated—dating here is for amusement only—a diversion and something to do rather than stay at home all the time. This probably sounds terribly confusing but all I really want to say is that I love you; I love you with all my heart & soul. Please try and remember this when you read about my daily adventures. It's true—my feelings have changed—I'm more sure that I want to spend the rest of my life with you and do all that I can to make you happy.*

*This is a terrible explanation but the best I am capable of right now. Do hope you understand and won't let your imagination run away with you. I really hope that you realize how much I love you, too. Can't say much more, can I. Please take care and drive carefully if there's snow. Do worry about you—will write more very soon—hope you do also.*

*Until then—all my love, Fran.*

*P.S. Believe me—I do love you.*

Por una mirada, un mundo;

por una sonrisa, un cielo;

por un beso... yo no sé

qué te diera por un beso.

[Gustavo Adolpho] Béquer

*[translation:*

*I don't know what I would give you*

*For a look… the world*

*For a smile… the sky*

*For a kiss, I don't know*

*what I would give you for a kiss.]*

I wrote back quickly, tucking into my envelope a scrap of scratch-pad paper that read: "Fran, dear, I had this letter sealed but when I got your letter today I wanted to insert this note. Please don't you be upset over what I said in that letter. I wrote it at a time when I was really down and I had been reading things into everything. I love you completely and any good love is built on trust. If I didn't believe in you all the way I wouldn't want anything to do with you. But since I do trust you I want everything to do with you—for the rest of my life. I love you, dear—don't worry about my imagination."

That settled the issue, though when I acknowledged her pending serenade by the Tuna, Paco's singing group, I joked that "I hope the Tuna aren't spawning." As Fran's letters went on, she went from being deeply homesick to not wanting to leave Spain. By February 27 she was writing, "Get awfully sad thinking about leaving here—only four days left—not nearly enough. It's so difficult to think of saying good-bye to everyone knowing that in all probability I'll never see them again. It's hard enough to leave someone when you know you'll be with them again but this is going to be too much. Did you feel like this when you had to leave France?"

Maybe I did, a little bit. But I was only 16 then and she was 20 now, a big difference in maturity level. I was happy that she came to enjoy her WTA so much, but I have to admit that I was also relieved to know her frenetic Spanish social whirl was ending.

Back at Notre Dame, I was still working hard to improve my grades. My second semester courses included Mass Media, Modern Culture, Philosophy of Man, Psychology, and Modern Fiction—a heavy but manageable load. I continued to work part time at the TV studio and managed the occasional weekend ski trips to a small hill near Sidney and a couple slightly bigger hills in Michigan. The former had the virtue of affording me the opportunity to see my family, not to mention free room and board during the trip. I had an occasional date but rarely saw the same girl twice.

I battled continuing problems with the Green Hornet, threatening to sell it on more than one occasion. The old Ford would generally get me where I was going, but she suffered from things like serious oil leaks and a bad cylinder. Meanwhile, my roommate Tom was enjoying his brand-new Triumph TR-4. I always felt cool just riding in it. We drove around much more often in the Triumph than in the Green Hornet except for a month or so when an accident kept the Triumph in the auto repair yard.

On March 5, the college girls bade farewell to their European families and met up for a two-week European tour. They visited Rome, Venice, Florence, Zurich, Vienna, and other spots before winding up in London for a few days. On March 18 they set sail from Southampton aboard the *SS United States*. She didn't offer the luxury of the *France,* but what she lacked in that department the *United States* made up for in speed. The fastest liner on the seas, she could cruise at a blistering 33 knots, enough to take a full day off the Atlantic crossing time.

Fran arrived in New York on March 23, 1964, coinciding with my spring break. She wanted me to meet her in New York and accompany her to Andover. As tempting as that was, I reasoned that her parents would be anxious to have her to themselves for a while. In addition, I had the opportunity to go home with Tom to Fort Lauderdale and I really didn't want to pass that up. I promised to come to Painesville the weekend of April 3 instead.

While I enjoyed the sun and sand of Ft. Lauderdale, Fran returned safely home. On March 29 she wrote me a letter on real paper—not onion skin! In it she talked about some awkwardness on the home front. "Think my family is a little disappointed in their oldest daughter—haven't talked about Europe or my trip for more than ten minutes," she wrote pensively. "It's much more difficult than I ever imagined—so many things happened that it's almost impossible for me to begin talking about it without having some initial questions to get things started." I'd had a similar feeling when I returned from France. My family wanted to know every detail about what I experienced but there was so much locked up inside my brain it wouldn't come out. Today, photos help jump-start travel stories, but since it took a week or two to get photos printed in 1964, it was impossible for Fran to show her family her photos before she returned to college on April 1.

Fran and I reunited on her campus on Friday, April 3. She still remembers my grand entrance to her dorm lobby, glowing with a Florida tan and wearing a baby-blue denim double-breasted sports jacket that was the height of fashion. More than one of the other girls in the dorm offered to leave with me but I only had eyes for Fran. We drove back to Sidney and spent the weekend there before returning to our colleges on Sunday evening.

It was, of course, a wonderful reunion. Fran and I both vividly remember the drive from Painesville to Sidney, spent with the radio cranked up loud and singing at the tops of our lungs to hits like the Beatles' "Love, Love Me Do." It was a beautiful Midwestern spring weekend, warm and with the tulips in bloom. Mom and Dad took us to dinner one evening, and some of my friends were home from school at the same time, so we had the chance to see them as well.

We had plenty of time to talk about what we'd each been doing for the last three months *and* catch up on our kissing—which we did plenty of. We got locked in such a long and passionate kiss at the train station that Fran nearly missed her train back to Cleveland, which had actually started to move by the time she boarded. "I still can't believe that final encore with the train Sunday," I wrote shortly afterward. "Hope you weren't too embarrassed to get in the car. Guess neither one of us was hearing too much from our heads that afternoon. Anyway, it's something we can tell our kids if they've got a sense of humor." Fran responded, "My ride was uneventful—one lady made a comment about almost missing the train but that's all."

In the following five weeks we would see each other three more times. It was difficult to take time away from our studies, but having been separated for so long, we couldn't help ourselves. More difficult was finding the cash to fund travel and proms, but this was a priority, so we managed.

Those visits took place against a sobering backdrop. That winter and spring saw a spate of marriages among people I knew, both friends at Notre Dame and former girlfriends. Some were planned, but some were not. Though I was crazily in love with Fran and dreamed of someday marrying her, neither of us wanted to marry while we were still in school. We were too immersed in our respective colleges to want to change. Today, it's conceivable that a young couple might marry, attend colleges hundreds of miles apart, and make it all work. In the America of 1964 that would have been virtually impossible. The thought of trying it never occurred to most people, and Fran and I were no exception.

The unplanned weddings therefore became a cautionary tale. As much as we wanted to have sex, they helped us remain mindful of the risks involved. As difficult as it was, abstinence seemed better than disappointing our parents and disrupting our educations. The lack of reliable birth control was a major factor, though not the only one. Only approved by the FDA in 1960, the Pill was not readily available to unmarried college girls. Even if Fran had been able to get a prescription for it, neither of us had yet come to grips with our Catholic religious scruples over artificial birth control. In one letter, I related the then-current joke about a new birth control pill approved by the Catholic Church: "The woman holds it firmly between her knees."

About that time, my father grew worried about the safety of the Green Hornet given the long trips I was making. Ready for a new car himself, he arranged for me to "inherit" his yellow Corvair, now dubbed the "Yellow Banana." I happily sold the Green Hornet and, since it was paid off, pocketed the small amount of cash from that deal. Given later safety studies, it's ironic that a used Corvair would be deemed the safer of the two vehicles, but at the time it was a reasonable conclusion.

Life at Mrs. Shaw's boarding house continued to be enjoyable. For me the freedom and relative quiet compared to dormitory living made it heaven on earth. We tried not to take advantage of Mrs. Shaw's good graces. But that spring, Chuck and I made 60 gallons of home-brew beer in our second floor "living room," intending to bottle and sell it at a profit. When Mrs. Shaw caught us in the act of mixing the ingredients, we tried to convince her that we were just creating bacteria for a biology experiment. She bought our story at first, though a week or so later when the house had begun to smell like a brewery, our "experiment" was consigned to her garage. Unfortunately, after we bottled our beer, the bottles began to explode. The whole venture literally ended with a bang, putting to rest another of my entrepreneurial ventures.

As the semester wound down I ramped up my studying even more and scrambled to find a summer job. It wasn't an easy task that year. Every kid over the age of 16 that I knew wanted to work in the summer, but temporary jobs were often hard to come by. That was especially true in South Bend in 1964. The nearby Studebaker auto plant had closed its doors just six months earlier, leaving hundreds unemployed. For an outsider, the competition for jobs was intense—rather like it is today in communities that are similarly hard hit by business and plant closings.

Because so many of my Sidney friends were either married or gone, I was determined not to go back to my home town for the summer. One idea was to work in Boston so I could be close to Fran. I also sent letters to a number of Cleveland radio and TV stations hoping someone would have an internship available.

My dad offered to circulate my résumé among his contacts. I had a brief ray of hope from an ad agency in Milwaukee, but it never went anywhere. Even Fran's father was doing some lobbying on my behalf with the ad agency he worked with in Boston. In deep frustration that nothing had come together, I took the only thing available in South Bend: a job as an encyclopedia salesman. Two of my roommates, Chuck Watson and Lou Esposito, were also staying in South Bend for the summer. There was an extra room in the house they had rented, so they were happy to have me join them and help with the rent.

As usual, Fran's classes lasted two weeks longer than mine. Despite this, we met up in Sidney to celebrate her birthday on June 5. We decided to spend the evening at Eddie's, a roadhouse in a village a few miles outside of Sidney. It had a jukebox, a dance floor, and an owner with few scruples about serving alcohol to well-behaved people who might not be of drinking age. However, since Fran had just turned twenty-one, she was now completely legal. (I had three months to go, though I looked older than my age.) We went with some friends, enjoying the chance to dance and talk about all that was going on in our lives. I then returned to South Bend to start the couple of days of classroom training that initiated my new "career."

Fran's roommate Janet was getting married on June 20 to Bill Darrow, a great guy who had just finished medical school. The wedding was in Elmira, NY, a long way away. But I didn't want to miss it or the opportunity to spend more time with Fran. The only way I could affordably get to Elmira from South Bend was by bus. I can assure you that getting there was *not* half the fun, to contradict the famous Cunard Lines slogan. In fact, it wasn't any fun at all. The trip took 24 grueling hours in a hot, smelly coach with seats designed for midgets. Still, the wedding was a wonderful event, and worth the sacrifice it took to get there. Afterward, I was grateful when some friends of Fran's offered me a ride to Cleveland, where I could catch a train for South Bend. But as always it was hard to say good-bye to Fran.

I reported for sales duty the following Monday morning, bound and determined not to fail. The job involved walking a prescribed neighborhood, dressed in suit and tie and carrying a heavy case of encyclopedia samples, from 10:00 a.m. until 6:00 p.m. It was hard going in the summer heat but in my second week, I made a cash sale—a real coup in a field where extended payments were the norm. I eventually succeeded in making one more sale, at which point I declared victory and left the encyclopedia business for good. The thing that finally did me in was the duplicitous method used to gain entry to someone's home. I hated having to tell people I was "conducting a survey" when I was really sneakily finding out if they were qualified prospects.

Now unemployed again, I began trying to find another job that would keep me in South Bend. Dad's former employer, the Oliver Corporation, happened to have a plant there. Through Dad's contacts, I managed to get hired as a shipping clerk in the department that printed and shipped product manuals and sales literature to Oliver dealers all over the country. As I told Fran, "the job is terrible, the pay is lousy, and they don't really seem to need me, but I'll stick with it if I have to." In the end, crushing boredom among other things made that impossible. Throwing in the towel, I returned to Sidney, where the lumber yard again hired me to unload boxcars for the rest of the summer. My job involved moving tons of two-by-whatevers out of the boxcars and into the yard. It was back-breaking, splinter-creating manual labor, but at least it was a job.

Meanwhile, Fran was working at the mental hospital again. She enjoyed the work despite its occasional dangers. Once, she learned that someone she had bathed the day before had attacked and seriously injured an aide the previous year. Fortunately, the patient was calm the day Fran worked with her.

That summer, our conversations about the future started to become more serious. We knew we were in love, and we began talking about marriage. There was no dramatic moment or formal proposal on bended knee. The momentous decision that we would like to get married came simply and naturally. At one point, I did ask, "Will you marry me?" Fran happily said "Yes."

We decided we would become engaged during our senior year and get married as soon as possible after graduation. Afraid our parents would object on the grounds that we were too young, we agreed not to tell them right away, but decided as well that if the proper occasion presented itself, we would take advantage of it. On a trip home in early July, I thought the time was right and broke the news to my parents. When I called Fran to let her know, she went ahead and told her folks. She filled me in on how that went in a lengthy letter written on onion skin she obviously was trying to use up. The letter is too long to print in its entirety but here is the key section:

*Saturday*

*July 4, 1964*

*Dearest Bob,*

*There was a beautiful sunset the other night—I took the car and went looking for a hill high enough above the trees and houses to see it but couldn't find one. Finally came home and went to my room. From there I could see the entire sunset and the mountains. I had forgotten how high up our house really is—it's been a long time since I just sat in my room and looked out the window. The whole episode made me realize how much there is right at your fingertips, and that so often you're apt to overlook it in search of finding it elsewhere. That's not to say that everything is here. You're not, and it's hard to be truly interested in anything without you here to share it.*

*I was so flustered and excited when you called. I scarcely let you say two words. And in my excitement I forgot to tell you how much I love you. I'm* sure you know it without my saying it, but I enjoy telling you as often as I can. I love you, Bob.

Your news certainly was surprising—it took me hours to settle down and go to sleep after talking with you. We're so fortunate that our parents are pleased with our plans. Yes, I've spoken to my mother and finally to Dad, too. We were sitting around having a drink the other night when Mom suggested I tell Daddy about my phone call. Had told Mom the morning after you called. Anyway, Dad eventually stopped trying to change the subject and I told him what we'd decided, and that you had already told your parents our plans.

Needless to say, I only half expected Dad's initial reaction. Won't go into details in a letter—have already told you his viewpoint—but I finally left the room practically in tears, then my parents argued. Later Dad sort of apologized and said he was very happy for both of us. Every day since then he's repeated his best wishes. I know he's sincere but still it hurt to have the initial announcement of our plans meet with an hour discussion and diplomatic lecture on economics. I know they're important and must be considered but it wasn't necessary right then.

Still, I doubt we'll really have any difficulty unless something really unexpected happens during the next 8 to 10 months. So my love, if you ever want to talk about our life with my parents, the biggest problems have already been aired. The next time they come up it won't be so one-sided, I'm sure. Now that I've told you all this, I think perhaps I've been a little too harsh and quick in speaking of my father. Forgive me for being somewhat disrespectful and over- sensitive.

Ever the practical man, her father was justifiably concerned about how his daughter would be supported if she married me right after graduation. Who knew if I'd have a job or if it would pay enough to support two? And who knew where it might be? Probably not near him, he feared. If she got married and started a family, would all of the education he had paid for be for nothing? Becoming a teacher, a secretary, or a nurse was what most women who worked did in the 1960s. Fran was being trained to teach, and we were confident she could do all the teaching she wanted to do.

We had no idea how or where we would earn a living, but our blind faith in each other and in the American economic system left us undeterred. Graduating from college in 1965 was very different than graduating today. Finding a good job then was neither automatic nor easy, but everyone I know who looked seriously for a job found one. Today, statistics suggest that barely half of all college graduates are able to find jobs in their chosen careers. I'm grateful that Fran and I didn't have to face that reality *or* the financial and emotional stress that goes along with it.

We had no answers to some of her father's questions, only complete faith that somehow the finances, along with everything else, would work out. Undaunted by her father's misgivings, I wrote: "It is too bad your father took it as he did at first but as long as he came around later that's all that counts. Sounds as though we have your mother to thank." Indeed, we did. Her mother loved me from the beginning. Truly happy for us, she used her powers of persuasion to calm her husband's fears.

My parents both accepted the news graciously. I had asked them to join me in the living room, away from my sisters' earshot, because I had some important news. As we sat, I said, "I want you to know that Fran and I have decided to get married right after we graduate. I know you might think we're too young, but we love each other and we know this is the right thing for the two of us."

I recall Mom speaking up first. She assured me that she found Fran a lovely young woman, notwithstanding an earlier comment that she didn't think Fran was my "type." (Mom sometimes shot from the hip before thinking about the impact of her remarks, and I had long ago learned to ignore it.) She added that she knew we had thought about our decision very carefully. When she told me she was very happy for us, I could tell she was entirely sincere. Characteristically, Dad was more reserved. He expressed his congratulations but also offered some advice. They were both concerned, like Fran's father, about the economics of our being married. Dad talked to me seriously to make sure I understood the responsibilities I would be taking on and the uncertainties that still lay ahead. I recall our discussion as being open and frank. I took his words to heart but only in the sense of doubling my resolve to succeed. I knew they had faith in me, and that was what counted.

At the end of August, I gladly bid the lumberyard job goodbye and headed back to Lake Winnipesaukee for a wonderful week with Fran and the Jordan family. I took advantage of the opportunity while there to formally ask Fran's father for his daughter's hand, permission he graciously granted. The week flew by. Fran and I, now officially engaged to be engaged, found precious moments when we could be alone together. Given that the family was living in the same small cabin as before, that required some ingenuity. But we managed. All too soon, it was back to college for our final year.

## CHAPTER THIRTEEN

*A*S WE ENTERED OUR FINAL YEARS OF COLLEGE IN SEPTEMBER 1964, one of our main preoccupations wasn't academic. During my end-of-summer trip to Lake Winnipesaukee, Fran and I had begun to discuss our engagement ring.

I of course knew nothing about such things, but equally naturally, Fran had been giving it a lot of thought. Knowing I didn't have much money, she kindly kept her expectations modest. She told me her preferences—white gold, not yellow; simple Tiffany-type setting; round cut stone—and left it in my hands.

At Lake Erie College, Fran received the honor of being named Dorm Head of her new dormitory, Avery Hall. Being the student Dorm Head made her the first contact for any girl who had a problem. Fran got her baptism by fire early on. This is from her first letter to me of the semester:

*Monday*

*September 21, 1964*

*Dearest Bob,*

*Seems like a year since Saturday even though it's been quite busy and time to relax has been scarce. Went back to Nemeth's tonight with Pam, Sally and "B" and those two crazy sophomores fed me martinis until my nose was numb. Just all of a sudden this afternoon everything got so very depressing but now I feel about ready to go to work.*

*Talked with the advisor of student teachers this afternoon and received a great shock. My Shakespeare class meets Tues. and Thurs. at eleven which means I'll be teaching two classes of Jr. Eng. before 11 and two classes of Fresh. Eng. after lunch until 3:30. I was sick—couldn't believe I had made such a ridiculous mistake. This term will be more hectic than previously anticipated.*

*Conducted my first dorm meeting last night—sort of a brief introduction for the freshmen and a traumatic experience for me. My hands were shaking so much while I talked and I couldn't even hold a cigarette. If there's no improvement in my self-confidence or whatever it is that makes one calm I'll be a nervous wreck before too many more meetings. But actually I love my job and already the rewards have been more than adequate. The freshmen in this dorm are really sweet and so enthusiastic. Hope their enthusiasm lasts.*

*How were your parents when you were home? Wrote mom and dad a long letter and told them we had decided on a setting for my ring—*

couldn't give them any idea of when I'd see it but maybe they'll enjoy the agonizing suspense too.

Going to bed now. Keep writing until I get your address. I miss you terribly and don't know how I'm going to last until the end of October. I love you, Bob.

*Wednesday*

*Hi again,*

*I'm so tired—finally settled down enough to go to sleep around 2:00 last night—only to be awakened at 5 a.m. by one of the freshmen. She had been awake all night with stomach pains—was afraid she had appendicitis! Had to wake up the dorm parents, call the Dr., stay with the girl until she calmed down, then take her to the emergency room at the hospital at 8. Pam and I have had two nights of uninterrupted sleep since we got back last week. If it keeps up like this I'll be numb to everything that happens around here.*

*Enjoyed talking with you so much last night. Actually we were quite good—only talked a half hour. After hanging up I was rather upset however; had forgotten to ask you to growl for me. Have the whole dorm listening to that song now.*

*Leaving for Cleveland now—told Janet we'd spend the afternoon with her. Sorry the first part of this letter repeated so many of the questions I asked last night. Will write again soon. I miss you and love you very much.*

*All my love,*

*Fran*

*P.S. The enclosed is from Nemeth's—*

The mention to growling referred to a popular song of the day. Roy Orbison's "Oh, Pretty Woman" features a throaty growl in admiration of the "pretty woman." Perfectly imitating that growl, I occasionally used it to express my appreciation for Fran, and she loved it.

That fall, Fran and I enjoyed the new luxury of some lengthy phone calls. The advent of telephone credit cards made it possible to make a call from any phone, having the calls billed directly to the card rather than having to fumble with change. We had to manage our usage so we didn't go broke, but given that Fran and I still had another year apart, it was still a modern convenience well worth taking advantage of.

Back in South Bend, the gang of five from Mrs. Shaw's had split up. Lou Esposito had graduated the previous June, while Chuck Watson and Gary Hosbein had moved to separate off-campus rooming houses. Staying together, Tom Franck and I wound up in the basement of a Notre Dame professor's home. Tom and I shared one of the basement's two finished rooms and two other students, Dick and Joe, shared the other. We lacked the separate "living room" we had enjoyed at Mrs. Shaw's but otherwise we were comfortable enough. The professor and his wife, Mr. and Mrs. Bobik, were welcoming people who tried to make us feel at home. We had our own basement entrance, however, so we didn't need or want to have much contact with them. We still ate all our meals out, and either took our dirty clothes to a laundry service or washed them ourselves at a laundromat. Most often, we used the laundry service, the laundromat being boring and time consuming.

I wrote back immediately.

ROBERT L. ZIELSDORF

1608 PORT JEFFERSON ROAD

SIDNEY, OHIO

9-22

Dear Fran,

First of all I want to apologize for my condition when I called you the

other night. I only set out to have a couple beers but after 1½ pitchers of beer and 2 martinis, I guess my lack of sleep and food caught up with me. Someday I'll tell all but right now there are more important things to say.

Such as: I love you. I'm not even going to try to describe the emptiness I feel when you aren't with me, but then you might know the feeling too.

Saw Jerry tonight. This afternoon he became the father of a girl. A baby one, I believe. Anyhow he was very proud and very high. I plan to visit his wife tomorrow after I register.

Time for bed, honey. I'll write again tomorrow when I've had time to unpack something besides my pen and paper.

I love you. Always,

Bob

P.S. Saw Bert Kasten today.

The cryptic P.S. in that letter was a tease. Fran knew that I was ordering our engagement ring, but everything else was a secret. Bert Kasten owned and operated a small jewelry store in Sidney. He was a friend of my parents, and I liked him a lot; over the years I had bought little things at his store, usually gifts for Fran or my mother. Mr. Kasten always gave me a special discount. When it came time to get serious about buying an engagement ring, it never occurred to me to look anywhere else.

I recall going into his store just before leaving for school and telling him in strict confidence that I wanted to buy an engagement ring for Fran. Although my parents knew Fran and I planned to get formally engaged, I hadn't told them when it would happen. It was important to me that Fran be the only one who knew I was purchasing a ring, though even she didn't know when I would give it to her. With confidentiality so important, I knew I could trust Mr. Kasten.

Naturally, he began by asking how much I planned to spend. I had been able to save around $700—not a huge amount even then, but hopefully enough for something respectable. Mr. Kasten gave me an education about diamond values and the color, cut, and clarity on which they are based. Once we settled on the design, he promised to find the biggest and best stone that fit my budget.

I wound up getting a nearly perfect half-carat round-cut stone—a good size in those days—mounted just as Fran wanted in a Tiffany-style white gold setting. I have no doubt that the ring was worth far in excess of whatever I paid. Although he never said so, I believe it was Mr. Kasten's special gift to us.

Wanting to preserve the element of surprise, I kept mum on all these details and drew the whole process out. Writing to Fran in late September, I began to set the stage for the surprise presentation. "By now you must be really busy if your whole schedule is in effect. If it helps you to relax you can console yourself in the thought that I'll be out to see you on October 9! I decided that I could never possibly wait until the 30th to see you, honey. And even though I won't be able to get home before then to see Mr. Kasten, I'm sure we can find some way to have fun. After all, we can't get engaged every weekend and I think it's kind of fun to watch you with your anxious pains," I wrote.

Expecting the ring to be ready in mid-October, the original plan was for me to go to Sidney to pick it up before my planned visit to Lake Erie College on October 30. Although no promises were made, Fran was hoping she would get the ring that weekend. Telling her I wouldn't be able to get the ring by October 9 was just a ruse. Based on Mr. Kasten's reassurances, I was actually fairly certain it would be in my hands by then.

Writing back with a long and newsy letter, telling me about her school life and asking how I was getting along in my new quarters, Fran finally got to the point. "When are you going home again—wouldn't you like to go down and come back with your parents for the Purdue game—huh?!? Some times I'm so anxious and filled with curiosity my toes curl and I have half-nightmares! The suspense is practically killing me. Maybe I have a secret from you too—until you write again and tell me you love me—remember I love you very much and think of you always. Take care my darling. All my love, Fran."

So my evil plan was working. In a September 30 letter, I gilded the lily: "Honey, I hate to disappoint you but I can't possibly get home before this weekend, and in fact, I can't see how I could manage it before the 31st. And even then, if I didn't like the ring for some reason it would take time to get it fixed—so you see, you might have to learn to live with your toes curled for a while."

As it happened, I didn't even wait until October 9. No sooner had I sent my September 30 letter than Fran called to tell me she had a ride to South Bend the weekend of October 2 with a friend who was heading to Chicago. That was a football weekend and every hotel room in the city was booked. Scrambling, I found a neighbor of the Bobiks who had a room to rent and made arrangements for her to stay there. I would have wanted to see Fran in any case, but now my eagerness was doubled. I already had the ring, and for all my kidding I was as anxious to give it to Fran as she was to get it.

As I remember it, Fran arrived too late on Friday night for us to do much of anything except get her settled in her rented room. The next day, October 3, we watched the Fighting Irish beat Purdue 34 to 15. It was the usual riotously exciting Notre Dame football experience, but even so my mind did stray to the big surprise I had planned for that night.

I told Fran we were going to have dinner in a nice restaurant in town. I can't recall the name of it, but it was a quiet, white-tablecloth establishment in a newer hotel near downtown South Bend. The ambience was perfect: subdued lighting around the room, candles on the table, soft background music, an attentive waitress, and a table for two in an out-of-the-way corner, without lots of curious on-lookers nearby.

After we got seated and ordered drinks, we chatted for a bit about the day's football game and how great it was that Fran was able to get to South Bend that weekend. Finally, the conversation turned to when I might get to Painesville and whether I would have the ring when I did. That was my cue.

Reaching into the pocket of my sport jacket, I pulled out the box with the ring. Handing it to her, I said, "There's no reason to wait any longer. I love you and would like you to marry me. Will you?"

Her expression moved from astonishment to realization as the reality sunk in. With tears welling in her eyes and her fingers trembling with excitement, she opened the box, took out the ring, and asked me to place it on her finger. When I did, she said, "Yes, I will marry you." Had we been alone somewhere, there might have been screaming and jumping up and down, but this wasn't the time or the place. Instead, I just got up, went to her side of the table and kissed her.

Naturally, neither of us can recall what we ate that night. We had no place to celebrate privately, so we had to make do with some smooching in the car on the way home. The following day, her ride back to campus appeared early, and all too soon she was gone. She wrote a few days later.

*Tuesday*

*October 6, 1964*

*Hello darling,*

*Been an engaged woman three days now but haven't had more than fifteen minutes to myself to think about my good fortune. Seems as though I just get comfortable and start daydreaming and someone knocks at the door or calls me to the phone.*

*I really do love my ring and wouldn't want it to symbolize anything but "forever!" It's still quite shocking to look at my left hand and see the diamond sparkling.*

*Had a pleasant trip back—slept a couple of hours and graded another set of papers. Arrived here about 4 p.m. In less than one minute after getting out of the car, about twenty girls came out yelling and screaming and kissing me and asking to see my ring. At dinner everyone in the dining room sang "congratulations" and for the rest of the night I just sat around and trembled. It's the general consensus, at least of my dorm, that the ring you gave me is one of the most beautiful that's ever been on campus. Naturally I believe this full-heartedly, but then I'm prejudiced. I know I should have it sized but still can't bear to think of taking it off and being without it for even a few days.*

*Janet was out last night. It won't be too convenient to stay with them Saturday night, so I'll probably have Betsy reserve a double room for you and her friend, Art Locker, at the motel for Saturday. Be able to tell you definitely when you get here.*

*Teaching is going well—believe the students are beginning to get used to me. Involves more work each day, but the rewards are amazing. I'm now two complete plays behind in Shakespeare and one unit behind in freshman General Studies. It's also at the point where four hours sleep a night feels good. Maybe this weekend you'll help me to grade a few sets of papers so that I can attempt to catch up on my reading.*

*Hope you're still not bored, and also that your friends were as happy for you as mine were for me and for our engagement. Funny thing, though, my toes still curl. Take care, my love, and drive carefully this weekend. I'll be watching for you about six-thirty. Until then, I love you and want to be with you very much.*

*All my love,*

*Fran*

*P.S. I love you, Bob. I'll say it forever and mean it for always.*

*Fran*

I did visit Painesville that weekend, the first of what would become many weekend visits. The increasingly frequent meetings changed our correspondence. We were writing fewer letters—and loving it.

Though I was now an engaged man, I was still a die-hard Notre Dame football fan as well—and the fall of 1964 was making history for the program as the "Era of Ara" dawned. Ara Parseghian was bringing Notre Dame football back to its glory days. Far exceeding the prevailing hope for "six and four in '64" by beating everyone in sight, his team was racing to become the top ranked team in the country. (Sadly, the 20-17 loss to rival University of Southern California at the end of the season shattered hopes of a national championship.) Fran came to Notre Dame a bit more than I traveled to Lake Erie College, in part because of the football schedule.

On October 17, I watched Notre Dame beat UCLA 24-0. On Sunday, I made a sudden decision to go home to Sidney for the day. As I told Fran, "Got up Sunday and it was such an ugly day that I didn't feel like sitting around in the cave. So at 2:30 I headed for home, got here at 6:00, had a home cooked steak dinner, did 4 ad layouts while watching TV, and I'm about to prepare to sleep in a comfortable bed for a change. I'll leave about 7:30 this morning and get back in time for my 11:30 class. Also—I'm now driving the Pontiac—the Corvair is going to the happy hunting grounds for bananas—wherever that is!"

My dad had come through again. The "Yellow Banana" had served me well but knowing how much highway driving I was doing, Dad thought I should be driving something more substantial. The Pontiac, dubbed "The Panther," was a black Bonneville convertible with red leather bucket seats that Mom had been driving for a few years. I couldn't have been more excited—it was a college man's dream car.

I drove it to Painesville the last weekend of October. Fran's mom and dad had come out from Andover for Parents' Weekend—Fran's younger sister, Nancy, now attended Lake Erie College as well, making it a "two-fer" for them. The following weekend, Fran visited South Bend. I let her drive the Panther back to LEC, expecting that she and a couple friends would drive it back to South Bend the weekend after. A freak snowstorm hit the day they left Painesville for the drive back, making the return trip a hair-raiser. As the storm dumped a foot of blowing snow on the Ohio and Indiana Turnpikes, all I could do was fret, sweat, and stew. There were of course no cell phones yet to keep me updated on her progress. When she finally arrived, hours late, she was safe but shaken. Her predictable train ride back at the end of the weekend was a welcome relief.

After her visit, I sent Fran a note with a small black bow enclosed. The note read: "The enclosed bow is a personal gift to you from Anna Maria Bobik, age 5, who likes me and thinks you are beautiful." The small black silk bow was attached to a bobby pin and meant to adorn a little girl's hair. Anna Maria, my landlords' daughter, had offered her personal treasure to a "big girl" she had met and admired.

In the midst of traveling to see each other that fall, Fran and I were both hitting our academic stride. Fran loved her student teaching and found she was quite good at it; she made the Dean's List that term. Although I just missed that honor, my grades were improving markedly. I loved my courses, especially the advertising-related ones. The WNDU-TV job wasn't open that term; fearing that anything else would cramp my style on weekends, I had chosen not to work that fall. Between the money I had saved from my summer job and the allowance I got from home, I didn't really need a job. But I did need some budget discipline. In early November, I announced my October phone bill to Fran: "$26.80 this month. Well this not only has to stop, it is going to. No more calls. For a while."

Always self-conscious about my "role" as the world's skinniest kid, I had been eating, as I wrote Fran, "like 2 horses" to get my weight up. I had reached 170 pounds at that point—an improvement, but not much for someone six feet, two inches tall. I was also making periodic stabs at exercise in an effort to get in better shape. "Joe and I decided to get in shape so we ran to Frankie's last night (for a beer). Somehow it seems we beat our own purpose but it felt pretty good to run about a half a mile in the rain. I'm going to play handball with Gary tomorrow—maybe that would be better."

As the weeks rolled along, Fran began to deal with two major issues. Most important, at least in her estimation, was planning our wedding. Invitations and announcements had to be chosen, printed, and addressed. Bridesmaids and ushers, a maid of honor, and a best man had to be selected and invited. Bridesmaids' dresses had to be chosen, not to mention the wedding gown. The church had to be scheduled, and so did venues for the rehearsal dinner and reception. Of course, her parents did much of the groundwork, but there was still plenty for Fran to do from school.

She was also thinking about where she would launch her teaching career—but naturally, that would be based to no small extent on where I would work. That issue was becoming a huge concern to me. I had started interviewing with the large corporations that visited the Notre Dame campus. Hoping to find a job in the advertising profession, I also started a targeted search. Although New York was where the big agencies and most of the action was, Fran and I had agreed that we were willing to forego its opportunities to avoid its expense and complications. Fran's father helped me network in Boston through the firm that did the advertising for his bank, I combed through the want ads in the *Chicago Tribune*, and I started sending resumés to every non-New York agency I could find, starting with the Dayton, OH, yellow pages. With six months to go, it was still early, but I was worried nonetheless.

Not that there wasn't a safety net or two. An old Milwaukee friend of my father, a general agent for Northwestern Mutual Life Insurance Company, was recruiting me. Visiting with him in Milwaukee, I took some aptitude tests to see if I was suited to be a sales representative for the company. Even though I told Fran afterwards that "I've decided my greatest potential actually lies in living in the Sahara and writing ..." I passed with flying colors. Selling life insurance, while a fine profession, didn't have a great deal of appeal. But at least it was an emergency fall-back in case all else failed, and as I wrote earlier, I had always loved Milwaukee.

And as I wrote to Fran: "I got an unusual offer today—to work for an international cinema magazine in Tokyo. This is for real! My Screen Arts professor, Mr. Fischer, knows the publisher or editor or somebody and he's always asking for some bright senior who is interested in films, etc. to work for him after graduation. And Mr. Fischer asked me today if I'd like to go. Might be fun for a year or two but I'm not sure it's practical either." Thus began a drama that took a few more months to conclude.

Though it wouldn't resolve our long-term needs, Fran and I were offered an unusual summer opportunity that really intrigued us. A friend of the Jordans named Janet Glendenning knew someone who conducted summer trips to Mexico for American teenagers. This "Mrs. O." was staffing what would be a two-month long caravanning experience for a couple of dozen participants. Though essentially chaperones, Fran and I would have the additional duty of driving the truck that pulled the Airstream trailer used as the group's headquarters and kitchen. Not a minor responsibility given that the tour went from New England across the United States to Mexico and then toured through the Mexican countryside. Nor were the accommodations luxurious: we would be camping out every night. Today there wouldn't be enough gold in Fort Knox to entice me to tackle this job. But back then, both Fran and I thought it sounded like a chance to experience something exotic and fun. We applied, but it took several agonizing months for Mrs. O. to officially confirm that we were in.

On the personal front, now that we were engaged and seeing each other practically every weekend, Fran and I found it harder and harder to be "good." We were having serious discussions about our attitudes toward sex, birth control and family planning.

Somewhere along the line we agreed that we both wanted a large family, settling on six children as a nice round number. Even so, birth control would be an issue we would have to grapple with even after marriage. Our Church insisted that artificial birth control was wrong. Though that policy was up for discussion during Vatican II, there were no signs that there would be a change.

I was lucky enough to have many chances to discuss religion and church philosophy at Notre Dame, often with priests, and those talks helped form my conscience on the subject of birth control. In addition, I had just started reading a new book by a Jesuit named Thomas D. Roberts, called "Contraception and Holiness," as part of my fall Theology course. Roberts offered common sense reasons why artificial birth control made sense and why using it should not be antithetical to leading life as good Catholics. I promised to, and did, pass it on to Fran when I finished reading. As I wrote to her, the first few pages "support what you and I have been saying all along. It's always nice to hear someone else share your opinion." Especially when that shared opinion happens to be published by a Jesuit priest. But though Fran agreed, she was still a bit tentative, and more cautious about going against Church dictates than I was.

Meanwhile, with the sexual tension building, it was becoming increasingly difficult to follow our resolution. This card seemed to say it all.

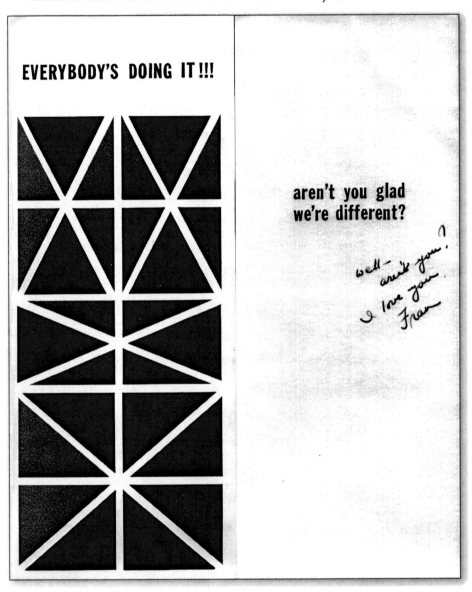

More and more of our friends were getting married or engaged—and more and more of our friends, married and unmarried, were having sex. Fran and I had many discussions about it but still felt that our will power would triumph.

Save for a ceremony that was still months away, we felt that we were spiritually married to each other. But the fear of an unwanted pregnancy, more than anything else, prevented us from giving in.

Despite the advent of the Pill, the "free love" era hadn't yet dawned, at least in our circles. Attitudes toward out-of-wedlock pregnancies hadn't changed all that much since our high-school years. Unmarried pregnant women were said to be "in trouble" or "in a family way." Since unmarried pregnant women and illegitimate births were not considered ordinary, the honorable thing for a young man to do was to make an honest woman out of the girl he got pregnant. Abortion was illegal, so even putting any moral issues aside, it was rarely an option.

In other words, an unexpected pregnancy would be a huge embarrassment, cause our parents great disappointment, and most certainly upset our nascent wedding plans. With all that in mind, Fran and I soldiered virtuously on.

Fran and I didn't spend that Christmas together. As I wrote, "After thinking it over it would be foolish for me to spend over $100 to come and see you when the money could go toward our honeymoon. I really wish I could—but I'm sure you understand."

In the same letter I announced that "I have a small surprise for you—Mom & Dad think that we might be taking a chance by keeping that dirty old Pontiac— you know how 5 yr old cars can be—so they will—if we wish—give us instead $1000 which we can apply to a new car which Dad can get us at cost. In other words—around April or so we could have a '65 Corvair (for example) for about $1200 which I would pay off after I start work. As much as I like the Panther, I'd feel a lot more secure with a new car, and we'd probably be better off with a more economical one at the same time. Please hurry out here, honey. I can't wait to talk to you about this."

Then I added: "I love you, Fran. When I saw the moon eclipse tonight I thought of you watching it too and cursed the miles between us. It's 240 times further from the earth to the moon than it is from me to you, yet I can see the moon anytime I want. It's just not fair."

Those words ended our 1964 correspondence. Though it had been a heart-warming and pivotal year, it ended on a comic rather than romantic note. I had my wisdom teeth pulled on December 22, a procedure done in the hospital to avoid the complications that could arise in an oral surgeon's office. But when Fran arrived in Sidney a few days after Christmas, she found me with a full-blown jaw infection. I looked like a squirrel with a face full of acorns. So much for lack of complications.

*Bob and Fran at Notre Dame Proms, 1964 & 1965*

# CHAPTER FOURTEEN

*P*LAYFUL AS IT SEEMED, FRAN'S FEBRUARY 1965 VALENTINE CARD TO ME hinted at a new reality. Her post-Christmas visit to Sidney six weeks earlier had marked a major turning point in our relationship. That week we finally succumbed to our greatest temptations—we made love. It wasn't planned. We simply took advantage of an opportunity. And it wasn't the last time our approach to premarital sex would change.

When Fran visited my family in Sidney, we would usually gather with my parents in our family room to chat or watch late night TV. Eventually Mom and Dad would say good night and leave the two of us alone. Most nights, we'd make out for a bit before going to bed—in our separate rooms—ourselves. When things got more intense than usual one night, I suggested to Fran that this would be our moment. A bit surprised, she agreed. I'm not going to discuss the details—as I said in the introduction, this book is about love, not sex. But naturally, it was a most exquisite experience.

Cruelly, though, we now found ourselves worried sick about what we had done and what the consequences might be. When we returned to college shortly after the first of the year we were both experiencing conflicting emotions: euphoria, depression, exhilaration, anxiety, worry. A volley of letters ensued almost immediately.

I wrote: "I can't think of anything to say to make you feel any more relaxed except maybe—relax!...I love you very much if that makes any difference."

Fran wrote to me that "It was wonderful and reassuring and happiness to talk with you last night. Wish we could have stayed on the phone for hours."

Fran continued to suffer intense anxiety as the days crept on and she waited for Mother Nature's verdict. Hearing her pain in one particularly intense phone call, I wrote in what I intended to be a classically philosophical tone, hoping she might find solace in my words: "...two humans gave in to what is called human but often denied said humans by the society they somehow inherited.... [our resolution was] pushed aside by the physical need of our young bodies. But more so by the psychological need of our young love. Beauty, love. This must be God. This must be heaven....the resolution is back. Giddiness...Fun. Love. So long, Depression. Where is God? Where is heaven? With beauty and love? Do not open until June 19. Respect. Unfulfilled psyches, but isn't the intellect always supposed to have control? There are no regrets—there will be no more depression....I love you, I miss you."

In less lofty tones but on the same themes, Fran wrote: "Being relatively alone leaves too much time for thinking and that in turn creates nervous tension. When I'm with you I can feel so much more relaxed and secure and right and justified. Sleep is no escape because I dream, and being awake makes me more aware of how long and lonely each day is...For all that's happened I feel no regret and no guilt because at the moment it seemed so perfect and right and natural....If I had talked to you tonight maybe I'd feel more relaxed....To repeat your wish—if only June followed January. If—if—if—Why is everything so conditional?"

To our profound relief, there were no unhappy physical consequences. We visited each other at least twice a month and we phoned frequently, the cost notwithstanding. Although the guilt and anxiety waned, we once again re-solved to avoid having sex. We thought it the right thing to do, but our resolve was strengthened by watching someone we both cared about forced into yet another unplanned marriage. We simply didn't want to suffer that fate with our own wedding only months away.

When Tom and I returned to South Bend in January, the Bobiks very nicely informed us they would like us to leave. Apparently our comings and goings at all hours were a source of disruption to their household. We could understand their position (we surely were not the quiet, studious types) but it came as quite a shock. After all, we thought, you have to expect some minor mayhem if you're going to rent a room to college seniors. Once we'd assimilated the news, we saw opportunity. We were avid *Playboy* readers who knew what a sophisticated bachelor pad was supposed to be, and Professor Bobik's basement wasn't it.

Read by most guys I knew at the time, *Playboy's* main draw was its photographs of beautiful women in various stages of nakedness. But it also published serious fiction and nonfiction, as well as sophisticated cartoons and jokes, giving rise to the familiar "I only buy it for the articles" line. Most of all, the magazine promoted an image many guys my age aspired to. Reading it, you could feel like a suave and sophisticated bachelor who had a spectacular city apartment, dressed in the best and latest fashions, read everything that mattered, knew just what cocktails to drink and what cigars to smoke, and of course had the world's most beautiful women at your beck and call. Even if you were, like me, a good Catholic boy who couldn't wait to commit to a good Catholic girl for life, it was a potent and appealing fantasy.

Notre Dame only allowed its students to live in university-approved off-campus dwellings. But having lived amid its regulations for over three years by then, Tom and I knew how to work around them. We asked the Bobiks to let us continue to use their address as our official residence as far as the University was concerned. That way we could find a real apartment, with Notre Dame remaining none the wiser. Somewhat to our surprise, the Bobiks agreed—no doubt to get rid of us as quickly as possible.

Within a couple of days we had located our new home: a furnished second-story walk-up in an old house south of downtown South Bend. Describing it as seedy would be an elaborate overstatement, unless you find worn-out linoleum floors, a 30-year old kitchen, a bathtub dark with ground-in grit, tattered furniture and sagging mattresses appealing. Hugh Hefner would *not* have been proud. We certainly weren't, but the rent was cheap, the place was basically livable despite its flaws, and it was immediately available. Best of all, our landlords were a nice blue-collar couple from West Virginia who weren't about to rat us out to Notre Dame.

My father was not a regular letter-writer. But he weighed in on this, in a letter so extremely rare that I actually saved it. A masterpiece of paternal advice, it had both an explicit message—about comporting myself properly so as not to get expelled from Notre Dame—and an implicit one, about abstinence.

THE PITTSBURGH HILTON

GATEWAY CENTER

PITTSBURGH, PA 15230

*Tuesday —*

*Dear Bob —*

*Here I am in Pitt again. Last week for the Compressed Air Institute and this week for a company meeting of general managers.*

Got the happy word while home last weekend that you have a new address. I have to admit to you that I secretly hoped you'd find a new place to live, but it was quite a shock to learn you had an apartment.

I assume that <u>no</u> apartments are on Notre Dame's approved list and this of course poses a problem I'm sure you have faced up to. If your former landlord hasn't in fact reported your move you may not have an immediate problem. But I can't contain myself from offering some follow-on advice.

I haven't been sure that you have regularly—or ever—equated your responsibility to save a buck for the happy event against the apparent desirability of getting together frequently. Now you have taken on a new responsibility—a more serious concern for whether you may or may not graduate!

Since Notre Dame is on record with respect to rules on housing, <u>any</u> charge against you leaves you out in left field. Any complaint registered against you would be a lot tougher to talk your way out of than any you have previously encountered. Tom will have to respect the cold fact that your situation is a lot more vulnerable than his.

Sooo—if Tom's gal and Fran visit South Bend you and Tom are going to have to be veritable prudes about the conditions under which they visit the apartment. Don't save a buck on such occasions. But beyond this there's going to be great temptations for parties— probably stag parties because you guys have an apartment. These are the most likely sources for a single complaint that could spell "fini."

*After all this guiding, I wouldn't urge you to move again. But I*

*would urge you and Tom to live 5 of the cleanest-nosed months you*

*have ever put in. And good luck to both of you.*

*Love,*

*Dad*

*P.S. Did Mom tell you we had sent a package to your old address a*

*day before you called to give your new one?*

Dad was dead right, of course, and I knew it. Tom and I didn't want to admit it out loud, but down deep we were aware of the risks. We made sure we didn't cross some invisible line that might cause problems with our *laissez-faire* landlords. We never threw the loud stag parties that Dad worried about, for example, just had the guys over on occasion for a fairly quiet beer and bull session. Tom had met and fallen in love with a Lake Erie friend of Fran's named Sue. When the girls visited South Bend together they could now stay with us, but we still tried to be careful not to cross an increasingly murky "line."

Despite our new privacy, Fran's frequent visits, and the approach of our wedding, we stuck to our no-sex resolution. Then, two months later, an amazing thing happened. The dermatologist I had been seeing fairly often had taken a personal interest in me, maybe because he felt bad that he hadn't cured my acne. Learning that I was going to get married, he asked about our plans for birth control. When I equivocated, he offered to give me a prescription so Fran could get the Pill. I surprised Fran with the news and she said she'd be willing to give it a try. Like many otherwise devout Catholics then and later, we remained committed to the Church even while skirting this particular rule.

With that, our resolution completely crumbled. We were past the guilt, and now there was no anxiety either. Life was good.

Tom and I quickly adjusted to apartment living. We reveled in having our own separate bedrooms, a living room with rudimentary TV and stereo, even kitchen facilities. Though neither of us was interested in cooking, it was a treat to fix cereal and toast, or even the occasional egg, for breakfast without having to go to a restaurant. We often had dinner in as well, even if it meant merely warming a can of spaghetti or some other prepared meal. We did the heating in the electric oven—though the technology had been invented, the first countertop microwave wasn't introduced until 1967.

Not that life there was glamorous. Just cleaning the filthy bathtub so it was usable presented a huge challenge. I wrote to Fran that "I just tried to clean up the bathtub because I'm feeling pretty damn grubby by now. I scrubbed it for 10 minutes and it still isn't clean. Gonna hafta get some SOS tomorrow and get the damn thing clean enough for my lily-white bod."

Even though our neighborhood was a far cry from the middle-class areas I had grown up in, Tom and I felt relatively safe, even somewhat inconspicuous. It was an easy drive to campus. I felt fortunate to have possession of the Panther, and treated it with appropriate care. I used it a lot, not only to get to campus but to get around town for visiting friends, eating out, and other fun. I also made frequent trips to Painesville and even to Sidney, so the miles were racking up. Getting the new car Dad had offered was still somewhere in the future.

While I was enjoying apartment living, Fran—still the Dorm Head—was suffering through her final year in a dorm. As she wrote, "The dorm is really noisy—someone is having a birthday party and we had a fire drill and it's almost the weekend and Pam's studying for a test, being anti-social and martyring, etc."

Another time she said that "It's so terribly cold here that it's really difficult to get warm enough to sleep. Think the dorm temperature is about 60 degrees and the wind comes in around the windows and actually blows the curtains."

It had been a long time since we had any word on our summer job from Janet Glendenning or the trip's organizers, the mysterious and uncommunicative O's. But in late January, Fran wrote: "Had a letter from Janet Glendenning. We're definitely going to Mexico—she wants to talk to us about some of the things we'll need, to quote Mom 'like sleeping bags.' I still haven't heard a thing from the O's—they seem like really weird-type characters. Guess our summer is all planned! At least we'll be able to write interesting and I'm sure humorous letters home. I still can't imagine myself sleeping outside on the ground."

In March I wrote to her about Dad's car promise. "Darling, Got a letter from Dad today. Loves Mexico and thinks we will too. They are in Puerto Vallarta now—you ought to get a card from there. Also, he's going to finance the balance over a 30 month period and make the 1st 6 payments if we'll let him have it for the summer. Sounds fair to me. What do you think?"

It was, of course, more than fair. We would have a new car to drive for the last couple months of school, we wouldn't have to worry about it while we were gone all summer, and it would be waiting for us when we returned and started our real lives, whatever and wherever they were going to be.

That continued to be an open question—and as time went on, an increasingly worrisome one. The closer we got to graduation and marriage, the more urgent it became for me to nail down a job. It would give us a means of support, but just as important, it would tell Fran where to start looking for a teaching position. Our summer jobs wouldn't generate much money, and we didn't want to return from Mexico without a job and a place to live waiting for us. My ongoing job search still had not produced anything concrete. I persisted in my blind faith that something would work out, but in the meantime did everything I could think of to make that something happen.

In February I followed up on the Tokyo job prospect my professor had told me about. Glenn Ireton was an American expatriate living in Tokyo; his *Movie Marketing* was a respected cinema industry trade journal, published in English with international readership. Beyond that I knew nothing. I was just intrigued by the prospect of living in Japan and working for a movie industry publication.

```
118 East Pennsylvania Street
South Bend, Indiana
February 4, 1965


Mr. Glenn Ireton
Editor and Publisher
Movie Marketing
Box 30—Central Post Office
Tokyo, Japan


Dear Mr. Ireton:
For three semesters I have been a student of
Mr. Edward Fischer at the University of Notre
Dame. I will graduate in June with a B.A. in
Communication Arts.
   Mr. Fischer mentioned that in past years you
have requested graduates interested in motion
pictures to work for you in Tokyo.
   I am interested both in magazine work and
motion pictures and the idea of working in
Japan is appealing to me. Mr. Fischer was
rather vague about the actual work involved
but did say it was of a general nature.
   The enclosed résumé should answer any
questions you have about what I have done.
   I will be married in June and my wife will
be qualified to teach high school English.
Also, I know nothing about the cost of living
in Japan, but I would expect to make enough to
live as I could in the United States on $6,000
to $7,000 per year. If you have room on your
```

staff and if you would be interested in me,
please let me know more specifically about the
duties involved. I would also like to know if
my wife would have an opportunity to teach in
Tokyo, and of course, about salary and living
expenses there.
    Thank you very much for your time, Mr.
Ireton. I hope to hear from you soon.

Yours truly,

Robert L. Zielsdorf

Mr. Ireton did offer me the job, but in three months of correspondence he was steadfastly inscrutable on the salary question. He wrote only that he would pay me a "living wage" plus my airfare to Tokyo as well as to Hong Kong, where I would get my work visa. He was helpful in suggesting places where Fran could apply for teaching jobs. But the "living wage" point left uncomfortable room for interpretation and to complicate things, the American "military mission" in Vietnam was ramping up by the month by that time. Military service seemed like a remote possibility to me, so I concentrated mostly on my post-college career. The Tokyo job offer forced me to think about the conflict. Married men were not being drafted but if that situation changed, I questioned the wisdom of finding myself half way around the world with a new wife and no money to get ourselves home. In spite of all that, I continued to pursue the position, not wanting to pass up what could be a golden opportunity.

When Proctor & Gamble, one of the country's biggest advertisers, interviewed on campus for a couple openings in their advertising department, I signed up for an interview with them. To my mind, their jobs would be right up my alley. An advertising career was my primary objective and a subject in which I excelled. I dreamed of someday opening a small advertising agency with Dick Cotterman, my Sidney High classmate. A job with P&G would be a huge step in that direction. Sadly, about a month after my interview, I learned that P&G wasn't interested in talking further with me. It was a huge disappointment, but my discouragement was lightened by hearing that the rejection did nothing to shake Fran's faith that I would someday be very successful.

I decided to consult with the head of the Notre Dame Communication Arts department, Thomas Stritch, to see if he could point me in a better direction. He made it clear that he had a firm policy of not doing that sort of thing, as he didn't want to be thought of as an employment agency for his students. Probably wise on his part, but no help to me.

Then, incredibly, a few days later he called me into his office. He had received a letter from a former student who was working for the Zurich-American Insurance Companies in Chicago. Leaving his job for another, the student was writing to see if Mr. Stritch could recommend someone to fill the opening. The position was Advertising Assistant and reported to the head of the Public Relations department, a Mr. Casimir Scheer. The job had no advancement potential but the letter said that Mr. Scheer was a true pro and that working for him would be the equivalent of getting a Masters degree in Advertising and Public Relations. Sounded good to me!

I sent off a letter and résumé and soon found myself in Chicago interviewing for the job. I felt it was a good interview and a good position, but the P&G experience had made me wary. Then it was back to South Bend to await news of my fate.

Fran and I decided that if the Chicago position came through, I would take it. If it didn't and nothing else arose, the Tokyo job would be the next choice. I therefore helped her write letters of application to schools in both cities: those in Tokyo based on Mr. Ireton's suggestions, those in Chicago based on throwing darts at a map. In late April I wrote to Fran, "Haven't heard anything from Chicago yet. It's about time for me to get really serious and go find a city and find a job. Wouldn't hurt to have something more to fall back on in case of a negative answer from Cas[imir Scheer]. Also saw an ad in a Chicago paper today from the agency in Dayton who wanted me to come down for an interview. Might not hurt to take him up on it. But I'm not so sure I want to live in Dayton."

The tension was mounting, but a few days later Casimir Scheer called, officially offering me a job at The Zurich. I would be paid $5,200 per year and would learn the advertising and PR business by writing press releases, developing point of sale materials for Zurich agents, and generally helping with whatever needed to be done. One non-negotiable point: I would have to start the Monday after I graduated. I could have a week off for my wedding and honeymoon but that would be it—no summer in Mexico. Mr. Scheer was desperate for help and would not give on either point.

Naturally, I accepted. I really wanted the educational experience that had been promised. Somehow we would make do on the salary—$100 a week went pretty far in 1965, even in a big city.

As it turned out, neither of us felt much disappointment over missing the Mexico experience. By May 5, I had made it official. "Called Janet and the O's and also wrote the O's," I wrote to Fran. "Janet was very nice. So was Mrs. O.— altho a bit shocked & therefore curt. Also wrote to Japan. It's really hard to keep turning down these exotic things and think about settling down in Chicago in less than 2 months."

Chicago is a big city, and Fran hadn't yet found a teaching job. Where would we live? My job was in the financial district in the Chicago Loop. If we lived in the city, which was the most exciting idea, Fran would have to teach in the city or commute to the suburbs. Agreeing that she should not work in the inner-city schools, it made sense for me to do the commuting. But even with that decided, we weren't sure where to look.

Once again, luck saved the day. Amid my hours combing want ads in the Chicago papers, I came across an ad for a four-bedroom bungalow available for the summer. Located in the far-south neighborhood of Riverdale, it belonged to married teachers who worked summers at a children's camp. They rented their house for those months to keep it occupied and earn some extra money. Fran and I thought it was a wonderful solution. It gave us a furnished, roomy and comfortable place for the summer. During that time, Fran would land her job and we would find a nearby apartment. All was right with the world.

Though it was hard to remember it at times, we were still at college. Fran and I continued to visit each other, attended the Notre Dame senior prom, and kept up with our class work. To be honest, I don't remember those final months of school very well. I was preoccupied with my job search and wedding plans, and with Fran and me speaking so much more there are few letters to remind me of our day to day lives. One letter from May does chronicle a TV Production class project that didn't go well. My fellow students and I were in a TV studio, charged with producing a five-minute segment for a children's show. Among other glitches, one of our "actors" failed to show and our special effects slides didn't work. It was just as well I hadn't aimed for a career in television production.

As the semester continued, the guys I knew had become aware that I was engaged and planning to get married right after graduation. One day, I ran into an acquaintance who asked, "Why do you want to get married so soon? These are the best years of your life. Why not enjoy the single life for a while?" My response was simple. "I've found the person I want to marry," I said immediately. "These *are* the best years of my life—and I want to spend them with her."

Of course, Fran and I kept on making wedding plans. In a process much more fun than seeking a job, we had to decide where to spend our honeymoon. Our first idea was Martha's Vineyard—affordable, on the water we both loved, and an easy drive from the wedding in Andover. This photo from a resort brochure is typical of the places we looked at.

As charming as that appeared, it wasn't long before an even more interesting idea came up.

*Tuesday*

*March 30, 1965*

*Hello darling,*

*Surprised to get another letter so soon? Just didn't feel like studying but did feel like writing to you to tell you about a really neat place we could stay from June 21 – 27. Tuni Woodrum, Sally's roommate, spent last summer working at the Chanticleer Inn on Nantucket and she really has*

*me interested in this place. As you know, Nantucket is another Island off*

*the cape, like the Vineyard, but seems to offer much more like dancing,*

*nightclubs, etc., plus sailing for $7.50 a day. I'm enclosing pictures, a floor*

*plan of the cottages, and the winter address of the Wileys who own the*

*inn. Want to write to them and see what they have to offer? Think we'd be*

*apt to have a lot of fun and the rates sound very reasonable. Tuni said you*

*might want to mention her name—she'll be there again this summer and*

*said she'd buy us dinner one night if we happened to be there....*

She had me at "sailing for $7.50 a day." Nantucket wasn't much harder to get to than Martha's Vineyard. I fired off a letter to Mr. Wiley to see if he had something I could afford.

Sometime after that, Fran told me that proper wedding etiquette dictated that the bride and groom present each other with a wedding gift. I was able to scrounge up enough cash to buy her a pearl choker—from Bert Kasten, naturally. I said nothing about it, planning to present it to her as a surprise shortly before our wedding day.

But when Fran asked me what I might like to receive, I was stumped. It had never occurred to me that *she* would give *me* a gift for our own wedding, and I had no clue as to what might be appropriate. But since she had asked, I had to give it some thought.

Abercrombie & Fitch, which I had enjoyed browsing during my many weekend visits to Chicago, saved the day. In the 1960s it was still a high-end sporting goods outfitter, rather than the stylish clothing store it has become since then. I never had the money to buy much, but I got a huge kick out of walking the aisles and dreaming about one day possessing some of those "big boys' toys" they sold.

That spring, the store was liquidating a gun collection—I believe it had been owned by the late editor of *Field & Stream* magazine. One of those guns had caught my eye because it was both unique and somewhat affordable. A Colt Frontier Scout 22-caliber revolver with pearl grips, it looked a lot like the cowboy cap guns I played with as a child. Colt had manufactured that model in homage to the guns the firm had made and sold in the 19th Century—the kind real cowboys once carried in the Wild West.

For a brief time I had considered buying it for myself, but it was far too big a purchase to contemplate seriously with our wedding and marriage approaching. When Fran asked about a wedding gift, it dawned on me that this was something I would cherish. Once Fran got over her surprise—it was obviously not your traditional token of love and esteem!—she agreed, asking me to buy it for her the next time I went to Chicago. I was touched by her willingness to "think outside the box" to get me something I really wanted.

Both Fran and I were extremely busy during April and May, yet the time seemed to drag on interminably. We were impatient to finish school, graduate, get married, begin our careers and start our life together. We were like little kids waiting for Santa Claus—the future just couldn't come soon enough. Slowly, though, everything fell into place. The wedding announcements and invitations were ordered, addressed and mailed. The wedding details were finalized, the attendants chosen, and the blood tests taken. In Nantucket, Mr. Wiley did indeed have a room we could afford, so the honeymoon was settled as well.

Classes and assignments were wrapped up and our friends and professors were bid farewell. Our eight-year correspondence was winding down, too. Fran's last letter to me was dated May 18.

*Tuesday*

*May 18, 1965*

*Dearest Bob,*

*Finally feeling normal after two long and fairly sleepless weekends. Last night I was so exhausted that I fell asleep about 10 and slept a full twelve hours. That ought to hold me pretty well, at least until after I write my senior seminar paper. Do want to have that done by Friday—then you can type it for me, huh?! It's supposed to be about 10 pages long—all creative writing with book notes only for specific references.*

*A notice came out in the bulletin this week announcing that all senior final exams would, or are, to be given on Friday, June 4 through Monday June 7. Don't have any idea what's going to happen in my English classes. Would be nice not to have any exams. Unless something freakish happens, our education exam will be June 2nd. Wish things for the end of the school year would be more definite. Have your heard any more about your exam schedule? It will be awfully disappointing if I can't make your graduation.*

*Have you had a blood test taken yet? Please send the results to Mom. I'll need them the week I'm home so I can file for our marriage license.*

*Oh—speaking of licenses—do you have my driver's license? Think I asked you to hold it for me when we went out over Lake Erie prom weekend. It could be in your blue denim blazer. If you have it, would you send it or bring it with you this weekend? It's the only decent identification I have. Don't know where it is if you don't have it.*

*Still have your argyle sweater. I forgot it this weekend. It's warm and smells like you. I like to wear it when I study in bed.*

*Nancy was over talking to me last night; she really believes she's in love. I hope if she's happy she is. Ken is awfully nice—I think you'll probably see him this weekend. Something about a party in Cleveland was mentioned.*

*I'm in American Fiction class now. It's the most boring 75 minutes of the week. Thank goodness the class only meets five more times. I can hardly wait to be finished with scheduled studying and reading and writing. It's hard to enjoy things that you know you have to do.*

*Went shopping yesterday—sent all the bills home. Wait till Mommy gets those. They know about your gun and it shouldn't be long before I get a check to pay for it. Please keep it put well away so nobody will handle it foolishly.*

*Have you heard from Mr. Wiley yet? Have you made ferry reservations for the car for June 20th? Do want to begin our life together—four weeks still seems like a very long time. Take care my love—I hope to see you this weekend. Let me know....*

*I love you and already miss you.*

*Fran*

My final letter to her was dated a week later.

May 25

Dear Fran,

I think the prom picture is great. In fact, I may give my copy to my parents.

Played poker again tonight. Was $5 down at one point but wound up winning 50 cents. Jack Murray was in the game. I found out he's flying home Sunday night. You might be on the same flight.

Guess what? No Theology exam! I've got nothing left to do but attend 2 or 3 classes and collect my diploma. Hot diggety dog. Doesn't make me too happy.

I'm feeling sorry for Tom. The guy really wants to marry Sue. He has realized a lot of his mistakes and she won't have him now. Think we might get up a petition on his behalf?

I love you, dear. Can't wait to see you. Friday seems a long way off and I miss you very much.

Bob

In early June, Fran received a letter from her father that serves as a fitting postscript to our correspondence. Its six handwritten pages shared family news, described the Lake Winnipesaukee cottage he had just purchased, and asked her to check loose ends on college bills he had received. The letter ended with this plaintive paragraph: "I'll see you when you arrive. It will be so good to talk with you. I find it hard to believe that you are going away and will miss you terribly. *C'est la vie* as the Frenchman says. I don't know what the Spaniard says but it would mean the same. I love you very much. Dad."

It was a brave and poignant acknowledgement, not just that Fran was step-ping out of his life, but of how much he would miss her. I sympathized with his feelings, and have since experienced them myself. But back then, my feelings were different. I just rejoiced in knowing that in mere days, Fran would be my wife, and *I* would not have to miss her any more.

My graduation ceremony was on Sunday, June 6. The next day I drove to Chicago to start my first career job at The Zurich. Mr. Scheer had agreed to give me the necessary days off for the wedding and a brief honeymoon. After I worked for about a week and a half, I drove to Andover in time to get married on June 19.

The festivities began with the rehearsal dinner, which my parents hosted the night before the wedding in an old mansion called the Lanam Club. The Saturday wedding ceremony and Mass at St. Augustine's Church was followed by a champagne reception at the nearby Merrimac Valley Inn. The wedding Mass had a special significance. Following Vatican II, Catholics were just being permitted to receive communion not only as bread but also as wine. That was the first time any of us had experienced the Mass that way.

The wedding was everything Fran wanted it to be. Her beautiful white gown had been hand-made for her. Fran's attendants were her sister, Nancy, and my sisters Julie and Lissa, while the best man was my Milwaukee friend Dan Harrigan. My Notre Dame friends Tom Franck and Chuck Watson and my Sidney friend Dick Cotterman, Fran's former roommate Janet Darrow and her 12-year-old cousin, Frank Burke, were all involved—we were truly surrounded by friends and family.

They say that every bride is beautiful, but Fran was radiant that day. Keeping with tradition, I had been forbidden to see her that day until she first appeared in the church. Seeing her for the first time in her gown, on her father's arm, was a stunning moment. Her dress, her veil, her flowers, her lovely face—all were in beautiful harmony. What I couldn't see was that she was holding on to her father's arm so tightly that she bruised it. Later, while we were kneeling in the sanctuary (still, in those days, with our backs to the congregation) she developed a sudden nosebleed. Luckily, she was able to discreetly stop the flow with the handkerchief I slipped her and no one was the wiser. It was one of those tiny moments that made the wedding seem real.

The reception her parents hosted was a great party and a fine meal. We left in mid-afternoon and drove to Wood's Hole, MA, to spend our first night as husband and wife. On Sunday morning we took the ferry to Nantucket Island and spent four nights at the Chanticleer Inn. Something of a joker, Mr. Wiley had directed us to a room with twin beds rather than the king we had requested. Watching to catch our reactions when we saw our room, he let us suffer for a few moments before leading us to the right place.

We had neither the time nor the money to stay long. From Nantucket, we drove to Lake Winnipesaukee, spent two nights with Fran's parents in the new cottage they had just purchased, and then drove to Chicago to start our life together in the rental bungalow that was our first, albeit temporary, home.

After eight years, writing letters might seem to be a hard habit to break. But the truth was that I didn't miss it one bit. We had spent eight years learning how important communication was to a good relationship, and by now had learned to communicate both in writing and verbally. Fran and I were both entirely ready to say a grateful and permanent goodbye to our lives as pen pals and begin our years as husband and wife.

*Bob, college graduation, 1965*

*Fran, engagement portrait, 1965*

*Bob & Fran's weddding, 1965*

# EPILOGUE

*F*RAN AND I HAVE BEEN MARRIED, AT THIS WRITING, FOR 48 YEARS. WE HAVE five children, three girls and two boys. Kristen, Beth, Matt, Rob, and Molly (in order of age, from oldest to youngest) are, of course, adults now. The oldest four are married, each to a great spouse. Together, they have given us ten grandchildren. Kristen and her husband Mike Schwartz live in Kansas and Matt and his wife Paulette live in Wisconsin. Beth and her husband David Alexander, Rob and his wife Kim, and Molly all live in Ohio. When we all get together, we number an impressive 21. Fran and I have been proud to watch all five of our kids grow up smart, energetic, responsible and with sound values. When we dreamed, long ago, of having a large family, we could not have asked for a better one than this.

My Zurich job lasted 18 months. When I found myself doing the same things repeatedly I decided it was time to move on. The *Chicago Tribune* offered me a job, but I wound up accepting a better opportunity in Dayton as a copywriter at The E. F. MacDonald Company. Eventually I became Director of Communication for the white paper group of the Mead Corporation. Fran and I were very happy raising our kids in Dayton.

But in 1976, the road suddenly forked. My friend Dick Cotterman went ahead and created the ad agency we had once dreamed of, inviting me to join him and a colleague as a full partner. At the same time, my father made me an interesting offer. Seven years earlier he had left the big corporate world to acquire a controlling interest in a small manufacturing business in Sidney; now struggling, the business needed marketing expertise Dad felt I could provide. If he succeeded in his attempt to buy out the other shareholders and I then joined him, he would sell me a twenty five percent interest in the business, which I would eventually take over from him.

As always in my career, I had Fran's full and unconditional support for whatever I chose to do. All my choices had strong positives as well as downside risks. I had an entrepreneurial itch that I was eager to scratch, so I ruled out staying with Mead. And there was something I saw in Dick's partner that warned me away from that choice. After much thought, I decided to go with Dad's offer. It turned out to be one of the best decisions of my life.

We moved our family from Dayton to Sidney in 1979 when our oldest was ready for eighth grade. In spite of my teenaged dislike of Sidney and the many promises I had made then to never return, I began to discover what a wonderful community it really was. For many reasons, Sidney became a marvelous place to raise our family and to operate a business. Fran and I recently sold our Sidney home, which had been in the Zielsdorf family since 1960. We now spend our winters in Vero Beach, FL, in a house on the water that our whole family loves. In the summer we're in our lakefront home in northern Michigan—another place designed to be a family magnet.

The company I shared with Dad made custom capital equipment for industrial bakers. Over my 30-plus years there, the business grew to be thirty times larger than when I started. It was a most satisfying career. A few years ago I decided to move on and sold it to a major public corporation. At the time, there were three of my family working for the business. It's gratifying that one of our sons-in-law, David, is still involved in managing the business. Our son, Matt, moved on in late 2012 to become president of a company in the Milwaukee area, and Rob left in mid-2013 to help grow a fine business in Sidney as Vice President, Sales.

Fran taught in a Catholic school in Niles, Illinois, a public high school in Dayton, and a Catholic high school in Sidney. For many years she was a full-time mom, focused on raising good citizens—a role in which she was a roaring success. In their different ways, each of our children is a true credit to the family, something I attribute both to their innate character and Fran's superb role model and mothering. She assumed many of the family and household management duties so I could focus on doing my job, advancing my career and building my business. This division of labor might seem a bit old fashioned in today's world, but it was the ideal business model for the "Zielsdorfs, Inc."

Over the years we have managed to stay in touch with many of the people mentioned in this book. Sadly, too many have since passed away. That long list includes both of my parents and both of Fran's, Dick Cotterman, my college roommates Tom Franck and Chuck Watson, and Dan Harrigan, of "Harrigan, you rat!" fame.

Tony Beck, who introduced us, is a retired Methodist minister in upstate New York. Chuck Eisenstein, who got me excited about Notre Dame, is retired and living in California. Steve Huxley, who gave me a glimpse of fraternity life, is a professor at University of San Francisco and also is the Chief Investment Strategist for Asset Dedication. Gary Hosbein, one of the five at Mrs. Shaw's house, is an attorney living in St. Joseph, MI. Jerry Houlihan, who shared my reconciliation trip to Cleveland, is an attorney in Miami, FL.

Fran's roommate and good friend, Janet Darrow, was recently widowed. She lives in New Jersey. Fran's friend, Bill Dalton, whose car she wrecked, lives in New Hampshire and writes a column for *The Andover Townsman*.

Fran and I have shared a long and happy marriage. While that didn't happen without effort on both sides, we are both grateful to have found our true soul mates at such an early age. That we could cultivate a strong friendship in spite of our youth and the miles that separated us for so long is both special and somewhat remarkable. Perhaps we owe the United States Postal Service a small debt for their role in our romance.

As the years roll on, I am increasingly appreciative of Fran's special kind of courage and grateful that she has been my partner, my friend, and my lover for so long.

Perhaps someday I'll write her a letter and tell her that.

# THE LAST WORD
## BY FRAN ZIELSDORF

*B*OB BEGAN WRITING THIS BOOK IN 2010. AT THE TIME, I NEVER SAW MYSELF contributing to the project beyond answering his questions about moments from our past.

Then, one of his mentors suggested that the book needed my perspective. At first, I felt hesitant—I didn't even want to show Bob what I'd written. But once I'd begun, it was a deep pleasure to revisit so many cherished memories, and to share my own feelings, from the sting of the "big chill" to the details of wedding planning.

~~~

My family was similar to Bob's in some ways and quite different in others. My parents were both born in Methuen, MA. Teenagers during the Depression, they were both college educated, the only ones to be so in their respective families. My mom, Marion, trained as a teacher, though she didn't work as a teacher until I was in college. My father, Bob, attended Boston College for both undergraduate and graduate work, on a scholarship for track and academics.

My father was about six feet tall and very athletic. His hair was always crew-cut in short, Army-issue style. Neither he nor my mom gained much weight over time; my dad retained his "Charles Atlas" build all his life. Even when he was in his 70s, he was fit, trim and tan. He was very successful in track and went to the Olympic Trials in Los Angeles in the early 1930s. Unfortunately, he got sick on the trip west and failed to qualify. He never mentioned that to me until I was in my late teens. I think he was embarrassed not to have done the job he was sent to do, and the fact that his qualifying times were as good as those of the athlete who won made it even more frustrating. In addition to being athletic, Dad could fix anything mechanical or electrical and build everything from toy boxes to shelving units.

If my mother stood up really straight she was 5' 4" inches tall. She was very beautiful—she had been voted "best looking" in high school and college—but never vain. I always thought she looked like a combination of Jane Wyman, Jane Wyatt from "Father Knows Best," and the Virgin Mary. High praise, I know, but true.

A quick and easy laugh was my mother's trademark. Molly, our youngest daughter, has that trait, as well as a facial resemblance to her. Though my parents both clearly loved us kids, it was far easier to know that from my mother than my father. She was just more affectionate, and took more time listening. Even with a house full of family she was unfailingly pleasant—I don't know how she did it.

For their era, my parents married relatively late—when she was 27 and he 30. My mother had already spent many months traveling cross country with her friends, and my dad had a good job by then. They married in 1940, bought a brand new house and settled down.

As my mom put it, my dad wasn't always right, but he was never wrong. He had the dominant personality of the pair. He would take over conversations as my mother quibbled, groused or complained under her breath. However, they seemed to get along well, offering each other what you might call checks and balances. They were openly affectionate. My dad always kissed her goodbye when he left for work in the morning and kissed all of us hello in the evening.

In my childhood home, the father was head of the family. There was a definite division of labor, about which nobody complained. Yet the message I got about gender roles wasn't simplistic. I was the eldest daughter, with no brother until I was 14, so my dad expected me to do anything a son could have done. He helped me develop a strong sense of personal capability; I discovered that I could do, learn, and be things not because I was male or female but because I was me.

Unlike Bob's, my parents were never particularly social. As a family we were close to relatives and a few neighbors. Family came first, always.

As Bob says, mine was an extended family. My grandparents lived with us, with their own bedroom and sitting room on the first floor. Throughout my childhood, my "Gram" was my favorite person and I loved having her in the house. My mom was also devoted to Gram, with whom she shared the household chores (Gram cooked, Mom cleaned).

When I was 12, my father's only remaining sister, Carolyn, moved in with us. A big section of the lower level was remodeled with a full bath so she had her own "apartment" in our house. She had never married or had a driver's license, but she went to work every day. An attractive, soft-spoken woman, she doted on all three of us kids. Much as I loved her, I saw her mostly at dinner so she didn't have much influence on me. That came mostly from Gram.

With my sister Nancy and my younger brother Bob, Auntie Carolyn's presence brought the household up to eight. We all ate dinner together every night at 6:15. My father held forth; my grandmother told stories about the years when my mom was still young and unmarried. Our kitchen's built in breakfast nook was the hub of our home. The phone was there and it was the place where we sat and visited. Ours was an informal, comfortable house—nicely furnished, but definitely not "decorated." I really didn't even know what that word meant back then.

As I read Bob's letters, it was interesting to hear about Bob's three sisters. I had one sister and one brother. My sister Nancy, three years younger than I am, was born after my father was discharged from the Army.

She was a beautiful kid, with very dark brown ringlets, green eyes, dimples and a quick, infectious laugh. From the beginning she was a tomboy, more interested in athletics than books. She became an accomplished horseback rider/jumper and competed at water skiing. She loved sleep-away camp and regularly brought home injured birds, squirrels, and other small animals. I always thought that she was very much like my dad, and very much my opposite. She was petite, dark, and athletic while I was tall, blonde and studious.

My brother Bob was born when I was in the eighth grade. He was born with Down syndrome, though it took my parents several months to acknowledge it. My mother had known that something was amiss, but the diagnosis wasn't given immediately and they waited for a professional opinion. My sense is that Dad was deeply disappointed. Their first son, a perfect-looking boy, had been stillborn—I still have the photograph that was taken of him—and now this new baby would not be able to follow in his father's footsteps either.

My parents did all the research they could, found good special classes and did the best they could to parent Bobby well. It was difficult, but he was deeply loved, and it helped that the little guy had three mother figures in the house thanks to the extended family that lived with us. Bobby was in private boarding schools while I was in high school and college, so I never knew him as well as my sister. Much closer in age to him, Bobby and my sister grew up together, while I saw him mostly on holidays. Today she is his legal guardian.

Bobby is at the high end of the Down spectrum, able to talk and take care of his own grooming. He loves to eat in restaurants and wishes he could drive. We keep in touch by phone, and he always says he loves and misses me. He is a bit withdrawn around "my" Bob; he was only 8 when Bob and I married and moved to the Midwest, so there wasn't much opportunity for them to develop a relationship.

~~~

When I met Bob I was 5'7" tall and weighed 128 pounds. I wore no makeup, had my hair cut in the popular "DA" and lightened it with lemon juice and Sun In. I had graduated as valedictorian of my eighth grade class and was pretty much a bookworm. I wasn't athletic and would rather read than move. And, I was shy.

Bob stood out at the party the night we met. First, because he was the stranger in the group. Even his friend Tony was fairly new, a transfer into our eighth grade class. The rest of us, 62 strong, had gone from kindergarten to junior high together.

Bob also stood out because he was taller than I was—about 5' 8". As I've said, I was already tall by that age, so his height was a big attraction. He had a weird haircut—he explained that his parakeet used the top of his head as a landing strip. I only found out later that his brown hair was naturally curly. He was dressed very nicely in the fashion of the day, didn't have the north Boston accent I was so familiar with, and seemed incredibly self-confident. After all, he had come from Pennsylvania all by himself!

The kissing game was as Bob described it. I really did elbow Geri out of the way to grab Bob's medal.

Like Bob's, my family was Catholic. As a family we attended Mass every Sunday, no matter where we were, and we always kept Lent. Boston College, where my dad had done his undergraduate and graduate work, was run by Jesuits, but his take on religion was way more liberal than my mother's. I was horrified when my father admitted to eating meat on a Lenten Friday during a business meeting! I was taught by Notre Dame nuns through eighth grade, so I was fully "indoctrinated." I'd even take lists of sins to the confessional every week so I wouldn't forget any. I was painfully aware of the effects of sin and the need for penance. God was everywhere and always knew what I was doing.

I remember our kiss well. Behind the pine tree, we leaned our heads together until just our closed lips met. His were so soft. Maybe we held the kiss three or four seconds. It doesn't seem like much until you count it out: one—one thousand; two—one thousand. That kiss was so nice. Then it ended, and we went back to the party to give all the other couples their turn.

That party was the only one I ever attended where we played kissing games. Lucky me!

I think Bob is right—he suggested that we write each other. I thought it would be fun to hear about life in another town and state. I saved every single letter or card Bob sent me right from the start, though I have no idea why. At the time we met, I definitely just wanted to be his pen pal, not his girlfriend. We were only 14, with four years of high school ahead of us. We wrote all the time about getting together, but it actually came as little surprise not to see each other often. York was far away from Andover. Milwaukee was really, really far. No matter how much we wrote about seeing each other I, for one, didn't expect a visit to happen. For all those reasons, thoughts of true love and marriage were definitely not on my mind.

Though I was not thinking about Bob romantically, I knew what I wanted some day. Being Catholic, I expected to marry a Catholic boy, and I believed marriage was forever. I would marry someone I could love for always and be willing to make reasonable concessions for marital harmony. From the time I was six or so, my favorite families all had lots of children. My mother's cousins each had six kids, my father's roommate had seven, and my elementary-school girlfriends' families were large as well. Even my favorite book, *The Five Little Peppers,* involved a large family. I knew I hoped to have lots of children once I married; when Bob and I talked about marriage, he was in agreement. (His best man was the oldest of ten.)

Like most kids, I would look at my parents' marriage and say, I won't put up with that, or my opinion will be equal to my husband's. In other words, I wanted all the good I saw in their marriage and none of the stuff that upset me. High goals, right? But it worked.

In the meantime, dating just seemed to be a normal thing to do. I was really curious about Bob's dates. The same thing went for asking about his opinions on "parking." It seemed like everyone who dated parked. It was a pretty innocent thing, at least in my circles. Sometimes it was just in your own driveway. If I did that, my mom, who always waited up for me, would flash the post light on and off after about 10 minutes.

I wasn't jealous about what he told me. And when it came to relationships and boyfriends, I valued his perspective. Bob and I were very open in our communication, and I believed he would be honest with me.

Bob mentions my two serious boyfriends, Donnie and Wally. I dated Donnie on and off during high school and into college. He was my favorite boyfriend, except for Bob, of course. We really liked each other, enough that we would date and part, then date again all four years of high school. There was a definite attraction, plus a lovely comfort level, in our relationship.

Donnie was about 6' 1," with sandy blond hair, blue eyes, a preppy style and black-rimmed glasses. I always knew when he was about to kiss me because he'd slyly reach up and take the glasses off. Handsome in a Richie Cunningham kind of way, he was well built but not an athlete. He was fun, kind, respectful and responsible—just an all-around nice guy.

Wally, my other high school boyfriend, was a completely different kind of boy. He was a junior when I met him during my sophomore year of high school. He was the first, and the only, "jock" that I dated: a three-letter man in football, basketball and baseball. I enjoyed dating someone in the athletic spotlight: it was thrilling to hear the student body cheer for my boyfriend! We eventually decided to go steady—again, my one and only "steady."

He was an inch or so taller than I was with an athlete's build and a swaggering walk. Handsome he wasn't, not even cute, but he had an ego, and his self-confidence in sports made him appear bigger and better looking than he was. Our backgrounds weren't similar—he was a Polish Catholic from a blue-collar family—but for a while that didn't matter. Neither did the fact that he was egotistical, jealous, moody and possessive. I was just infatuated. For a while, nice-guy Donnie couldn't quite compete!

We dated for about 18 months; I would say that I was happy about half of the time. My parents never liked him and finally forbade me to see him more than once a week. It was a difficult, emotional split, but overdue. Honestly, I was relieved, even though it was difficult to be alone again. Bob's comment—"I imagine you are happy without Wally by now"—showed real insight. I *was* happy. Wally was the boy I was thinking of when I wrote to Bob asking "why do boys who say they like you act so mean?" Ours was an intense relationship, but ultimately not a rewarding one.

As Bob writes, there was a time during which I felt caught between Wally and Donnie. Wally and I had ended our relationship. I started dating Donnie again. Wally had a new girlfriend, but he still called me, talked with me between classes, and insisted I go to the prom with him. He didn't like my dating anyone else and in turn, Donnie didn't like Wally hanging around me. It was uncomfortable and unpleasant. Bob commented, but could provide no help.

〜〜〜

Bob's text is so tactful about how I looked when he came to see me in the hospital after my car accident. In truth, I was incredibly embarrassed to be seen in that condition. The top of my head had been shaved so that a metal cap could be screwed into my skull for traction. I couldn't move my arms or legs; my private nurses had to brush my teeth, but they hadn't tweezed my eyebrows! To have Bob see me like this after three years of separation was traumatic.

At that point, I didn't know if I'd ever be able to move my body again. But with the optimism of a 17-year-old, I wasn't too worried.

I think Bob and his friends visited for about 20 minutes. Then he leaned over my bed and kissed me—me with no hair, no makeup, not even normal pajamas. His lips were still so soft, so nice. It got me thinking of him as someone who could be more than my pen pal.

From my accident to my discharge from Mass General was a full month. I hadn't walked for almost a month but the surgery had restored all movement to my limbs. I used the quiet time to reflect on who I was and who I wanted to be. I think I made some significant decisions: for example, to be less self-centered, kinder to my mom, and more involved in everyday family life. I changed hugely in attitude, demeanor and outlook from that accident. To discover that I would recover fully and could go on to try to achieve my goals was a lightning bolt.

From the date of my discharge from the hospital, it was only six weeks before school started. I wasn't as strong as I thought and a full load of college prep courses was too much for me that first semester after the accident. I hated that and felt like a quitter, but physically, I just couldn't do it. I wore a huge leather and metal neck brace until Thanksgiving week. It was an embarrassment. I had no dating life that fall, but I did have lots of visits from friends and, of course, letters from Bob.

Bob's subsequent visit to Andover was, of course, a much more important milestone. He arrived the Friday evening after Thanksgiving with his buddy Tony, who had introduced us, and a mutual friend named Tom. Bob looked good—

he was so relaxed and easy going. To me, he seemed to ooze self-confidence, something I definitely lacked. I was so anxious, I had complete deodorant failure.

The four of us ate a leftover Thanksgiving dinner, during which the boys carried most of the conversation. Eventually Tony and Tom left. My family left Bob and me alone to get reacquainted. The next day my dad allowed Bob to drive our car. I showed him my school and the local teen hangouts. When we went to dinner with my parents on Saturday evening, Bob was amazingly comfortable talking to them. That really impressed me, though when he spilled water all over my mom's cashmere suit I realized that he was more nervous than he looked.

That same night, we went to a great party. My best boy friend (not boyfriend!) Billy commented that "Fran, this one's a keeper." I was thinking the same thing.

Afterward, we spent a while parked and exchanged a few kisses. I felt "tinglings" I'd never felt before. After writing for so long, we knew each other better than we would ever have guessed. I wanted this boy in my life even though he lived so far away. We declared our newly discovered love, and I gave him my class ring.

He left the next afternoon for Ohio. I confided to my mom that I hoped to marry Bob some day. She may have thought I was crazy, but kindly didn't say so.

However, marriage still seemed very far in the future. For the time being, it was planning for college that was the priority.

Since turning 13, I had always wanted to go away to college. I even dreamed for a while about going to Hawaii, though my father immediately nixed that idea. I also thought about studying in Europe, but both the finances and the logistics were too daunting. When I learned about Lake Erie College, it really fit the bill. Every junior spent a winter term in Europe, not just language majors, and the cost of the trip was included in the tuition. The school immediately became my first choice.

Of course, it would have been nice to attend a school closer to Bob's. But we both felt we had years for that. A chance to study abroad was more compelling at that time. The fact that "LEC" was a woman's college was attractive too—actually, I only applied to women's schools. At the time I was applying I felt as though I'd had enough of boys, and I do mean *boys*. The prospect of not dating was a welcome relief.

Off went my application forms, my English composition, my SAT scores and my highest hopes. When I learned that I had been accepted, those were happy days.

Getting ready for college was fun, especially shopping for clothes. I felt some anxiety about leaving home, but at that point it was never overwhelming.

That summer's best times were spent at Lake Winnipesaukee. Vacationing there was great. Just our nuclear family came, and everyone relaxed, maybe because it *was* just our nuclear family!

The lake was, and is, the most beautiful place I've ever been. The lake itself is crystal clear, 28 miles by 10 miles. The water is dotted with 128 islands and surrounded by three mountain ranges and lots of quaint little New England villages complete with white church steeples. I always loved the water activity at the lake and the smell of pine needles warmed by the sun. We had stayed in the same cabin community for nine years—fourteen cottages nestled under the pines on the water—so it was a kind of second home, well-loved and familiar at a time when my life was about to change dramatically.

Then, suddenly, summer was over and it was time for the drive to college. Even though I hadn't been too anxious earlier, I was terrified of being left on my own. My mom knew that if offered the chance I would have gone back home with them.

The college was founded by Baptists in the mid-nineteenth century. It wasn't a big campus, especially compared to Notre Dame, and the student body averaged around 400. Once I had met my wonderful roommates and lots of other freshmen, I felt that my prospects of being happy there were good, so I settled in quickly.

Like Notre Dame and most other schools of the time, LEC had strict rules and regulations. If you left the dorm after 8 p.m., you signed out. Freshmen had to be signed back in by 11 p.m., 12:30 on weekends. Weekly College Meeting was required, as was class attendance. I remember feeling safe and secure, and I loved not having males around.

Not seeing Bob much that year was disappointing, but to be expected. Notre Dame was an 8-hour train ride from Lake Erie College. It would have been a 6-hour drive, but that was mostly a moot point. Students were not allowed to have cars on campus until they were seniors, and I never had a car of my own there.

Among the many new experiences of my freshman year of college was my first meeting with Bob's parents. As he writes, I arrived on Thanksgiving morning, eight hours late due to train delays and feeling nervous and exhausted. I still don't know how Bob figured out exactly when the train would finally get in—he must have stayed up calling the New York Central all night.

The Zielsdorf house astounded me. It was huge, professionally decorated—*everything* went together—and gorgeous. Bob's mother impressed me even more: she was so very elegant, polished, self-assured, and socially charming. Frank, Bob's father, was easy-going, relaxed and soft spoken. My first impressions of them were good. But I never felt that I quite made the grade with Mrs. Z. I remember her asking if her girls could help me fix my hair—but it was "fixed" already!

The Zielsdorfs were very, very social. They belonged to the country club set, traveled extensively, and enjoyed an evening cocktail. In contrast, my parents never traveled without the family and, at that time, didn't drink. Meeting Bob's family was a whole new experience for me.

Over the years, I realized that Mary Zielsdorf was somewhat similar to my dad in personality, while Frank was more like my mom. I always felt that Bob's dad accepted and liked me. But even later on, when it came to his mother, I felt like I had to prove something—like I wasn't quite enough "as is." I suspect Bob's sisters might have felt the same about their mom. I think that to Mary, friends and a full social calendar just rated higher than family. There was nothing I can remember being easy about my mother-in-law. She was never nosy or intrusive, nor deliberately mean. But she often spoke without thinking first, and it wasn't easy to know where you stood with her.

Compared to my dad with his tight control of family finances, Bob's parents were incredibly generous with gifts. My family was financially comfortable. We had nice birthday and Christmas presents, new clothes, good food, two cars, TVs and a yearly vacation. Still, our household ran on a budget—money for food, clothing, gas, and so on was allocated from each paycheck—and I never remember Dad giving my mother a lavish gift. There were several occasions when I was truly overwhelmed with the Zielsdorfs' gift giving. But generous as they were with gifts, they were sometimes less so with time. With their social schedule, there wasn't much time for family.

Bob talks about the breach in our relationship we came to call "the big chill." Naturally, it's a moment in our relationship I remember vividly—and just as naturally, my perspective of it is very personal.

I can't recall ever having been as angry, humiliated, and embarrassed as when my parents and I showed up in Sidney and Bob wasn't home. The trip added 9 hours to our already long 11 ½ hour trip back to Andover, making his absence an even greater insult.

This was a side of Bob I'd never known from five years of writing. In my opinion, he was—all at once—self-centered, rude, thoughtless, inconsiderate and totally boorish. How had all that escaped me? Who was this Sharon? Did I mean anything to him any more?

Furious as I was, I still didn't want to end our five-year relationship. We had declared our love 18 months earlier, so that would have been a *very* big step. I decided that I would be civil but not loving. I was too hurt. We'd just have to wait and see. Our correspondence cooled significantly. I spent the summer getting closer to Donnie. He and I started dating again about a month before I left for college. This time it felt different—we were very taken with each other, and that fall his letters declared that he loved me.

I felt no reason to share this with Bob. He and I had our own special relationship, and in my mind, we were all too young to be committed. Donnie was somewhat aware of Bob, as I had told him we were writing. He had met Bob at a party during that Thanksgiving visit to Andover. During the times when I didn't know exactly where I stood with Bob, Donnie was right there—as kind and sweet as ever, and not treating me with total disregard. When I was home from school, we spent hours together. It was never physical, but we loved each other. I learned how to knit and made him three sweaters—but I didn't make any for Bob!

In hindsight, I'm so grateful that Bob ended the stalemate we were in—first by writing to tell me he was tired of the nasty, snide and sarcastic letters I had been sending, and then by announcing he was coming to see me. I had never wanted to end our correspondence; I was just smarting from the Sharon incident. His firmness forced us to resolve things.

That weekend in Cleveland, we spent hours after dinner talking: trying to repair our relationship, regain trust, and figure out what we each wanted to be to the other. When Bob said that he'd like to marry me one day, it was unexpected and overwhelming. That honest comment helped me face the truth. We were compatible, we loved each other, we knew each other more deeply than we had even realized, and we really had the foundations for a long-term relationship. While I loved Donnie, I also knew in my heart that I wasn't right for him. My strong will would have made him miserable; because I loved him, I had to let him go. These were some of the things I mulled over as I returned to school that Sunday night.

Poor Donnie had the misfortune to call me that night. He thought I sounded funny and asked what was going on. Admitting that I had spent time with Bob that weekend, I broke the news that our relationship had begun again. Hurting Donnie was not what I wanted, but it *was* what happened. In a ten minute phone call our relationship was over. I hated myself. In the long run it would be best for all of us, but that night was awful.

Bob and I were pinned in October 1963. It was a complete surprise to me. I was wearing a wool dress—in my favorite preppy style, of course. I remember the actual pinning itself somewhat differently than he does. The pin was supposed to rest right over the heart. When Bob went to pin on the Notre Dame flag he just couldn't do it. I think it came too close to a kind of touching we weren't doing. So as I recall, I pinned it on myself.

Bob's parents were at Notre Dame with friends from Sidney for a football weekend at the time we got pinned. I remember joining them at a round table for dinner. Everyone seated there could see everyone else, so my pin was obvious as soon as I removed my coat. Bob announced that we had great news—we were pinned. No effusive congratulations followed; in fact, it was an awkward moment. Finally, Bob's dad said "That's great!" and the Zielsdorfs' friends followed suit. I'm sure Bob's mother chimed in too, but I have no memory of that. Obviously, Bob hadn't given his parents so much as a clue that he had bought me a pin. They had to have been as surprised as I was. I hoped they would still like me.

After dinner, I called my parents from a pay phone to share the news. My mom was clearly excited, while my dad was quiet. Phone calls then were so expensive that we couldn't talk long. I had to wait for a letter and just hope they would both be pleased for me.

Neither the Zielsdorfs nor my own parents had committed to their future spouses at such a young age. Looking back now, I can understand why they would have felt cautious about our seriousness with each other.

~~~~

Pinned and with the "big chill" a distant memory, I felt secure in my relationship with Bob as I planned for my Winter Term Abroad. That was my main reason for choosing Lake Erie College, as I've mentioned. But as the time to leave for Spain grew closer, I was filled with doubts. Would my language skills be adequate? Could I still survive on the $5 a week I had to spend? How often would I see the other 11 girls in the Valencia center? Would my host family be nice?

The months just before I departed felt stressful. My beloved grandmother was in failing health, and there was talk of sending my brother away to a special school. I knew there might be many changes before I came home again. And there was so much to do as I planned and shopped for my four months in Europe. I had lived away from home for two years by then; I was no longer an integral part of dinner-table conversations and everyday events. But this would be a new kind of separation. The headaches I had at that time were the manifestations of all of this tension.

It did turn out to be a challenge, but also an exciting time. Valencia was on the Mediterranean but not a resort town. American naval vessels would dock there. My Spanish family was kind. We lived in an apartment building with a doorman/mailman. It wasn't fancy, but though it was damp and cold, it was adequate. Bob has described the apartment well, though he didn't mention something I still remember: that the little refrigerator always had chicken feet in it!

Meeting Spanish university men was also fun, especially since most of them spoke a little English. We got together in groups in the afternoon. The main meal of the day was eaten at home around 1 p.m. The shops all closed for siesta then, reopening around 4:30. That was our social time, when we young people got together in groups before going home again by 9:30 for the evening meal. We talked, danced, and sang along with the Beatles, a brand new group from London at that time. I discovered paella, tortillas and cheap red wine. It wasn't really as much of a social whirl as it must have sounded from my letters. But the chance to spend time with kids our age was fun, and along the way I learned a lot about cultural and social differences.

Lake Erie students attended daily classes at the University as well as group meetings, cultural tours and excursions. On the one long weekend our group had for travel, we flew to Madrid. We had a marvelous time, though I can remember having to get used to the fact that the bathrooms in our hotel were at the end of the hallways and shared with other guests. From Madrid, one friend and I traveled to Toledo, which had been the home of the painter El Greco for over 40 years. His painting of St. Peter brought me to tears, moving me as no artwork ever had. Several weeks after that excursion, my Spanish sister Amparano and I went with friends to a beautiful seaside town called Benidorm, which is now a resort but was much quieter then.

As Bob mentions, our correspondence created the occasional moments of misunderstanding while I was away. But most of it was lovely. After so many years of writing as platonic pen pals, I was touched to see how romantic Bob's letters could be. "God, I miss you, Fran. So many little things happen during the day that I want to tell you. I keep wishing that you were right beside me," he wrote in one letter. "I love you so much that if you ever let one day go by without saying "I love you, Bob," it would really crush me. Don't worry about boring me, Fran…you will never bore me, and until God runs out of stars, I'll love you," another said. We were already pinned, but these declarations were new, and I don't remember Bob saying things like this out loud. I still re-read those letters frequently, and cherish them all.

Returning home after my Winter Term Abroad, I hardly knew where to begin describing my trip. Seeing and being with my family again felt so good, and it was fun to give them all the little gifts from Spain that I had chosen. Yet I also felt disoriented. Having just spent four months in a foreign country, I was now back among people who had never been to Europe. How could I possibly communicate all of my experiences? Here at home things had been happening too, of course, and I was totally "out of the loop." For a while, I felt a need to retreat, be alone, and organize my thoughts.

But I didn't feel confused about Bob. Once we were finally together again, our thoughts turned to being together always.

We actually started talking about being engaged during a visit to Lake Winnipesaukee in the fall of 1964. We were celebrating Bob's 21st birthday. We decided that we would marry as soon as we graduated from college, in June of 1965.

He asked my opinion on the shape of the diamond in the engagement ring and whether the setting should be platinum or gold. Then he shocked me with the news that he had already selected a ring, which he would give me after school started. I was so thrilled that I would have been at Notre Dame every weekend. Unfortunately (or not!), I had student teaching from Monday through Friday that fall along with regular classes—a big responsibility.

Bob told me in every letter that September that the ring wasn't ready yet. I was *not* feeling very patient. Then one Friday, a friend offered me a ride to South Bend—her boyfriend was driving to Chicago. When I called Bob and asked if he could see me that night, of course he said yes. So there we were, with a completely unexpected weekend together ahead of us. I had no hopes of seeing the ring, as he hadn't a clue that I would be there.

On Saturday night, Bob suggested that we go out to dinner at a nice restaurant in a local hotel. Unusual, but it sounded like a nice change. Before dinner arrived, Bob pulled a little box out of his sport coat pocket and handed it to me. I was flabbergasted—how could this be? I only found out later that he had gotten the ring a couple of weeks earlier and planned to give it to me the following weekend, during our scheduled visit.

The ring was lovelier than I had ever imagined, white gold with raised prongs holding a sparkling diamond. To make it even more beautiful, he had selected it himself. I felt faint as Bob slid the ring on my finger. My stomach was full of butterflies, my hand was trembling, and my heart felt like it was bursting with love. There were no dramatics, just the simple "will you marry me?" Finally, we were officially engaged to be married.

I called my parents from a pay phone to share our great news. I had already let my mom in on our wedding plans. (She had promptly gotten us a coffee percolator with her Green Stamps!) Telling my dad had been harder. I had waited until August, a mere ten months before the planned date. He wasn't happy, pleased or excited. Mom intervened after I left the room, crying. Thanks to her help as well as a bit of time to "process," Dad was better, even congratulatory, the next week. By the time I called to tell them that our engagement was official, both he and Mom were thrilled.

Then there were Bob's parents. As it happened, they were in South Bend with the same friends who had been with them the weekend we were pinned. We met them for brunch on Sunday and announced our engagement. Again, a big surprise for them. Bob had never mentioned that he was buying a ring, even though they knew we were planning a wedding for the following June. I have to say, surprise sure made my future in-laws quiet!

Even after Bob and I were committed to each other, we chose to keep our relationship non-physical, to wait for our marriage. But the more often we began to see each other, the more difficult that became. One winter night when Bob said he'd like to make love to me, it seemed like the right thing. We loved each other completely. And we had been writing for seven and a half years—crazy in love for over a year, and committed emotionally for life since summer.

Birth control wasn't yet readily available then, at least for me. I was fine for a couple of weeks afterward, but then guilt and fear of pregnancy surfaced. I was a wreck. What if I got pregnant? What about our parents, our final five months of school? Literally ill with worry, I continued to go to classes, attend meetings, and write letters. Thank God we dodged the proverbial bullet, but neither of us wanted to be in that emotional state again.

That February, someone near and dear to both of us got pregnant and had to marry. That was like a huge alarm bell in our heads. There was no way we wanted to be in that situation. We held back after that for what seemed like months. It wasn't quite as difficult as it might have been, just because there were so few places we could be alone and intimate.

At the time Bob and I got serious, what I knew about birth control would have fit on a business card. What I was very aware of was that the Catholic Church was dead set against it. Bob took a more liberal attitude than I did toward this issue, probably because of his opportunity to meet more liberal priests at Notre Dame.

When we were taking our required pre-marriage counseling, the priest in Ohio informed us that if he thought we were using birth control or even thinking about it, he would notify our home church pastors and forbid the marriage. Strong words indeed! They sure made me afraid of contraception, though I figured that I might still be willing to try the pill after we were married.

Planning the wedding was fun, though it had its challenges. The year Bob and I got engaged, my sister, brother and I were all in private schools, so the family budget was tight. My father allowed as how I could have $1,500 for my wedding—in total, for everything. I really was grateful and determined to make it work.

At the time, if you wanted to be married in Church at Mass, the ceremony had to take place before noon. That was fine with me. Having a luncheon with a champagne toast but no open bar meant big savings.

For the wedding gown, Mom took me to the shop where she had bought her own dress some 26 years before. The owner put together a beautiful sheath gown—no excess, expensive fabric—and a custom-made veil that touched the floor. Since she was also supplying the five bridesmaids' dresses, my mom's outfit and my going away ensemble, she gave us a great deal. My gown was $150, and I loved it.

Dad knew someone who would give him a bargain on thermographed, not engraved, invitations. I selected a photographer who would supply us with an album of 24 photos at a price that fit our budget.

All this was done over Christmas break. By the time I went back to school, we had confirmations on everything but the rehearsal dinner—the Zielsdorfs' responsibility—the reception, and the flowers. When I returned to Lake Erie College, Mom worked hard to tie up all the loose ends. Our cake was copied from one in *Brides* Magazine, while the wedding flowers were a replica of those in my parents' wedding: beautiful cascades with not-so-expensive flowers. All in all, I knew it would be wonderful and beautiful and simple *and* in my budget.

The wedding was lovely. Bob's parents had said not to expect many of their friends because of the distance from Ohio and Wisconsin to Massachusetts. In the end, we had 75 wedding guests—a very manageable number, and one that allowed us to talk to everyone.

My parents later surprised me and planned for cocktails and a catered dinner at our home the night of the wedding. Their close friends, the out-of-town guests and the members of the wedding party and their dates were all invited. When Bob and I stopped at my house before heading off on our honeymoon, we were both touched by the spectacular spread my parents had arranged.

My dad had what we then called "conniptions" over my wedding gift to Bob: the ivory-handled pistol he described in the book, which cost a full hundred dollars. Dad said he'd never heard of a bride gifting a groom, but he gave me the money I needed to buy it—he had clearly mellowed a bit by then! Bob gave me a beautiful set of pearls. My bridesmaids received gold signet rings, while the groomsmen got oversized steins. I remember that Bob's roommate Tom filled his with gin and tonic.

After leaving the reception, we drove to my house, where Bob attempted to wash all the shaving cream and confetti off the car. Then it was a few hours' ride to Woods Hole, where we would board the ferry to Nantucket in the morning. We stopped along the way to see my brother, who was enrolled at St. Colletta's School.

In retrospect, I wonder why we didn't hop into bed after checking into the motel. But we didn't. Maybe we were so used to holding off by then a little more waiting seemed natural. After putting our suitcases in the room, Bob left to find a car wash so he could finish cleaning the car so that we wouldn't be such conspicuous newlyweds. While he was gone, the hotel manager rang the room and asked for Mrs. Zielsdorf. Thinking he wanted my mother-in-law, I quickly replied, "She's not here."

We had a lovely dinner before finally returning to our room. I had purchased a fabulous peignoir set and was anxious to wear it, like Doris Day did in her movies. I never found out if Bob liked it or not!

Nantucket was glorious. We sailed, swam, biked, hiked, and picnicked. We only had three days. Then we were off to Lake Winnipesaukee to say goodbye to my parents before we moved to Chicago.

~~~

Bob describes the way our correspondence wound to an end. By the time we stopped writing, we were extremely focused on our marriage and our future. I can't remember thinking that I'd miss getting Bob's letters; instead, I was just looking forward to not having to say goodbye every weekend.

On several of our anniversaries, Bob has written me a letter. They always make me cry with happiness.

We've always talked about our strange pen pal courtship. Our kids grew up hearing about it, and now our grandkids. When anyone asks how we met, they get the whole story.

When the idea of this afterword arose, Bob playfully said he would give me "the last word." But of course, one of the things our correspondence helped teach us is that in a good relationship, *neither* partner truly has the last word. There is always room for questions and responses, and always time for dialogue and deeper understanding—whether that dialogue is spoken from a few feet away, or sent long distance via Post Office and "sealed with a kiss."

# ACKNOWLEDGEMENTS

*S*O MANY HAVE PROVIDED HELP AND ENCOURAGEMENT FOR THIS PROJECT that I hesitate to start naming names for fear I will overlook someone. Having said that, I fearlessly proceed, apologizing in advance to anyone I have forgotten.

The idea that the letters Fran and I wrote to each other could be the basis for a book first occurred to me perhaps 35 years ago. When I occasionally voiced the thought aloud I never failed to get a positive reaction. When I retired from business in 2008, I decided it was time to re-engage my right brain, and so the long-dormant book idea started to become a reality.

Step one was to take a memoir writing course taught by Suzanne Fox at the Vero Beach Museum of Art. Suzanne would become my mentor, coach, editor, and friend. When I outlined the book concept to my classmates they universally encouraged me to proceed. Later, whenever the subject would come up, it was invariably met with great enthusiasm by both friends and strangers. Dan Malovany, editor of a baking industry trade magazine, loved the idea and contributed his thoughts and ideas. A host of others were so supportive that I couldn't possibly have wavered in my resolve to proceed.

This work is truly a team effort. Suzanne Fox guided me every step of the way, providing chapter-by-chapter feedback, guidance with several revisions, highly professional editing, and an education on the mysterious (to me) ways of the book publishing industry. Bob Dilenschneider, a Notre Dame classmate and CEO of The Dilenschneider Group, added his own encouragement and an introduction to Mel Parker. Mel, of Mel Parker Books, was enthusiastic as well, offered hugely insightful suggestions for improving the first draft, and became my literary agent. The painstaking scanning of the letters and envelopes and the complex book design were both done by cj Madigan of Shoebox Stories. I appreciate her scrupulousness and the similarly careful efforts of Nancy Brown, my former assistant, who transcribed the letters and proof-read the manuscript. And of course, many, many friends have expressed their support in so many ways.

My family have given me tremendous joy—and waited patiently for the finished book to appear. (Along the way, I purposefully glossed over certain youthful indiscretions so that family could read the book with a minimum of embarrassment.) This work is a champagne toast to Kristen and Mike Schwartz, Beth and David Alexander, Matt and Paulette Zielsdorf, Rob and Kim Zielsdorf, and Molly Zielsdorf. It is also a ginger-ale toast to our grandchildren: Gillian and Nate Schwartz; Matthew and Jack Alexander; Ellie, Erin, and Megan Zielsdorf; and Abby, Alex, and Charlie Zielsdorf.

In his novel, "Franny and Zooey", J.D. Salinger's Zooey is at one point going to appear on the radio. His friend, Seymour, counsels him to shine his shoes and Zooey asks why. He is told to do it for the Fat Lady. Zooey eventually forms his own mental image of the mythical Fat Lady, and he always shines his shoes for her before going on the air. My grandson, Jack Alexander, is a talented writer with a particularly strong interest in following this project. As I wrote,

Jack became my Fat Lady, my muse. When writing, I wrote for Jack—my way of shining my shoes before going on the air. I am grateful for his inspiration.

I have shared my appreciation for Fran elsewhere in this book. Here, let me just say that her tremendous moral support throughout this undertaking and her terrifically insightful "Last Word" have truly helped make this book far more than it otherwise would have been.

Finally, to all of the others whose positive energy contributed to *Sealed with a Kiss*, a profound *Thank You.*

CPSIA information can be obtained
at www.ICGtesting.com
Printed in the USA
LVOW10s1541041017
551170LV00012B/1167/P

9 780991 317400